THE JOHN HARVARD LIBRARY

A Brief Narrative of the Case and Trial of

JOHN PETER ZENGER

Printer of The New York Weekly Journal

By

JAMES ALEXANDER

Edited by Stanley Nider Katz

THE BELKNAP PRESS OF
HARVARD UNIVERSITY PRESS
Cambridge, Massachusetts
1963

Distributed in Great Britain by Oxford University Press, London

Library of Congress Catalog Card Number 63-19133

Printed in the United States of America

CONTENTS

INTRODUCTION

INTRODUCTION

For nineteenth-century historians, the trial of John Peter Zenger for seditious libel in 1735 constituted the first chapter in the epic of American liberty. For them it was a "notable struggle between [the colonists'] arbitrary ruler and their persecuted fellow citizen." The outcome was believed to have thrown terror into the hearts of "the partisans of royal prerogative in England and America" who recognized it as "a dangerous triumph of popular reason and will over the authority of judicial canons and forensic pendantry."[1] George Bancroft was particularly emphatic: Zenger's *Journal,* he wrote, was founded "to defend the popular cause," and the printer's acquittal caused all colonial Americans to exult in the "victory of freedom."[2] Even the arch-Federalist Richard Hildreth believed that the Zenger trial "vindicated" the freedom of the colonial press, while the nationalist John Fiske thought that Zenger's lawyer had opened the way for a vital reform of the law of libel: "Hamilton may be said to have conducted the case according to the law of the future, and thus to have helped to make that law."[3] Modern textbooks of American history continue to describe the trial as one of the foundation stones of the freedom of the press, and as an important victory of the popular will over the tyrannical attitudes of aristocratic government.[4]

But recent investigations of the trial and the surrounding circumstances bring all of this into question. Zenger and his associates, it becomes clear, were neither political democrats nor radical legal reformers. They were, in fact, a somewhat narrow-minded political faction seeking immediate political gain rather than long-term governmental or legal reform. Nor was the case itself a landmark in the history of law or of the freedom of the press in the sense in which it has been discussed. The reformation of the law of libel and the associated unshackling of the press came about, when they did, as if Peter Zenger had never existed.

Yet, for all of this, the case remains an episode of great historical importance. For, viewed in its full contemporary context, it reveals not the conclusion but the origins and sources of change: it allows us to see in dramatic detail the nature of the forces developing in the early eighteenth century which would end, two generations later, in the transformation of both politics and the law.

i

The arrival in August 1732 of William Cosby as governor of New York set in motion the train of political events that concluded in the trial of John Peter Zenger. Prior to Cosby's arrival "Party differences seemed over and every thing seemed to promise an easier administration than any governor had ever met with in this place." [5] But after only a few months of Cosby's rule such optimism had been shattered. It was the old story: "A governor turns rogue, does a thousand things for which a small rogue would have deserved a halter: And because it is difficult, if not impracticable, to obtain relief against him; therefore it is prudent to keep in with him, and join in the roguery, and that on the principle of self-preservation." [6]

The cause of the change seemed obvious. Cosby was a "rogue governor" to many New Yorkers from the moment he stepped ashore. He was quick-tempered, haughty, unlettered, jealous, and above all greedy: it was his greed that brought him the greatest difficulty. Determined to use his position to restore his ebbing fortunes, he was interested only in those aspects of the governorship that brought in money, and particularly in the sale of the various provincial offices at his disposal. The jobs were in any case not very lucrative, and the Governor's manipulation of them cost him dearly in terms of the good will of New Yorkers. Those in his coterie were delighted at the prospect Cosby held before them, but a number of important freeholders, already agitated by the economic decline of the colony, were antagonized. Their antagonism quickly gave birth to an organized opposition to the Governor's influence.

The immediate origins of the opposition lay in the dispute over "Van Dam's salary." Rip Van Dam, a New York merchant of Dutch extraction, had assumed the executive powers in New York after the death of Cosby's predecessor by virtue of his office as senior member of the provincial Council. According to tradition, which had not always been observed, Van Dam ought to have set aside half his salary for the incoming governor, and Cosby, backed by the authority of an instruction of the Privy Council, claimed this share immediately upon arriving in New York. Van Dam refused to part with the money, however, unless, he said, Cosby gave him in return half the perquisites of the governorship which had devolved upon him in England before his departure for America. Van Dam estimated his income to have been £1975.8.10 and Cosby's £6407.18.10; he could hardly have been astonished, therefore, when Cosby refused to accept the bargain.[7]

Cosby turned to the courts to recover the money he felt was due him. But which court should he use? If he brought a common law action in the Supreme Court of New York, he would have to submit himself to a jury of New Yorkers, and it seemed unlikely that a strange and already unsympathetic governor would receive much support from twelve of Van Dam's countrymen. On the other hand, he could not ask the Court of Chancery for an equitable remedy since in New York the governor acted as chancellor. Surely he could not hear his own suit. His solution was to ask the Supreme Court, whose judges were his appointees, to act as a court of equity. The Supreme Court was technically empowered to sit in this capacity, calling itself an Exchequer Court, and there were local precedents for such a course of action.[8] On the other hand, no Court of Exchequer had sat in New York for many years, and there was popular opposition to it on the grounds that it was unnecessary and politically dangerous. New Yorkers, like most Americans, opposed all sorts of equity jurisdiction, preferring legal proceedings that were based upon the common law and upon legislation. Courts of equity, which were originally based on conceptions of abstract justice, relied upon the discretion of the judges and sat without juries. The resulting law, it was felt, was less predictable and less responsive to public feeling than were the rulings of the common law courts.

Despite these popular attitudes, Cosby pressed on with the suit. He ordered the Attorney General to bring an information against Rip Van Dam and in December 1732 he joined the Council in enacting an ordinance establishing a Court of Exchequer in New York.[9]

The case came up for argument before the three judges of the Supreme Court in April 1733. Van Dam's lawyers immediately argued against the exercise of equity jurisdiction by the Supreme Court sitting as a Court of Exchequer. The Chief Justice, Lewis Morris, agreed with them and delivered a long discourse attacking the propriety and legality of such a court. His associates on the bench, James De Lancey and Frederick Philipse, however, disagreed. Morris promptly rebuked them and then went to the extreme length of publishing his discourse.[10] Governor Cosby was understandably provoked and, in August 1733, dismissed Morris from the Supreme Court and raised Justice De Lancey to the chief justiceship. But Cosby had pulled the tiger's tail, for Lewis Morris was the foremost politician, as well as one of the wealthiest inhabitants, of New York. The Van Dam case soon sank into the background as Morris rallied his friends for a campaign to destroy the Governor.

The conflict with Cosby came at a peculiarly important point in the history of the Morris family's fortunes. The family had long commanded respect in both New York and New Jersey.[11] Lewis Morris, lord of the manor of Morrisania in Westchester County, had been chief justice of New York since 1715 and assemblyman from 1710 to 1728, during which time he had been the "first minister" to Governors Hunter and Burnet. His son Lewis, Jr., had served in the New York Council from 1721 to 1729. But the administration of Governor Montgomerie (1728–1731) marked the beginning of decline in the family's political fortunes, for Montgomerie had replaced Morris, Sr., as his principal adviser and suspended his son from the Council; the Philipse family had succeeded the Morrises as the leaders of the Assembly. By 1732 the chief justiceship was the last vestige of the Morrises' political ascendancy in New York, and its loss seemed an intolerable affront.

Lewis Morris, therefore, joined Rip Van Dam in opposition to Governor Cosby, using the salary-court dispute as the focus for an organized effort to drive Cosby out of New York. The controversy had already alienated many Dutch New Yorkers and drew them to Morris' side. Among these antigubernatorial partisans were the wealthy New York City merchant, Gerardus Stuyvesant, Philip Livingston, second lord of Livingston Manor, who was closely allied to the Dutch by marriage, and a number of Albany traders. Van Dam's lawyers, James Alexander and William Smith, also rallied to the side of the judge who had upheld their contentions, as did the politician and scientist, New York's surveyor general, Cadwallader Colden. All these men had at least one thing in common: they had been excluded from the small group (concentrated especially in the Council) which was benefitting from the Governor's control of political appointments and land grants. Colden, Alexander, Smith, and the Morrises were also united in a land speculation involving an area along the Connecticut boundary known as the Oblong. Their claims to title to the land had been challenged by Cosby's crony, Francis Harison, and the Governor later turned against them personally when he accepted Harison's suit to vacate their title in his Court of Chancery.[12]

Lewis Morris seems a most unlikely character to have led a popular political party, for, as Colden explained, he was not by temper "fitted to gain popularity." [13] Nevertheless, the stagnation of the province and the Governor's unpopularity enabled Morris to mold New York's strongest opposition party since the revolutionary days of Jacob Leisler. He and his son ran for the Assembly in October and November 1733, and were resoundingly elected despite the dubious tactics employed by Cosby's sheriff in an effort to defeat them.[14] This success was followed in October 1734 by the election of all but one of a slate of Morrisite candidates for the Common Council of New York City.

Securely placed where they could effectively criticize Governor Cosby, the Morrises and their allies commenced an unrelenting campaign of censure. None of Cosby's early missteps was allowed to go unnoticed. His illegal acceptance of a gift of £1000 offered him by the Assembly of New York in gratitude for his opposition to certain English legislation was played up, as was his near-treasonous mistake of allowing a French sloop, based in Canada, to provision in the port of New York. The opposition was particularly indignant over Cosby's destruction of the "Albany Deed," an Indian land grant which had ceded a tract near the city to its magistrates. Morris and his friends also argued that Governor Cosby had wrongly taken part in the legislative proceedings of the Council, that he had not summoned all the councilors to meetings (meaning, of course, that he had ignored Colden, Alexander, and Livingston), that he had abused his position as chancellor, and that he had appointed indigent strangers to be county sheriffs.[15]

In the by-elections and municipal elections of 1734, the Morris party, if such an informal group can be called a party, stood for the impartial administration of justice, the independence of the three branches of the provincial government, the appointment of qualified and genuinely local officials, and the protection of private property rights—a "popular" program. These points were equally attractive to freeholders in town and country and to the artisans of New York City, especially in a time of economic distress, and the Morrisites played for both groups. They loudly proclaimed themselves "constitutionalists," boasting of their attachment to George II, the House of Hanover, and the Glorious Revolution, and stigmatizing Governor Cosby as an unconstitutional tyrant.

Cosby's response to the formation of this opposition was to complain that his opponents sought "to lead weak and unwary men into *tumults* and *sedition,* to the *disturbance* of the *public peace,* and to the endangering of all *order* and *government.*"[16] He wrote his patron, the Duke of Newcastle, secretary of state, that "the example and spirit of the Boston people begins to spread amongst these colonies in a most prodigious manner," and that the Massachusetts difficulties were "spirited up from home by Mr. Pulteney and that faction." [17] The administration's newspaper reiterated the association of the Morrisites with the contemporary English opposition, which it branded "not national, but personal":

> The contention is not, now, between the government and the people, or between the King and the nation, nor between the ministry and the people; but between the gentlemen in power, and certain gentlemen out of power; and the strife is, *who shall be the greatest.*[18]

The Morrisites did not seem to mind the association, for they adopted Pulteney's slogan of "King George, Liberty, and Law."

Thus, by 1734, a full-scale opposition faction had been created in New York. Outside of the Westchester and New York City election successes, however, the new party made little headway. For Cosby was able to retain firm control of the Council and the provincial courts, and he succeeded in preventing the Assembly from turning against him. The opposition then resorted to its last hope: to force the recall of the Governor by the ministry in London. Late in 1734 they sent Lewis Morris to England to plead not only the case for his own restoration to the bench but also for the Governor's removal on the grounds of incapacity for his office.[19] And they launched a newspaper, the *New York Weekly Journal,* in the hope of finding popular support in the colony and of stirring up criticism of the Governor.

ii

The printing press had begun to exercise an influence on American politics in the early years of the century, and the Morrisites had been quick to seize upon the printed word as a political weapon. Cadwallader Colden, author of the history of the Six Nations, had been Governor Burnet's chief propagandist, and most of the leaders of the group were experienced pamphleteers even before 1733. Both Lewis Morris and Rip Van Dam had committed their complaints against Governor Cosby to print, although Van Dam's pamphlet had been the work of his lawyers, Alexander and Smith.[20] It became apparent, however, that although pamphlets were useful vehicles for the presentation of extended trains of thought, they were not so well suited to the rigors of political infighting. A less formal means of expression was needed to quicken the tempo of their criticism of Cosby, to lower the level of their attack and, not least, to hide their identities.

Cosby's opponents were hampered, however, by the fact that New York's sole newspaper, William Bradford's *New York Gazette,* was "a paper known to be under the direction of the government, in which the Printer of it is not suffered to insert anything but what his superiors approve of, under the penalty of losing £50 per annum salary and the title of the King's Printer for the Province of New York." This situation was transformed on November 5, 1733, however, with the publication of the inaugural issue of the *New York Weekly Journal,* America's first party newspaper, which quickly proved to be a powerful weapon "of invective and satire against the Governor." [21]

The *Weekly Journal* was printed and published at the modest print shop of John Peter Zenger. Zenger had come to New York as a boy of thirteen, one of that forlorn company of Palatine Germans that emigrated via England in 1710. His father had died on shipboard during the journey and, soon after their arrival, his mother had apprenticed the child to New York's public printer, William Bradford, to learn the trade. After serving his eight years, young Zenger had set out for Maryland to make his fortune as the public printer to the colony, but he soon returned to New York and a year's partnership with Bradford. In 1726 he hung out a sign over his own printing shop, where he produced polemical tracts, theological works, and a good many books in Dutch. He was still virtually unknown when the Morrisites hired him to print their newspaper in 1733, and in their employ, he remained only what he had been trained to be, a printer. The guiding genius and effective editor of the *Journal* was James Alexander, who had defended Van Dam and was soon to represent Zenger in his legal difficulties.[22]

The missionary zeal of Alexander and his friends made the *Journal* a lively and imaginative newspaper. Each issue contained several essays, reprinted from either English or American sources or composed especially for Zenger's paper. Among the English essayists, the *Journal* was fondest of Addison and Steele and the radical libertarians Trenchard and Gordon.[23] Essays composed by the Morrisites themselves were generally presented as pseudonymous letters to the editor from subscribers. The heart of the case against Cosby was offered in such letters, which ranged from abstract discussions of government policy and administration to vicious personal attacks on the Governor and his cronies.

Finally, in addition to foreign and domestic news, the *Journal* included paid advertisements. These too were read carefully, if only because Zenger frequently inserted sham advertisements which abused the Cosbyites in the grossest terms. These were, in fact, the *Journal*'s substitute for political cartoons. Once, for example, the paper carried a request for the return of a lost spaniel, described in such a way as to be identified immediately by readers as Cosby's publicist, Francis Harison. Later, the Governor himself was similarly described as a monkey; and another time a notice announced the arrival, immediately preceding Zenger's libel trial, of a "choice parcel of new authorities" imported from "God knows where."[24] Alexander thus transformed virtually every department of the *Journal* into a vehicle for criticism of the Governor. Occasionally he printed a few lines of dashes in a letter critical of Cosby, explaining that, "Something is here omitted, for which I beg my correspondent to excuse, as not safe for me to print"; but on the whole the *Journal* was looking for trouble.[25]

Even a duller man than William Cosby would have realized that the *Journal* had been deliberately created as an instrument of propaganda. He complained to the Board of Trade that he had found James Alexander "to be at the head of a scheme to give all imaginable uneasiness to the government by infusing into and making the worst impressions on the minds of the people. A press supported by him and his party began to swarm with the most virulent libels." He also charged that Lewis Morris' "open and implacable malice against me has appeared weekly in false and scandalous libels printed in Zenger's *Journal*," and that Morris sought to prejudice the minds of "a deluded and unreasonable mob." The technique was well known:

> There is nothing more common with writers of seditious libels than for them to tell the world they speak the sentiments of the people, thereby endeavoring to persuade them that it is their interest alone which they labor.

Van Dam, Alexander, and Morris, the Governor said, were trying to entice him into a "paper war to justify the proceedings of the court, my own conduct, and His Majesty's authority, which ought not to be prostituted to the censure of the mob," but he vowed that he would not fall into the trap.[26] He did not, if what he meant was that he would not publish letters or pamphlets against the opposition in his own name. He did not need to, for the *Gazette* was at hand to speak for him.

Bradford's paper did not deign to notice the *Journal* for the first two months of its existence. However, it came to the Governor's defense at the beginning of January 1734, when a correspondent took great pains to dissociate Cosby ("the Father of his People") from the corrupt Governors Coote (Bellomont) and Cornbury, while ascribing the *Journal*'s most recent criticism to "a parcel of griping lawyers" who were disappointed at losing the chance to exploit the fraudulent Albany Deed.[27] Thereafter, the tempo of the *Gazette*'s attack quickened, producing a "paper war" which ended only with the Zenger trial and Cosby's death.

Bradford countered Zenger's Trenchard and Gordon by reprinting some of the standard English defenses of the established order, such as Collier's *Moral Essays,* Hooker's *Laws of Ecclesiastical Polity,* Clarendon's *History of the Rebellion* and, above all, the *Spectator*.[28] Bradford's correspondents, like Zenger's, vigorously defended their champion and rebutted articles in the *Journal*. They were particularly scornful of the *Journal*'s journalistic standards. One letter alleged that Zenger misquoted Cato, abusing Trenchard and Gordon's meaning by patching together extracts from their pieces which he admired. Another deplored Zenger's wild use of large type, which altered the meaning of essays he reproduced in the *Journal*. And another condemned Zenger's "vile" advertisements "as secret arrows that fly in the dark, and wound the reputation of men much better than others."[29]

Cosby was quickly convinced that the *Journal* was becoming influential among the citizens of New York and that it posed a real threat to the maintenance of public order and to the permanence of his administration. The teeth of the opposition would have to be drawn if he was to survive.

iii

The leaders of the New York opposition party found the slogans of free speech to their taste and interest. In a manifesto on the freedom of the press which was printed in the second and third numbers of the *New York Weekly Journal* they wrote that in a constitutional monarchy criticism by the press is a necessary safeguard against those unlawful ministers who were beyond the reach of ordinary legal action:

For if such an overgrown criminal, or an impudent monster in iniquity, cannot immediately be come at by ordinary justice, let him yet receive the lash of satire, let the glaring truths of his ill administration, if possible, awaken his conscience, and if he has no conscience, rouse his fear, by showing him his deserts, sting him with shame, and render his actions odious to all honest minds.

Thus a free press can make highly placed criminals cautious and possibly bring them within the scope of ordinary justice; and it is therefore "not only consistent with, but a necessary part of the constitution itself." True, honest men may sometimes be defamed by an unrestrained press, but that is a small price to pay for the opportunity to weed out "evil ministers." And since truth always prevails over falsehood, an honest man's reputation cannot be permanently stained by such lies. Above all, liberty itself is based upon free discussion:

The loss of liberty in general would soon follow the suppression of the liberty of the press; for it is an essential branch of liberty, so perhaps it is the best preservative of the whole. Even a restraint of the press would have a fatal influence. No nation ancient or modern ever lost the liberty of freely speaking, writing or publishing their sentiments, but forthwith lost their liberty in general and became slaves.[30]

But what was this liberty "of freely speaking, writing, or publishing" in the eighteenth century? In England, the only major restraint on the freedom to print was the law of libel: "The liberty of the press consists in printing without any previous license, subject to the consequences of the law."[31] The law of seditious libel was intended to protect the government from defamation which would threaten public tranquillity and security. Any publication, whether true or false in its allegations, which contained "written censure upon public men for their conduct as such, or upon the laws, or upon the institutions of the country" and hence tended to bring the government into disrepute, was liable to prosecution under this concept.[32]

By the early eighteenth century the common law courts of King's Bench had assumed jurisdiction of such prosecutions, and juries were therefore involved. The judges of King's Bench, however, reserved to themselves the power to decide whether words were libelous and permitted the jury to decide only the facts of publication and innuendo: whether the offensive words had in fact been "communicated abroad" and whether they actually referred to the people or institutions as charged. The jury's verdict was thus "special," restricted to a few questions of fact, rather than a "general" verdict of guilty or not guilty. If the publication censured the leaders, laws, or institutions of England, the royally appointed judges were almost sure to find it seditious, and the author and publisher guilty.

The English common law crime of seditious libel was acknowledged to be in force in colonial New York, even though no statute of seditious libel was on the colony's books.[33] But American law and procedure were not uniform or consistent, and there was a tenuous American tradition of claims by men accused of seditious speech that juries were the proper judges of their crimes. William Bradford, curiously enough, had used the argument that juries were judges of law as well as of fact when he was charged with publishing a seditious Philadelphia newspaper in 1692. Fifteen years later, when an itinerant clergyman, Francis Mackemie, tried in New York for unlicensed preaching with intent to pervert the church and government of the province, admitted preaching the sermon but claimed that he had not thereby broken the law, the Chief Justice permitted the jury to return a general verdict. Yet neither of these cases had established respectable precedents against English practice, and it seems fairly certain, therefore, that a man who criticized Governor Cosby should have expected the same treatment by the Supreme Court of New York that a critic of George II would have received from the King's Bench.[34] This, at any rate, was the position taken by the defenders of the Cosby administration.

Bradford's *Gazette,* responding in February 1734 to the *Journal*'s manifesto on the freedom of the press, enunciated the virtues of the law of libel. Particularly concerned to mock the idea that the press was the safeguard of all English liberties, he argued that printing was as much within the purview of the law as "natural speaking." Both ordinary men and printers are responsible for the harmful effects of their speech, he said, and " 'tis the abuse not the use of the press that is criminal and ought to be punished." [35] The *Gazette* reminded Zenger's essayists of the contemporary English law, which admitted that a man could not be prevented from speaking his mind but declared that he could not be exempted from the legal consequences of his speech.

Encouraged by the prospect of a debate on a subject close to Morrisite hearts and hopes, the *Journal* replied to Bradford's legalism with an implicitly radical statement on press freedom. It argued for nothing less than the abolition of legal penalties for libel:

> I agree with the Author that it is the abuse, and not the use of the press, is blameable, But the difficulty lies who shall be the judges of this abuse . . . Make our adversaries the judges; I don't well know what will not be a libel; and perhaps, if we be the judges it will be as difficult to tell what will. I would have the readers judges: but they can't judge if nothing is wrote.[36]

Bradford disdained to reply to this extreme assertion, until the September 1734 election successes encouraged Zenger to print two effusive ballads and an epistolary report of the election. Then the *Gazette* mildly retorted:

For men of sense and judgment will always be able to distinguish truth from passion, and among them, consequently, the Author of a report, really false and groundless, must do himself much more prejudice than the person he would injure by his calumnies.[37]

A few weeks later, when the Morrisite attack had become even more intense, the *Gazette* took a less permissive tone. No restraint ought to be put upon the press, Bradford wrote, except "what is sufficient to prevent the grossest abuses of it, abuses that dissolve society, and sap the very foundation of government." The two broadside songs, which by then had become evidence against Zenger for libel, were obviously such gross abuses of freedom of the press, Bradford said, "but with regard to abuses of a less flagrant nature, I had rather see such permitted, than the liberty itself abridged."[38]

Alexander's response to this Cosbyite sally proved that the opposition party could not ultimately bring itself to deny the validity of the existing law of libel. An essay in no. 53 of the *Journal* admitted that certain kinds of speech were punishable—which, of course, had been Bradford's argument all along.

It is true, that abuses that dissolve society, and sap the foundations of government, are not to be sheltered under the umbrage of the liberty of the press.

But, the writer continued, the broadside songs were harmless stuff:

If they will fix determinate meanings to sentences and even blanks, which the Authors have not fixed, and to which other meanings can with equal justice be applied; I would be glad to know wherein this liberty of writing consists?

He also felt that the Governor had misinterpreted Zenger's "Continuance of the Middletown Papers" when he singled it out as libelous speech, for this essay was "purely argumentative upon political points, without the least syllable of an indecent reflection upon anybody."[39] The *Journal*'s position was, therefore, that although some speech was criminal, its speech was not.

The editor of the *Journal* offered his readers little more precision in liberalizing the meaning of the law of seditious libel than he did on the freedom of the press. He was certainly less direct about the substance of the law than about its procedural aspects. The long introductory essay on the freedom of the press seems to imply that no restrictions on speech are consistent with constitutional government, and the letter in no. 15 is reasoned along similar lines. The implication of these statements would seem to be that even false speech does not endanger government or society, perhaps because truth cannot be obscured by falsehood. This impression is intensified by no. 18 of the *Journal,* which reprinted Cato's famous letter on libeling, one of the first English publications to favor the test of truth: "The exposing therefore of public wickedness, as it is a duty which every man owes to truth and his country, can never be a libel in the nature of things."[40] But then, despite all of this, the essay in no. 53 goes to the opposite extreme by definitely ruling out the test of truth, admitting that any speech which endangers the state or society ought to be punished.

On the procedural aspects of the law of seditious libel, though, the *Journal*'s view was clearer and more consistent: it favored an expanded role for the jury in libel prosecutions. The jury system had become the center of controversy during Governor Cosby's Exchequer proceedings against Van Dam, and an early number of the *Journal* indicated the Morrisite admiration for juries.[41] During July and August 1735, when the Zenger jury was actually being chosen, the paper returned to the subject with two reprints. One, which had originally appeared in the English *Craftsman* when its editor was on trial for libel, praised trial by jury and a new English law which guarded against packed juries and abusive treatment by judges.[42] The second, part of a tract on juries by Sir John Hawles, which was published on the day of the Zenger trial in order to have the maximum impact on the New York jurors, argued that although juries were generally judges of fact, they occasionally judged questions of law "as it arises out of, or is complicated with, and influences the *fact.*" When law and fact are inseparable the jury must determine both and, in any case, must avoid a verdict of "only guilty of the fact." [43] The *Journal*'s implied support of the view that law and fact are inseparable in cases of libel aligned the paper with the most advanced reformers of the procedural law of libel.

Confusion on the substance of the law of libel, advocacy of procedural reform and hesitancy on absolute freedom of the press—on the whole, the *Journal*'s position seems to have been one of support for freedom from prior restraint, subject to the future punishment of the law, as judged by a local jury. The Morrisites were slightly ahead of contemporary American thinking on the subject of libel, but hardly the radical exponents of free speech which history has held them to be.

If the *Journal*'s conception of freedom of the press was not radical according to the standards of 1735, was the content of the newspaper as criminal as Governor Cosby contended? A brief glance at the issues proscribed by the administration shows that Zenger printed criticism of the governing regime in at least three forms: satire, reportage, and essays on government. The two broadside songs celebrating the New York City municipal elections are typical satire, while numbers 7 and 49 are good examples of reportage, describing the French sloop incident and the municipal elections.[44] The songs implied that Cosby was disrespectful of the law, while the articles tacitly accused the Governor of treachery to the colony and of political skulduggery.

The *Journal*'s attacks were not always so direct, however. The "Middletown Papers," which criticized Cosby's use of adjournment and prorogation of the Assembly, seem to be what Zenger claimed they were, serious essays on the problems of government.[45] No. 13, however, suggested that the Governor's behavior endangered the liberties and properties of New Yorkers and threatened them with "SLAVERY," while no. 23 openly called Cosby a tyrant: "Who is then in that Province that calls anything his own, or enjoys any liberty longer than those in the administration will condescend to let him do it?"[46] If we except the "Middletown Papers" in nos. 47 and 48, then, all the issues of the *Journal* which Governor Cosby singled out were openly and severely critical of his government in New York. They contributed to the effectiveness of an opposition party in the colony at a time when the notion of a "loyal opposition" did not exist. By the standard of Lord Mansfield, as well as of James De Lancey, John Peter Zenger was in fact a libeler, for words which posed a threat to the security of the government were understood to be criminal, and the Cosby administration clearly felt itself menaced by Zenger's *Journal.*

iv

Zenger had been publishing the *Journal* for two months when Governor Cosby decided to still its voice. The first step occurred when newly promoted Chief Justice James De Lancey charged the January 1734 Grand Jury on the law of libel and asked them to return indictments for the seditious libels which had recently been circulating in the province. The nineteen grand jurors, though they unquestionably knew that De Lancey alluded to the products of Zenger's press, refused to act. Undaunted, the Chief Justice brought the subject of libels before the next Grand Jury in October. In the intervening months, the Morrisites had won the important New York City municipal elections, and Zenger had published his broadside to celebrate the victory. De Lancey asked the jurors to present the two "scandalous" songs for indictment, which they did. But unfortunately for the administration, the jurors protested that they found it impossible to discover the identity of the author, printer, or publisher of the broadside.[47]

Thwarted, Cosby then tried to bring the authority of the Assembly and the Council into play against Zenger's press. The Governor singled out four particularly obnoxious numbers of the *Journal* (7, 47, 48, 49), and managed to get the Council to request the Assembly's concurrence in an order to burn the newspapers. The Assembly refused to cooperate, however, and the Governor and Council were forced to carry out the vendetta against Zenger on their own. Asking the Governor to withdraw, on November 2, 1734, the Council decided that the four issues of the *Journal* were indeed seditious, and agreed on a course of action: that the four *Journals* be burned; that the Governor proclaim a reward for the discovery of the authors; "That Zenger the printer thereof be by order of this Board taken into custody by the Sheriff and committed to prison"; that the Attorney General prosecute the printer and authors when they were discovered; and that the Attorney General examine all the issues of the *Journal,* submitting to the Council "the particular places or paragraphs in each of them" which tended to sedition.[48]

The Council's order to burn the newspapers was delivered to the New York Court of Quarter Sessions on November 5, but the Morrisite Common Council refused to have anything to do with it. The Governor's personal powers were sufficient to carry his plan through, however, and on November 17 the Sheriff imprisoned Zenger. He was arrested on the Council's warrant which charged him with printing and publishing seditious libels which tended to raise factions and tumults in New York, inflaming the minds of the people against the government, and disturbing the peace. Zenger's arrest jolted the Morrisites, since they knew that if he were convicted and his press silenced, their most potent weapon would be lost. The opposition party came to the printer's defense and at this point dispatched Lewis Morris to London to argue its case before the officials of the Crown.

The leading Morrisite lawyers, James Alexander and William Smith, initiated Zenger's defense by applying for a writ of *habeas corpus,* which would free the printer on bail. On November 23 they presented their arguments before Chief Justice De Lancey in a crowded courtroom, contending that the defendant ought to be freed on moderate bail, since he swore that he was not worth more than £40, "the tools of his trade and his wife and children's wearing apparel excepted."[49] De Lancey, who had signed the warrant for Zenger's arrest, imprudently announced to the spectators that "if a jury found Zenger not guilty, they would be perjured."[50] He then set bail at £400 although there was no precedent in New York history for such excessive bail. Unable to raise the sum, Zenger remained in the city jail until the conclusion of his trial, eight months later.[51]

Bradford's *Gazette* rejoiced in Zenger's tribulations and caustically suggested that the printer's friends were not sufficiently concerned with his plight to raise bail.[52] In reality, of course, the Morrisites could have found the money, but they were shrewd enough to value the sympathy aroused by the news of Zenger's hardships. They exploited his imprisonment in the same way that subsequent political factions capitalized on the jailings of John Wilkes and Alexander McDougall. James Alexander was even able to continue the regular publication of the *Journal,* so that his friends had little to lose, unless Zenger's conviction forced the closing of the paper.

Even after Zenger's arrest, Cosby was faced with the problem of how best to bring charges against him. Hopefully, he asked the Grand Jury to find an indictment for seditious libel, but, despite the efforts of a newly appointed and more tractable sheriff to find pliable jurors, they refused to act.[53] Therefore, on January 28, 1735, Attorney General Richard Bradley filed an "information" charging Zenger with seditious libel for printing and publishing parts of his 13th and 23rd *Journals.* The "information" was a device by which the government could initiate prosecutions independently of a Grand Jury, and it was generally regarded as a high-handed, unfair procedure which undercut the popular basis of the jury system. In an admittedly political trial, this procedure doubtless alienated many otherwise neutral New Yorkers, and made the prosecution even more unpopular.

Smith and Alexander immediately took up their cudgels and spared no effort to convert Zenger's defense into an impeachment of the Cosby administration. Their tactic was, in the words of Smith's historian son, "to puzzle the prosecutor" by questioning "the authority of his judges."[54] The defense lawyers offered exceptions to the commissions of the two Supreme Court judges, De Lancey and Frederick Philipse, which the judges received for consideration on April 15, 1735. The principal point of the exceptions was that the two commissions ran "during pleasure" rather than during "good behavior" as did the comparable commissions of the judges of King's Bench in England. They also alleged that the commissions wrongly entitled the judges to exercise the jurisdiction of Common Pleas as well as of King's Bench, that the commissions were founded on neither the common law nor the statute law of England or New York, and that the commissions were invalid because they were not granted with the "advice and consent" of the New York Council. By implication, the defense was charging Governor Cosby with tyrannically flouting the laws of England and New York and of setting up personal henchmen with unlawful powers to control the judicial system of New York. On April 16, as if in confirmation of the Morrisite insinuations, Chief Justice De Lancey refused to hear the exceptions in court, and, on the 18th he disbarred Smith and Alexander.

The reasons for the attack on the judges are not difficult to understand. The Morrisite lawyers, not anticipating disbarment, had jumped at the chance to document the case against Governor Cosby which they had initiated in Van Dam's trial. Further, the law and legal institutions, symbols of governmental stability, were the watchwords of the Morris constitutionalist program; [55] and, in addition, if the trial should result in a conviction of Zenger, the issue of the judges' commissions would provide ground for appeal. Finally, the Morrisites particularly detested De Lancey and Philipse: De Lancey because he had usurped Lewis Morris' place on the bench, and Philipse because his family had supplanted the Morrises in domination of the New York Assembly.

The reasons for the disbarment are less obvious: it was an extraordinarily high-handed course for the youthful Chief Justice to have taken, and it can have done very little to increase the popularity of the prosecution. It can probably be explained as a tactic to deprive Zenger of competent legal counsel, since there were few lawyers in New York at the time and probably none so skilled as Smith and Alexander.

Surprised by De Lancey's stroke against his counsel, Zenger petitioned the court on April 18 to appoint a lawyer for him. The Chief Justice obliged by naming John Chambers, a competent lawyer but a Governor's man, who pleaded Zenger not guilty to the information and moved for a struck jury. Procedure for striking a jury required that the clerk of the court choose forty-eight names from the list of New York freeholders, then allowing the prosecution and defense to challenge twelve names each. In this way, twenty-four men were chosen, out of whom the final twelve might be selected without injustice to either party. As it turned out, the clerk produced a list which the defense recognized as including nonfreeholders, former magistrates displaced in the September elections, and tradesmen in the Governor's employ. Zenger's friends objected to this ruse, and on July 30 the Chief Justice ruled that the names of jurors should be properly struck from the Freeholders' Book in the presence of counsel. The men finally chosen for Zenger's jury are notable only for their obscurity, which suggests that they represented the faceless Morrisite majority of the 1734 New York City elections rather than the merchant friends of Governor Cosby.[56]

Although Chambers had avoided a packed jury, Zenger's friends were afraid that the court-appointed lawyer would not be so effective in court. The scarcity of New York lawyers and their political commitments to Cosby forced the Morrisites to look for a more satisfactory replacement for Smith and Alexander. They found the man they wanted in Pennsylvania, where the proprietary system had engendered a vigorous, recurrent and articulate opposition to arbitrary colonial government. In a brilliant stroke, Alexander engaged Andrew Hamilton of Philadelphia to defend Zenger. Reputedly the best lawyer in America, Hamilton had been a dominant figure in Pennsylvania politics since 1717, and in recent years had found himself in bitter opposition to the proprietary governor of the colony. "He had," Smith's son wrote, "art, eloquence, vivacity, and humor, was ambitious of fame, negligent of nothing to ensure success, and possessed a confidence which no terrors could awe."[57] A professional associate and friend of James Alexander, from whom he frequently borrowed law books, Hamilton must have been sympathetic from the outset to the political dilemma of the Morrisites.[58]

He was not, on the surface at least, a likely person to speak in defense of the freedom of the press, for in Philadelphia in 1729 he had participated in the prosecution of Andrew Bradford for seditious libel. But the two situations were significantly different. Bradford's newspaper, originally founded by his father, William, the New York editor, had libeled the Pennsylvania Assembly, of which Hamilton was the Speaker, and the lawyer's vindictive attitude stemmed from his advocacy of legislative independence. Furthermore, Andrew Bradford had been conducting a bitter political vendetta against Hamilton since 1733, when the lawyer had fallen out with Governor Gordon.[59] The chance to strike out against Bradford's father, combined with his old friendship with the antigubernatorial party in New York, must have been too good to miss.

Zenger's trial finally took place on August 4, 1735. After the Attorney General read his information, Chambers delivered his opening speech, and the stage seemed set for a weak defense of the printer.[60] When Chambers had concluded, however, Andrew Hamilton rose dramatically from his chair in the City Hall courtroom, and announced to the youthful Chief Justice that he would participate in Zenger's defense. Armed with years of courtroom experience and a well-prepared brief, speaking with the daring of one indifferent to the local political contests, Hamilton made short work of convincing the sympathetic jury of Zenger's injured innocence.[61] When the arguments were concluded at the end of the day, it took the jury only a few minutes to return a verdict of not guilty. "Huzza" rang out for Zenger and Hamilton.

V

John Fiske aptly characterized the Zenger defense when he said that Andrew Hamilton conducted the case according to "the law of the future," for it is quite apparent that the law of 1735 was squarely against him. Procedurally, Attorney General Bradley took the traditional view that only the question of Zenger's publication of the papers was to be left to the jury. Libelousness, he said, was for the judges to decide. And the Chief Justice agreed with him that the law of New York was accurately stated by the 1606 Star Chamber case, *de Libellis Famosis,* which held that true statements could be libelous.[62] But Hamilton chose to address himself to the jurors, arguing that the court's law was outmoded and that the court was usurping the rights of the jury. Specifically, he maintained that truth was a defense against an accusation of libel, and that the jury had the right to return a general verdict where law and fact were intertwined.

Hamilton contended that falsehood is the principal thing which "makes a libel" and offered a long string of legal citations to try to prove his point.[63] Bradley's citations, he said, were Star Chamber law, which had died with that court in 1641.[64] Still further flying in the face of contemporary English practice, he alleged that restricting juries to special verdicts would render juries "useless," and that "where matter of law is complicated with matter of fact, the jury have a right to determine both."[65] Juries in murder and trespass cases, he argued in logical analogy, heard evidence on all the questions involved and returned a general verdict. Hamilton, like the reformers who followed him, had a strong case logically but a weak case in terms of contemporary English legal practice.

At the root of the Zenger defense, however, was Hamilton's exposition of the right of citizens to criticize their rulers. Identifying Zenger with the men in the jury box, Hamilton remarked that the crowded courtroom itself proved that the trial, which had been instigated by the Governor and his Council, concerned issues which were not mentioned in the information against Zenger. He played upon local loyalties by contending that the law of seditious libel was intended to protect the King and his ministers rather than the governors of the American colonies. Pressing the case further, he suggested that what is good law in England is not necessarily good law in America, where self-help was the proper rule of conduct.[66] Inch by inch, he drove the jurors to see that the dreary English authorities cited by the prosecution were inapplicable in the American situation, where governors and governed were not so far apart.

Arguing politics rather than law, Hamilton declared that the right to criticize government rests on the assumption that the state exists to protect each person's liberty and that the rulers of the state are merely the guardians of the public good. The formation of the state creates political power which may be used for good or ill. When the state fails and political power threatens to destroy individual rights, the citizens therefore need not obey their magistrates:

> When the representatives of a free people are by just representations or remonstrances made sensible of the sufferings of their fellow subjects, by the abuse of power in the hands of a governor, they have declared . . . that they were not obliged by the law to support a governor who goes about to destroy a province or colony.

Hamilton observed that it is the magistrates who have the easiest access to political power, and the best safeguard against their misuse of power is public criticism:

> It is a right which all freemen claim, and are entitled to complain when they are hurt; they have a right publicly to remonstrate the abuses of power, in the strongest terms, to put their neighbors upon their guard against the craft or open violence of men in authority.

Freedom of criticism will prevent the commission of social evil "by making a governor sensible that it is in his interest to be just to those under his care." For, when magistrates openly abuse their trust, the outraged public will withdraw its cooperation and the magistrates will be powerless. To this end, it is the social duty (and "natural right") of each citizen to guard against the perversion of power, restrained only by law.[67] And the law forbids only *false* criticism.

Hamilton drove his argument for free speech closer to home by insisting that it was peculiarly important in the American colonies where governors, representatives of the Crown, cannot be brought to justice for their misdeeds.[68] The governor's political power generally allows him to control local assemblies and courts, and therefore to dominate the very institutions which ought to limit his power. Free speech is, therefore, the American's best method of rousing legislators to their sense of duty and of warning governors to behave responsibly. In the American colonies, as in all states, however, the basic restraint upon unjust action is the law. In a free society, the jury system prohibits the neglect of the laws, ensuring that popular rights will not be abused in the courts:

> Jurymen are to see with their own eyes, to hear with their own ears, and to make use of their own consciences and understandings, in judging of the lives, liberties or estates of their fellow subjects.

Among the laws which juries must guard most jealously is that which protects all but false criticism of the magistrates, who otherwise may overstep their bounds and threaten the liberty of the citizens.[69] Free speech and jury trial are thus the bastions of individual liberty in America, the bulwarks against lawless power.

The force of Hamilton's argument for free speech rested upon his sense of the difference between government in England and in America. The sovereign King of England had an undoubted right to a severely protected sphere of action. The American governor, however, was merely the local representative of the King. It seemed logical that he was entitled to less freedom of action than a sovereign, and that he was therefore more open to criticism.[70] Furthermore, American sovereignty appeared to reside in the people, especially as their assemblies came to dominate colonial government. The absenteeism of the King and his imperial administrators combined with the colonial experience of self-government, therefore, to produce an American sense of popular government which far outran the whiggery of England.

Hamilton, like the Morris party, sensed this popular spirit and mobilized it in defense of Zenger. Although his argument in the case has long been regarded as the masterpiece of early American legal argument, it was singularly weak law. His citations in support of truth as a defense are altogether unconvincing, and neither history nor law justified his glorification of the jury's role in libel cases. But the rhetoric by which the Philadelphia lawyer expounded the freedom of speech was designed to appeal to the twelve plain jurymen, and to accord with their experience of government. The law was against him, but the law was out of step with public opinion, and he saw to it that Zenger was tried by the public rather than by the law.[71]

vi

The Anglo-American world reacted noisily to the news of Zenger's acquittal. Newspapers and correspondence carried word of the trial throughout the Atlantic community, and the publication of the *Brief Narrative* in June 1736 ensured that the tale would be told in all its Morrisite glory.[72] The challenge sent forth by Alexander's pamphlet was accepted most willingly in the West Indies. There, a comprehensive reply to Hamilton's argument was composed by a Barbadian in 1737.[73] The author, who called himself "Anglo-Americanus," was obviously a well-trained lawyer. Developing an English barrister's technical view of the Zenger case, he found little difficulty in exposing the fragility of Hamilton's legal argument. His refutation of the contention that truth is a defense against accusations of seditious libel was a strong, orthodox exposition of the law of libel. He ruthlessly examined the citations offered by Hamilton on this point, and demonstrated that most of them were inapplicable since they turned on questions other than those of truth. The basic point, Anglo-Americanus said, was simply that the state as well as the individual has a right to protect itself from injurious criticism.[74]

This idea was as much political as legal, and the bulk of the pamphlet was devoted to an argument against Hamilton's politics. Zenger's lawyer, Anglo-Americanus wrote, "seems to be above having his points of law decided by the authorities of the law; and has something in reserve . . . This is what he calls *the reason of the thing,* but is truly and properly a sketch of his own *politics.*" The correct reasoning, the pamphlet claimed, rested on the belief that the law is concerned with the maintenance of the social fabric rather than the moral worth of individual acts. Therefore "human laws do not strictly regard the moral pravity of actions, but their tendency to hurt the community, whose peace and safety are their principal objects." On this analysis, citizens have no "right" to publish truthful complaints, since even truth may prove disruptive to the state. Complaints ought to be addressed to the magistrates rather than to one's neighbors, since the liberty of the press "is not to be trusted in the hands of every discontented fool or designing knave." [75]

Hamilton had argued that the colonists had no other means of redress for the actions of a tyrannical governor than the freedom of public criticism. Anglo-Americanus denied that this was so, maintaining that the proper remedy for colonial injustice is a complaint to the imperial administration in England. He taunted the Morrisites, whose mission to London had been a failure, with the assertion that "if one half of the facts contained in Zenger's Papers, and vouched for true by his counsel, had been fairly represented and proved at home" the Crown would have dismissed Cosby from his post.[76] Respect for the laws and institutions of the empire, he said, is the surest guarantee of colonial justice. The rule of law protects both the social order and the rights of the citizens, but where the two conflict, the stability of the state must take precedence.

The Barbadian *Remarks* drew a quick retort from James Alexander, who further underlined the political nature of the Zenger defense.[77] Alexander, like Hamilton, argued for an expanded definition of legally free speech and, similarly, based his position upon an analysis of the nature of popular government. He asserted that free speech is "a *principal pillar*" of a free society: it prevents the government from becoming tyrannical by subjecting the actions of the magistrates to a searching *"popular examination."* Since truth always overcomes falsehood in the open field, unimpeded criticism of the rulers will check their evil inclinations. Free speech, then, is the constitutional method of keeping a popular government in harmony with the ideals of the people.

Alexander looked to history to prove his case. He described the repressive effect the introduction of restrictions on free speech had in ancient Rome, a lesson the Tudor and Stuart kings of England had learned: "THOSE of the British Kings who aimed at despotic power, or the oppression of the subject, constantly encouraged prosecutions for words." The most despotic of English kings, Charles I, limited the freedom of the press in order to ignore Parliament and subvert the constitution, but his repression made the Civil War inevitable. The conclusion of history is clear: "THAT WHOEVER ATTEMPTS TO SUPPRESS EITHER OF THOSE, *OUR NATURAL RIGHTS*, OUGHT TO BE REGARDED AS AN *ENEMY* TO LIBERTY AND THE CONSTITUTION."

The New York lawyer also surveyed the history of the English laws of libel. He ascribed the rigorous Star Chamber version of the crime to the absolutist inclinations of James I, especially the pernicious doctrine that the truth of a statement increased its libelousness. James's sons and grandsons perpetuated the crime of seditious libel, but the harsh Stuart doctrine was finally destroyed in 1688, when the seven bishops were acquitted by their jury. Alexander admitted that, even after the Glorious Revolution, some kinds of speech were generally considered to be criminal: false criticism of the government, for example. But he stoutly maintained the right of fair criticism: "to expose the evil designs or weak management of a magistrate is the duty of every member of society." [78] After 1688, he argued, truth had become a valid defense and the jury the rightful judge in prosecutions for libel.

Thus, both friend and foe of the Zenger defense recognized that its strength lay in the realm of political theory. Neither Hamilton nor Alexander could counter the legal objections of Anglo-Americanus, and they did not really try to do so. They argued on what Alexander called the "passionate" level against the traditionalist conception of free speech. They appealed to popular notions of government and society, and cited first principles ("the constitution") rather than the law. Neither lawyer, we may guess, was under any illusion about what the law of libel actually said, but they both had firm convictions about what it *should* say—and they were confident that ordinary New Yorkers would agree with them. In the words of one of Hamilton's admirers, "If it is not law it is better than law, it ought to be law, and will always be law wherever justice prevails." [79]

vii

The little courtroom in New York's City Hall reverberated to the cheers of the crowd when Zenger's acquittal was announced by the jury foreman. In contemporary eyes it was a great victory, not for Zenger and the *New York Weekly Journal,* but for Hamilton and the Morrisite party. Zenger languished another night in jail, while the Morrisites feted Andrew Hamilton at the Black Horse Tavern.

The Morrisites, however, were soon to find that they had won a battle, rather than the war. They maintained their control over the government of New York City, but failed to win over either branch of the provincial legislature, and Governor Cosby remained their implacable enemy. The lone Morrisite hope was that the ministry in England would restore Lewis Morris to his judgeship and recall Cosby, but here too they failed, for Morris was given virtually no help toward reinstating himself. Furthermore, when Cosby died in early 1736 the ministry appointed the councilor George Clarke, Cosby's principal adviser, to succeed him.

Confronted with this rebuff, the Morrisite leaders alienated their popular following by grasping greedily for the spoils of the Clarke administration. Morris, the leader of the opposition, salvaged his own career but ruined his reputation by accepting the governorship of New Jersey, which was separated from New York in 1738. James Alexander and William Smith were quietly reinstated to the bar in 1737. Within a few years of Zenger's trial, there was nothing in New York politics to show that the Morrisite opposition had ever existed. If it had truly sought to put New York politics on a popular basis, it had failed.

The role of the Zenger trial in the legal history of colonial New York was only slightly more significant. The case was not considered to have established a legal precedent, but it did have an important practical effect on the administration of the law of libel in the colony. It underlined the *power* (although not the *right*) of juries to return general verdicts and therefore to acquit men the judges thought were libelers, and, as a consequence, it rendered seditious libel prosecutions uncertain to succeed when they were unpopular, and hence limited their usefulness. Thus when in 1770 Alexander McDougall, a leader of the Sons of Liberty, was indicted by the Grand Jury for libeling the New York Assembly, his supporters arranged for the republication of the *Brief Narrative*. The result of this suggestion of a restaging of the Zenger trial was that the prosecution, on a convenient excuse, was dropped. Although the law remained as it had been stated by Attorney General Bradley and Chief Justice De Lancey, it was too obviously out of step with public feeling to be effective in jury trials.[80]

The Zenger trial, however, while it significantly contributed to neutralizing seditious libel in the armory of weapons used to restrict speech, by no means guaranteed respect for freedom of the press in colonial New York. In effect it transferred the location of the principal threat to free speech from the courts to the legislature. For the Assembly, standing upon its privileges and dignity, cowed printers and authors into a cautious exercise of their liberties by threatening to try them before its own bar, between 1747 and 1770.[81] Still, progress had been made, for it is one thing to be prosecuted and judged by one's elected representatives and quite another to be assailed by the surrogates of the Crown.

In England too the trial received considerable contemporary attention but created no legal precedent. Like the trial of the seven bishops in 1688, it was considered to be a politically motivated legal anomaly. More than thirty years after Hamilton's speech to the jury, Lord Mansfield and Sir William Blackstone were united in agreeing that freedom of the press meant no more than freedom from prior restraint subject to the subsequent punishment of the law.[82]

Not everyone agreed with Mansfield and Blackstone, however, and the demands for reform of the law of seditious libel became louder as the century grew older. Trenchard and Gordon, writing as Cato, had inaugurated the reform tradition as early as 1721, but the English counterpart of the Zenger trial did not occur until 1752, when a jury disregarded its instructions and returned a general verdict of not guilty in a case where publication was self-evident.[83] The subsequent trials of John Wilkes and the Dean of St. Asaph (in which Mansfield enunciated his famous dictum) dramatically illustrated the inadequacies of the law and aroused a widespread public dissatisfaction which finally resulted in the passage of a reform act in 1792.[84] Fox's Libel Act, as it was called, granted the jury the power to return a general verdict "upon the whole matter put in issue" and freed them from the obligation to find the defendant guilty "merely on the proof of the publication by such defendant."[85] This act brought English procedure into line with Hamilton's demands of 1735, but the substance of the law was not reformed until 1843, when Lord Campbell's Act proclaimed that truth could be pleaded in defense of a prosecution for seditious libel.[86] It was therefore more than a century after the Zenger trial that Hamilton's contentions were made law in England, and neither Hamilton nor the Zenger case appear to have been cited by the English reformers. English law had simply caught up with public feeling, which demanded a considerable freedom for the discussion of public affairs.[87]

Nor can it be shown that the Zenger case led to reform of the federal law of libel in post-Revolutionary America. So far as the federal government was concerned, the First Amendment's guarantee of the freedom of speech and the press proved to be insufficient protection for daring newspaper editors. Whatever the intentions of the framers, the amendment certainly failed to prohibit the federal courts from entertaining prosecutions for seditious libel under the Federalist Sedition Act of 1798. But it was, oddly enough, this law that introduced an important reform of the common law of libel, a reform that comprehended all the changes that had been demanded in the course of the century by critics of the harsh English tradition. Henceforth, decreed the Federalists, truth was a defense, juries could judge the law as well as the fact, and, what is more, the intent of the speaker (as well as the tendency of his speech) was a criterion for judging libelousness.[88]

But in this realization of Andrew Hamilton's principles his name was never mentioned and the safeguards he espoused were of little use to Jeffersonian critics of the Adams administration. Judges required defendants to prove the truth of their words rather than showing them to be false; they overawed partisan juries into returning convictions; and they frequently assumed the power to determine the criminality of the publications. Americans learned the lesson which the French Revolutionary disturbances had taught English believers in Fox's Libel Act—that juries and the standard of truth were not a reliable defense against *popular* prosecutions for seditious libel.

The Sedition Act lapsed with Federalist rule in 1800, but the Jeffersonians, who had developed a sophisticated philosophy of the freedom of the press during their years of persecution by the federal courts, themselves turned persecutors. The party of Jefferson mercilessly hunted down Federalist printers and brought them to trial for libel in the state courts. But when the Federalist-Jeffersonian animus died out in the early years of the new century, the federal government ceased to use its powers against the press. After 1800 there was no federal libel statute, and in 1812 the Supreme Court ruled that there was no criminal common law in the United States, so that the law employed against Zenger could never again be appealed to in the federal courts.[89]

The states, like the federal government, ceased to prosecute for seditious libel during the first half of the nineteenth century, but not before they had attempted to retain the common law crime. New York did not reform its antiquated libel laws until after the Revolution; the law remained as it had stood on April 19, 1775. The result was that when the Jeffersonians in 1804 brought a seditious libel charge against a Federalist newspaper editor, Harry Croswell, the truth of his publication could still not be advanced as an argument for his defense, nor could the jury decide the tendency of his words. Confronted with a Jeffersonian bench and jury, Croswell was convicted.

Alexander Hamilton was Croswell's lawyer, and while he conducted the defense in the spirit of his Philadelphia namesake, he discussed the Zenger case only in the appeal, and only to refute the lower court's use of De Lancey's charge to the jury as a precedent:

Zenger's case has been mentioned as an authority. A decision in a factious period, and reprobated at the very time.

A single precedent never forms the law. If in England it was fluctuating, can a colonial judge, of a remote colony, ever settle it? He cannot fix in New York what was not fixed in Great Britain. It was merely one more precedent to a certain course of practice . . . Why are our courts to be bound down by the weight of only one precedent? . . . This is to make the colonial precedent of more weight than is in England allowed to a precedent of Westminster Hall.[90]

Hamilton defended the standard of truth, suggesting that a proper definition of permissible speech was "truth, with good motives, for justifiable ends." The higher court sustained him and freed Croswell.

So convincing was Hamilton's argument for reform of the common law of libel in the Croswell case that the state legislature incorporated his definition of free speech in its statute of 1805. Thus, seventy years later, the Morrisite defense of Zenger, which had been bad law in 1735, became good law in New York—although the Zenger case itself had been cited only negatively, to argue that De Lancey's pronouncement had not created a precedent. During the course of the nineteenth century, virtually all the states of the union accepted this Hamiltonian definition of freedom of the press.

viii

Thus the Zenger case did not directly further the development either of political liberty or of freedom of the press in America. The Morrisite party was a self-interested political faction which truly represented neither "freedom" nor "the popular cause." Zenger's acquittal marked one of its few significant political victories, and it ceased to exist a year after the trial. Likewise, although the Morrisites got Zenger off, Alexander and Hamilton were unable to change the law of libel. The case did not set a legal precedent, though the New York press benefited from public recognition of the power of a jury to return a general verdict, which in fact made future seditious libel prosecutions too risky for governors to attempt.

The fame of the case is, however, by no means undeserved, for the arguments brought forward in Zenger's defense represent an early appreciation of the emerging popular basis of American politics, full recognition of which would ultimately lead to reforms both of politics and law. In pursuit of their narrow aims the Morrisites articulated the connection between law and politics in a popularly based society. The colonial New York law, so accurately stated by Bradley, De Lancey, and Anglo-Americanus, was based upon the premise that the state, in the form of the Crown and its servants, was sovereign and immune from criticism. The law as the Morrisites propounded it was posited on the diametrically opposed notion that the government was the servant of the people and that open criticism was one of the important ways in which magistrates could be kept responsible to them. Hamilton, while apparently contending that the law was on his side, was actually arguing that it ought to be so. Thus Hamilton, Alexander, and Anglo-Americanus were agreed that the issue was one of political theory rather than law, but their conceptions of politics conflicted since one was based on English and the other on American political experience. Contemporary New Yorkers fleetingly glimpsed this distinction and, moved by the Morrisite rhetoric, acquitted Peter Zenger. The theory was too advanced for the time, however, and could not be realized in continuing political action or incorporated into law in 1735.

Because of the insight it stimulated into the popular aspect of American political life, the Zenger case has always served as a useful symbol of the development of political freedom in America. Whenever the popular basis of politics has appeared to be threatened, Alexander's pamphlet has been recalled, and the unassuming and unheroic Zenger has come to symbolize the idea that personal freedom rests upon the individual's right to criticize his government.

Thus the Zenger case, though it did not directly ensure the freedom of the press, prefigured that revolution "in the hearts and minds of the people" which was to make an ideal of 1735 an American reality, and it has served repeatedly to remind Americans of the debt free men owe to free speech.

A NOTE ON THE TEXT

A LETTER from Andrew Hamilton to James Alexander sheds some light on the composition of the *Brief Narrative*. Writing on March 18, 1736, Hamilton reported that he was sending Alexander the draft of "Mr. Zenger's trial." "When I first wrote you I intended to revise it by my notes but being interrupted with business I neglected and at last being in hopes that you was not like to obtain Mr. Chambers' and Mr. Atty.'s argument, your design of publication was over." Alexander was apparently pressing him for his account of the trial, however, and Hamilton therefore sent it, "ill done as it is," rereading it only once. He asked Alexander to "alter and correct it agreeable to your own mind," and requested that Captain Norris, Lewis Morris' son-in-law, "correct the language for it wants much." [1]

The idea of publishing a report of the trial was therefore doubtless Alexander's, and most of the composition was probably his. The account of the exceptions to the Supreme Court judges' commissions, for instance, uses the same text as does the *New York Weekly Journal,* which Alexander was almost certainly composing during Zenger's imprisonment.[2] The account of the trial itself, however, is quite different than the *Journal*'s, and it is probably Alexander's reworking of Hamilton's rough draft.[3]

On September 27, 1735, Zenger announced that the *Brief Narrative* was in the press, and would be published "with all imaginable speed," but Hamilton's delay in preparing his notes set the publication date back by many months. The *Journal* of June 21, 1736, advertised the pamphlet as "just published." It was soon reprinted in Boston and circulated throughout the English colonies in North America. At the same time it was extensively distributed in England. Four or five editions were published in London in 1738, the year in which *Areopagitica* was reprinted for the first time.[4]

Interest in the *Brief Narrative* did not die with the Zenger affair. It was reprinted fifteen times before the end of the century, and is surely deserving of its reputation as "the most famous publication issued in America before the *Farmer's Letters*."[5] Its reappearance after the 1730's increasingly marked stages in the struggle for freedom of speech or for popular government. Its republication in London in 1752 was part of the defense of William Owen against the charge of seditious libel, and in 1765 accounts of the two trials were published in a single pamphlet, while the seditious libels of John Wilkes were still being actively discussed.

Similarly, the second New York edition of the *Brief Narrative* was published by John Holt in 1770 during the abortive attempt to convict Alexander McDougall of a seditious libel against the New York Assembly. Holt's *New York Journal,* the namesake of Zenger's paper, defended McDougall by asserting the principles of Andrew Hamilton against the "infamous Star Chamber doctrine of libels" which "Liberty herself, in the form of ZENGER," had destroyed.[6] After the Revolution the republication of the pamphlet continued to mark such occasions. When Sir Thomas Erskine, the foremost English reformer, conducted a brilliant defense of the Dean of St. Asaph in a 1784 seditious libel trial, his reward was the publication of an edition of the *Brief Narrative* inscribed in his honor. And a reissue in Boston in 1799 expressed the reaction of Jeffersonian newspaper editors to John Adams' Sedition Act.

In nineteenth-century America the *Brief Narrative* suffered an eclipse, but it has re-emerged strongly since the turn of our own century.[7] Livingston Rutherfurd, a descendant of James Alexander, produced a book on the Zenger case in 1904 which included a literal reprint of the 1736 edition of the pamphlet. The Works Progress Administration turned out a manifold reproduction in 1940, and the Rutherfurd edition was reprinted in 1941.[8] Interest continued in the post-World War II era, when the concern for internal subversion once more threatened to restrict the freedom of speech: new editions of the *Brief Narrative* were issued in 1954 and 1957.[9]

The present edition supplements the *Brief Narrative* with the other major documents of the Zenger case. It is also the first to attempt a full identification of the documents, people, and ideas that appear in the pamphlet. It seeks in this way to explain the case more completely than before by restoring it to its original context.

Since the Rutherfurd edition continues to provide an accurate literal text, in the present edition the spelling and capitalization have been modernized, and the punctuation somewhat simplified, in order to provide a more readable text. Obvious petty errors of typography have been silently corrected; however, Zenger's prolific italicization has been left unchanged except where it was used to refer only to direct quotations (now enclosed in quotation marks) or to proper names.[10] The original footnotes are indicated by asterisks and appear at the foot of the page; the present editor's notes are specified by arabic numerals and appear as a group at the end of the book. Specific references to the *Brief Narrative* are always to the volume in hand. Legal citations have been expanded to recognizable length, but have been left in legal form; all other references are in standard scholarly form. All dates are written as though the new year began on January 1 rather than March 25, as in the old style. Thus, March 15, 1733/4 becomes March 15, 1734. The editor's additions to the original notes are enclosed in square brackets; square brackets in the text, however, enclose original writing. The indented bracketed passages in the text of the *Brief Narrative* are James Alexander's explanatory comments on the events described in the narrative of the trial, inserted so as to leave the legal arguments unimpeded. The Latin translations have been made by Bernard S. Smith.

Permission to reprint the *Brief Narrative* and the various items in the appendices has been gratefully received from the Rare Book and Manuscript Divisions, New York Public Library, and Mr. John Rutherfurd; from the New-York Historical Society; from the Rare Book Division, Library of Congress; and from the Commonwealth Fund.

A Brief Narrative of the Case and Trial of

JOHN PETER ZENGER

Printer of The New York Weekly Journal

A Brief Narrative of the Case and Trial of

JOHN PETER ZENGER

Printer of The New York Weekly Journal[1]

As there was but one printer in the Province of New York that printed a public newspaper, I was in hopes, if I undertook to publish another, I might make it worth my while; and I soon found my hopes were not groundless: My first paper was printed November 5th, 1733, and I continued printing and publishing of them, I thought to the satisfaction of everybody, till the January following; when the Chief Justice[2] was pleased to animadvert upon the doctrine of libels, in a long charge given in that term to the Grand Jury, and afterwards on the third Tuesday of October 1734 was again pleased to charge the Grand Jury in the following words:

Gentlemen; I shall conclude with reading a paragraph or two out of the same book concerning libels; they are arrived to that height that they call loudly for your animadversion; it is high time to put a stop to them; for at the rate things are now carried on, when all order and government is endeavored to be trampled on; reflections are cast upon persons of all degrees, must not these things end in sedition, if not timely prevented? Lenity, you have seen will not avail, it becomes you then to enquire after the offenders, that we may in a due course of law be enabled to punish them. If you, Gentlemen, do not interpose, consider whether the ill consequences that may arise from any disturbances of the public peace may not in part lie at your door?

Hawkins, in his chapter of libels,[3] considers three points: *1st. What shall be said to be a libel. 2ndly. Who are liable to be punished for it. 3rdly. In what manner they are to be punished.* Under the 1st. he says, § 7. *Nor can there be any doubt but that a writing which defames a private person only is as much a libel as that which defames persons entrusted in a public capacity, in as much as it manifestly tends to create ill blood, and to cause a disturbance of the public peace; however, it is certain that it is a very high aggravation of a libel that it tends to scandalize the government, by reflecting on those who are entrusted with the administration of public affairs, which does not only endanger the public peace, as all other libels do, by stirring up the parties immediately concerned in it to acts of revenge, but also has a direct tendency to breed in the people a dislike of their governors, and incline them to faction and sedition.* As to the 2nd point he says, § 10. *It is certain, not only he who composes or procures another to compose it but also that he who publishes, or procures another to publish it, are in danger of being punished for it; and it is said not to be material whether he who disperses a libel knew anything of the contents or effects of it or not; for nothing could be more easy than to publish the most virulent papers with the greatest security if the concealing the purport of them from an illiterate publisher would make him safe in the dispersing them: Also, it has been said that if he who hath either read a libel himself or hath heard it read by another do afterwards maliciously read or report any part of it in the presence of others, or lend or show it to another, he is guilty of an unlawful publication of it. Also, it hath been holden that the copying of a libel shall be a conclusive evidence of the publication of it, unless the party can prove that he delivered it to a magistrate to examine it, in which case the act* subsequent *is said to explain the intention* precedent. *But it seems to be the better opinion that he who first writes a libel, dictated by another, is thereby guilty of making of it, and consequently punishable for the bare writing; for it was no libel till it was reduced to writing.*

These, Gentlemen, are some of the offenses which are to make part of your enquiries; and if any other should arise in the course of your proceedings, in which you are at a loss or conceive any doubts, upon your application here, we will assist and direct you.

The Grand Jury not indicting me as was expected, the gentlemen of the Council proceeded to take my *Journals* into consideration, and sent the following message to the Grand Assembly:

Die Jovis, 3 ho. P.M. *17th of* October, 1734.[4]

A message from the Council by Philip Cortlandt, in these words, *to wit.*

That Board having had several of Zenger's *New York Weekly Journals* laid before them, and other scurrilous papers, tending to alienate the affections of the people of this Province from His Majesty's government, to raise seditions and tumults among the people of this Province, and to fill their minds with a contempt of His Majesty's government: And considering the pernicious consequences that may attend such growing evils, if not speedily and effectually put a stop to. And conceiving that the most likely method to put a stop to such bold and seditious practices, to maintain the dignity of His Majesty's government, and to preserve the peace thereof, would be by a conference between a committe of this Board, and a committee of the Assembly; it is therefore ordered, That the gentlemen of this Board, NOW ASSEMBLED, or any seven of them, be a committee to join a committee of the House of Representatives in order to confer together, and to examine and enquire into the said papers and the authors and writers thereof.

Which message being read.

Ordered, That the members of this House, or any fourteen of them, do meet a committee of the Council at the time and place therein mentioned.

Die Veneris, 9 ho. A.M. 18 October, 1734.[5]

Mr. Garretson from the committee of this House reported that they last night met the committee of the Council on the subject matter of their message of yesterday to this House; and that after several preliminaries between the said committees, the gentlemen of the Council reduced to writing what they requested of this House and delivered the same to the chairman, who delivered it in at the table, and being read, is in the words following:

At a committee of the Council held the 17th of October, 1734.

PRESENT [6]

Mr. Clarke	Mr. Livingston	Mr. Cortlandt
Mr. Harison	Mr. Kennedy	Mr. Lane
Dr. Colden	Mr. *Chief Justice*	Mr. Horsmanden

Gentlemen;

The matters we request your concurrence in are that Zenger's papers, No. 7, 47, 48, 49, which were read, and which we now deliver, be burnt by the hands of the Common Hangman, as containing in them many things derogatory of the dignity of His Majesty's government, reflecting upon the legislature, upon the most considerable persons in the most distinguished stations in the Province, and tending to raise seditions and tumults among the people thereof.[7]

That you concur with us in the addressing the Governor to issue his proclamation, with a promise of reward for the discovery of the authors or writers of these seditious libels.

That you concur with us in an order for prosecuting the printer thereof.

That you concur with us in an order to the Magistrates to exert themselves in the execution of their offices, in order to preserve the public peace of the Province.

By Order of the Committee. Fred. Morris, Cl. Con.

Mr. Garretson delivered likewise to the House the several papers referred to in the said request.

Ordered, That the said papers be lodged with the Clerk of this House, and that the consideration thereof and the said request be referred till Tuesday next.

Die Martis, 9 ho. A.M. 22 October, 1734.[8]

The House according to order proceeded to take into consideration the request of a committee of Council delivered to a committee of this House on the 16th instant, as likewise of the several papers therein referred to. And after several debates upon the subject matters, it was *Ordered* THAT THE SAID PAPERS AND REQUEST LIE ON THE TABLE.

The Council finding the General Assembly would not do anything about it, they sent the following message to the House:

Die Sabbati, 9 ho. A.M. 2 November, 1734.[9]

A message from the Council by Mr. Livingston, desiring this House to return by him to that Board the several seditious *Journals* of Zenger's No. 7, 47, 48, 49, which were delivered by a committee of that Board to a committee of this House, the 17th of October last, together with the proposals of the committee of that Board delivered therewith to a committee of this House; and then withdrew.

On Tuesday the 5th of November, 1734, the Quarter Sessions[10] for the City of New York began when the Sheriff delivered to the Court AN ORDER, which was read in these words:

At a Council held at Fort George, in New York, the 2nd of November, 1734.

PRESENT

His Excellency William Cosby, Captain General and Governor-in-Chief, etc.

Mr. Clarke	Mr. Livingston	Mr. Cortlandt
Mr. Harison	Mr. Kennedy	Mr. Lane
Dr. Colden *	Mr. *Chief Justice*	Mr. Horsmanden

Whereas by an order of this Board of this day some of John Peter Zenger's Journals, entitled The New York Weekly Journal, containing the freshest advices, foreign and domestic, *No.* 7, 47, 48, 49, *were ordered to be burnt by the hands of the Common Hangman, or Whipper, near the pillory in this city, on Wednesday the 6th instant, between the hours of eleven and twelve in the forenoon, as containing in them many things tending to sedition and faction, to bring His Majesty's government into contempt and to disturb the peace thereof, and containing in them likewise, not only reflections upon His Excellency the Governor in particular, the legislature in general, but also upon the most considerable persons in the most distinguished stations in this Province. It is therefore ordered that the Mayor and Magistrates of this city do attend at the burning of the several papers or Journals aforesaid, numbered as above mentioned.* Fred. Morris, D. Cl. Con.

To Robert Lurting, Esq., Mayor of the City of New York, and the rest of the Magistrates for the said City and County.

Upon reading of which ORDER, the Court forbad the entering thereof in their books at that time, and many of them declared that if it should be entered, they would have their protest entered against it.

On Wednesday the 6th of November the Sheriff of New York moved the Court of Quarter Sessions to comply with the said order, upon which one of the Aldermen offered a protest, which was read by the Clerk and approved of by all the Aldermen, either expressly or by not objecting to it, and is as followeth:

Whereas an ORDER has been served on this Court, in these words.

[The order as above inserted.]

And whereas this Court conceives they are only to be commanded by the King's mandatory writs, authorized by law, to which they conceive

* N.B. Doctor Colden was that day at Esopus [now Kingston, N.Y.], 90 miles from New York, though mentioned as present in Council.

they have the right of showing cause why they don't obey them, if they believe them improper to be obeyed, or by ORDERS, which have some known laws to authorize them; and whereas this Court conceives THIS ORDER to be no mandatory writ warranted by law, nor knows of no law that authorizes the making the order aforesaid; so they think themselves under no obligation to obey it: Which obedience, they think, would be in them an opening a door for arbitrary commands, which, when once opened, they know not what dangerous consequences may attend it. Wherefore this Court conceives itself bound in duty (for the preservation of the rights of this Corporation, and as much as they can, the liberty of the press, and the people of the Province, since an Assembly of the Province and several Grand Juries have refused to meddle with the papers when applied to by the Council) *to protest against the* ORDER *aforesaid and to forbid all the members of this Corporation to pay any obedience to it,* until it be shown to this Court that the same is authorized by some known law, which they neither know nor believe that it is.

Upon reading of which, it was required of the Honorable Francis Harison, Recorder of this Corporation, and one of the members of the Council (present at making said order) to show by what law or authority the said ORDER was made; upon which he spoke in support of it, and cited the case of Doctor Sacheverell's sermon, which was by the House of Lords ordered to be burnt by the hands of the Hangman, and that the Mayor and Aldermen of London should attend the doing of it, To which one of the Aldermen answered to this purpose; That he conceived the case was no ways parallel, because Doctor Sacheverell and his sermon were impeached by the House of Commons of England, which is the Grand Jury of the nation, and representative of the whole people of England: That this their impeachment they prosecuted before the House of Lords, the greatest court of justice of Britain and which beyond memory of man has had cognizance of things of that nature, that there Sacheverell had a fair hearing in defense of himself and of his sermon. And after that fair hearing, he and his sermon were justly, fairly and legally condemned; that he had read the case of Dr. Sacheverell, and thought he could charge his memory that the judgment of the House of Lords in that case was that the Mayor and Sheriffs of London and Middlesex only should attend the burning of the sermon, and not the Aldermen; and farther he remembered that the order upon that judgment was only directed to the Sheriffs of London, and not even to the Mayor, who did not attend the doing it; and farther said that would Mr. Recorder show that the Governor and Council had such authority as the House of Lords, and that the papers ordered to be burnt were in like manner legally prosecuted and condemned, there the case of Doctor Sacheverell might be to the purpose; but without showing that, it rather proved that a censure ought not to be pronounced till a fair trial by a competent and legal authority were first had.[11] Mr. Recorder was desired to produce the books from whence he cited his authorities, that the Court might judge of them themselves, and was told that if he could produce sufficient authorities to warrant *this* ORDER, they would readily obey it, but otherwise not. Upon which he said he did not carry his books about with him. To which it was answered, he might send for them or order a Constable to fetch them. Upon which he arose and at the lower end of the table he mentioned that Bishop Burnet's pastoral letter was ordered by the House of Lords to be burnt by the High Bailiff of Westminster; upon which he abruptly went away, without waiting for an answer or promising to bring his books, and did not return sitting the Court.[12]

After Mr. Recorder's departure, it was moved that the *protest* should be entered; to which it was answered that the *protest* could not be entered without entering also the ORDER, and it was not fit to take any notice of IT, and therefore it was proposed that no notice should be taken in their books of either, which was unanimously agreed to by the Court.

The Sheriff then moved that the Court would direct their Whipper to perform the said ORDER; to which it was answered that as he was the officer of the Corporation, they would give no such *order*. Soon after which the Court adjourned, and did not attend the burning of the papers. Afterwards about noon, the Sheriff after reading the numbers of the several papers which were ordered to be burnt, delivered them unto the hands of his own Negro, and ordered him to put them into the fire, which he did, at which Mr.

Recorder, Jeremiah Dunbar, Esq., and several of the officers of the garrison attended.[13]

On the Lord's Day the 17th of November, 1734, I was taken and imprisoned by virtue of a warrant in these words:

At a Council held at Fort George in New York, the 2nd day of November, 1734.

PRESENT

His Excellency William Cosby, Captain General and Governor-in-Chief, etc.

Mr. Clarke	Mr. Kennedy	Mr. Lane
Mr. Harison	*Chief Justice*	Mr. Horsmanden
Mr. Livingston	Mr. Cortlandt	

It is ordered that the Sheriff for the City of New York do forthwith take and apprehend John Peter Zenger for printing and publishing several seditious libels, dispersed throughout his *Journals* or newspapers entitled *The New York Weekly Journal, containing the freshest advices, foreign and domestic;* as having in them many things tending to raise factions and tumults among the people of this Province, inflaming their minds with contempt of His Majesty's government, and greatly disturbing the peace thereof; and upon his taking said John Peter Zenger, *to commit him to the prison or common gaol of the said City and County.*

Fred. Morris, D. Cl. Con.

And being by virtue of that warrant so imprisoned in the gaol, I was for several days denied the use of pen, ink and paper, and the liberty of speech with any persons.—Upon my commitment, some friends soon got a *habeas corpus* to bring me before the Chief Justice, in order to my discharge or being bailed; on the return whereof, on Wednesday the 20th of November, my counsel delivered exceptions to the return, and the Chief Justice ordered them to be argued publicly at the City Hall on the Saturday following.

On Saturday the 23rd of November the said exceptions came to be argued by James Alexander and William Smith of counsel for me, and by Mr. Attorney General and Mr. Warrel[14] of counsel against me, in presence of some hundreds of the inhabitants; where my counsel (saving the benefit of exception to the illegality of the warrant) insisted that I might be admitted to reasonable bail. And to show that it was my right to be so, they offered *Magna Charta, The Petition of Right* 3 Car., *The Habeas Corpus Act* of 31 Car. 2, which directs the sum in which bail is to be taken to be "according to the quality of the prisoner, and nature of the offense." Also 2nd Hawkins, Cap. 15 § 5, in these words, "But Justices must take care that under pretense of demanding sufficient security they do not make so excessive a demand as in effect amounts to a denial of bail; for this is looked on as a great grievance, and is complained of as such by 1 W. & M. Sess. 2nd, by which it is declared *that excessive bail ought not to be required.*"[15] It was also shown that the seven bishops, who in King James the IInd's time were charged with the like crime that I stood charged with, were admitted to bail on their own recognizances, the Archbishop in £200 and each of the other six in £100 apiece only. Sundry other authorities and arguments were produced and insisted on by my counsel to prove my right to be admitted to moderate bail, and to such bail as was in my power to give; and sundry parts of history they produced to show how much the requiring excessive bail had been resented by Parliament. And in order to enable the Court to judge what surety was in my power to give, I made affidavit *that* (*my debts paid*) *I was not worth forty pounds* (*the tools of my trade and wearing apparel excepted*).

Some warm expressions (to say no worse of them) were dropped on this occasion, sufficiently known and resented by the auditory, which for my part I desire may be buried in oblivion: Upon the whole it was *ordered that I might be admitted to bail, myself in £400 with two sureties, each in £200 and that I should be remanded till I gave it.* And as this was ten times more than was in my power to countersecure any person in giving bail for me, I conceived I could not ask any to become my bail on these terms; and therefore I returned to gaol, where I lay until Tuesday the 28th of January, 1735, being the last day of that term; and the Grand Jury having found nothing against me, I expected to have been discharged from my imprisonment: But my hopes proved vain; for the Attorney General then charged me by *information* for printing and publishing parts of my *Journals* No. 13 and 23 as being *false, scandalous, malicious, and seditious.*[16]

To this information my counsel appeared and offered exceptions, leaving a blank for inserting the judges' commissions, which the Court were of opinion not to receive till those blanks were filled up. In the succeeding vacation the judges gave copies of their commissions; and on Tuesday the 15th of April last, the first day of the succeeding term, my counsel offered these exceptions; which were as follows:

The Attorney General, *v.* John Peter Zenger	On information for a misdemeanor.

Exceptions humbly offered by John Peter Zenger to the Honorable James De Lancey, Esq., to judge in this cause.

The Defendant comes and prays hearing of the commission by virtue of which the Honorable James De Lancey, Esq., claims the power and authority to judge in this cause, and it is read to him in these words:

George the Second, by the grace of God, of Great Britain, France and Ireland, King, Defender of the Faith, etc. To our trusty and well beloved James De Lancey, Esq. We reposing special trust and confidence in your integrity, ability and learning, have assigned, constituted and appointed, and we do by these presents assign constitute and appoint you the said James De Lancey, to be Chief Justice in and over our Province of New York, in America, in the room of Lewis Morris, Esq., giving and by these presents granting unto you full power and lawful authority to hear try and determine all pleas whatsoever, civil, criminal and mixed, according to the laws, statutes and customs of our Kingdom of England, and the laws and usages of our said Province of New York not being repugnant thereto, and executions of all judgments of the said Court to award and to make such rules and orders in the said Court as may be found convenient and useful, and as near as may be agreeable to the rules and orders of our Courts of King's Bench, Common Pleas, and Exchequer in England. To have hold and enjoy the said office or place of Chief Justice in and over our said Province, with all and singular the rights, privileges, profits and advantages, salaries, fees and perquisites unto the said place belonging, or in any ways appertaining, in as full and ample manner as any person heretofore Chief Justice of our said Province hath held and enjoyed, or of right ought to have held and enjoyed the same, to you the said James De Lancey, Esq., for and DURING OUR WILL AND PLEASURE. In testimony whereof we have caused these our letters to be made patent, and the great seal of our Province of New York to be hereunto affixed. Witness our trusty and well beloved WILLIAM COSBY, Esq., our Captain General and Governor-in-Chief of our Provinces of New York, New Jersey, and the territories thereon depending in America, Vice-Admiral of the same, and Colonel in our Army, at Fort George in New York, the twenty-first day of August, in the seventh year of our reign, *Anno Domini* 1733.

Which being read and heard, the said John Peter Zenger, by protestation not confessing nor submitting to the power of any other person to judge in this cause, doth except to the power of the Honorable James De Lancey, Esq., aforesaid to judge in this cause, by virtue of the commission aforesaid, for these reasons, *viz.*

1st. For that the authority of a judge of the King's Bench in that part of Great Britain called England by which the cognizance of this cause is claimed is by the said commission granted to the Honorable James De Lancey, Esq., aforesaid, only *during pleasure;* whereas that authority (by a statute in that case made and provided) ought to be granted *during good behavior.*

2nd. For that by the said commission, the jurisdiction and authority of a justice of the Court of Common Pleas at Westminster in that part of Great Britain called England is granted to the said James De Lancey, Esq., which jurisdiction and authority cannot be granted to, and exercised by, any one of the justices of the King's Bench.

3rd. For that the form of the said commission is not founded on nor warranted by the common law, nor any statute of England, nor of Great Britain, nor any act of Assembly of this colony.

4th. For that it appears by the commission aforesaid that the same is granted under the seal of this colony by His Excellency William Cosby, Esq., Governor thereof; and it appears not that the same was granted, neither was the same granted, by and with the advice and consent of His Majesty's Council of this colony; without which advice and consent, His Excellency could not grant the same.

Wherefore, and for many other defects in the said commission, this Defendant humbly hopes that the Honorable James De Lancey, Esq., will not take cognizance of this cause by virtue of the commission aforesaid.

Was signed, {James Alexander.
William Smith.

The exceptions to the commission of the Honorable Frederick Philipse, Esq., were the same with the foregoing, including therein his commission, which is in these words:

George the Second, by the grace of God, of Great Britain, France and Ireland, King, Defender of the Faith, etc. To our trusty and well beloved Frederick Philipse, Esq., Greeting: Whereas it is our care that justice be duly administered to our subjects within our Province of New York and territories thereon depending in America; and we reposing especial confidence in your integrity, ability and learning, have assigned, constituted and appointed, and we do by these presents assign, constitute and appoint you the said Frederick Philipse to be Second Justice of our Supreme Court of Judicature for our Province of New York, in the room of James De Lancey, Esq., giving and granting unto you the said Frederick Philipse full power and authority, with our other justices of our said Supreme Court, to hear, try and determine, all pleas whatsoever, civil, criminal and mixed, according to the laws, statutes and customs of our Kingdom of England, and the laws and usages of our said Province of New York not being repugnant thereto, and executions of all judgments of the said Court to award and to act and do all things which any of our *justices of either Bench, or Baron of the Exchequer in our said Kingdom of England* may or ought to do; and also to assist in the making such rules and orders in our said Court as shall be for the good and benefit of our said Province; and as near as conveniently may be to the rules and orders of our said Courts in our said Kingdom of England: To have, hold and enjoy the said office or place of Second Justice of our said Province of New York, together with all and singular the rights, privileges, salaries, fees, perquisites, profits and advantages thereto, now or at any time heretofore belonging, or in any wise of right appertaining; unto you the said Frederick Philipse, for and *during our pleasure*. In testimony whereof, we have caused these our letters to be made patent, and the great seal of our said Province of New York to be hereunto affixed. Witness our trusty and well beloved WILLIAM COSBY, Esq., our Captain General and Governor-in-Chief of our Provinces of New York, New Jersey, and territories thereon depending in America, Vice-Admiral of the same, and Colonel of our Army, etc., at Fort George in New York, the twenty-first day of August, in the seventh year of our reign, *Anno Domini* 1733. Fred. Morris, D. Secry.

Tuesday the 15th of April, 1735.

Mr. Alexander offered the above exceptions to the Court, and prayed that they might be filed. Upon this the Chief Justice said to Mr. Alexander and Mr. Smith that they ought well to consider the consequences of what they offered; to which both answered that they had well considered what they offered and all the consequences. And Mr. Smith added that he was so well satisfied of *the right of the subject to take an exception to the commission of a judge, if he thought such commission illegal*—that he durst venture his life upon *that point*. As to *the validity of the exceptions* then offered, he said he took that to be *a second point;* but was ready to argue them both if their Honors were pleased to hear him. To which the Chief Justice replied that he would consider the exceptions in the morning; and ordered the Clerk to bring them to him.

Wednesday, the 16th April, 1735.

The Chief Justice delivered one of the exceptions to the Clerk, and Justice Philipse the other, upon which Mr. Smith arose and asked the judges whether their Honors would hear him upon these two points.* *1st. That the subject has a right to take such exceptions if they judged the commissions illegal. 2ndly. That the exceptions tendered were legal and valid.* To which the Chief Justice said that they would neither hear nor allow the exceptions; *for* (said he) *you thought to have gained a great deal of applause and popularity by opposing this Court, as you did the Court of Exchequer; but you have brought it to that point that either* we must go from the bench, or you from the bar: *Therefore we exclude you and Mr. Alexander from the bar;* and delivered a paper to the Clerk and ordered it to be entered, which the Clerk entered accordingly and returned the paper to the Chief Justice; after which the Chief Justice ordered the Clerk to read publicly what he had written; an attested copy whereof follows:

At a Supreme Court of Judicature held for the Province of New York at the City Hall of the City of New York on Wednesday, the 16th day of April, 1735.

* This first point is largely treated on in the arguments of Van Dam's counsel, in support of their plea to the jurisdiction of the Supreme Court, printed here above a year before that, from page 14 to 35, to which no answer has as yet appeared; which argument contains also some part of the arguments necessary to support the 2nd point. [See the Introduction, n. 20.]

PRESENT

The Honorable James De Lancey, Esq., Chief Justice.
The Honorable Frederick Philipse, Esq., Second Justice.

James Alexander, Esq., and William Smith, attorneys of this Court, having presumed (notwithstanding they were forewarned by the Court of their DISPLEASURE if they should do it) *to sign, and having actually signed and put into Court, exceptions in the name of John Peter Zenger; thereby denying the legality of the judges their commissions; though in the usual form* and the being of this Supreme Court. *It is therefore ordered that for the said contempt, the said James Alexander and William Smith be excluded from any farther practice in this Court, and that their names be struck out of the roll of attorneys of this Court.*

per Cur'. James Lyne. Cl.

After the order of the Court was read, Mr. Alexander asked whether it was the order of Mr. Justice Philipse as well as of the Chief Justice? To which both answered that it was their order; upon which Mr. Alexander added that it was proper to ask that question *that they might know how to have their relief:* He farther observed to the Court, upon reading of the order, that they were mistaken in their wording of it, because the exceptions were *only to their commissions,* and *not to the being of the Court* as is therein alleged; and prayed that the order might be altered accordingly. The Chief Justice said they conceived the exceptions were against the being of the Court. Both Mr. Alexander and Mr. Smith denied that they were, and prayed the Chief Justice to point to the place that contained such exception; and further added that the Court might well exist though the commissions of all the judges were void; which the Chief Justice confessed to be true: And therefore they prayed again that the order in that point might be altered; but it was denied.

Then Mr. Alexander desired to know whether they *overruled* or *rejected* the exceptions; the Chief Justice said he did not understand the difference; to which said Alexander replied that if he *rejected* the exceptions, then they could not appear upon the proceedings, and in that case the Defendant was entitled to have them made part of the proceedings by bill of exceptions: But if they *overruled* them, then by so doing they only declared them not sufficient to hinder them from proceeding by virtue of those commissions, and the exceptions would remain as records of the Court, and ought to be entered on the record of the cause as part of the proceedings. The Chief Justice said they must remain upon the file to warrant what we have done; as to being part of the record of the proceedings in that cause, he said, you may speak to that point tomorrow.

Friday, April 18th, 1735.

Mr. Alexander signified to the Court that on Wednesday last their Honors had said that the counsel for Zenger might speak to the point concerning the *rejecting* or *overruling* of Zenger's exceptions on the morrow: To which the Chief Justice answered that he said, *You may get some person to speak to that point on the morrow, not meaning that the said Alexander should speak to it, that being contrary to the order.* Both Mr. Alexander and Mr. Smith said they understood it otherwise.

They both also mentioned that it was a doubt whether by the words of the order they were debarred of their practice as counsel as well as attorneys, whereas they practiced in both capacities? To which the Chief Justice answered that the order was plain, *that James Alexander, Esq., and William Smith were debarred and excluded from their whole practice at this bar, and that the order was intended to bar their acting both as counsel and as attorneys, and that it could not be construed otherwise.* And it being asked Mr. Philipse whether he understood the order so; he answered that he did.

Upon this exclusion of my counsel I petitioned the Court to order counsel for my defense, who thereon appointed John Chambers, Esq., who pleaded *not guilty* for me to the information. But as to the point *whether my exceptions should be part of the record as was moved by my former counsel,* Mr. Chambers thought not proper to speak to it; Mr. Chambers also moved that a certain day in the next term might be appointed for my trial, and for *a struck jury;* whereupon my trial was ordered to be on Monday the 4th of August, and the Court would consider till the first day of next term whether I should have a struck jury or not, and ordered that the Sheriff should in the meantime, at my charge, return the Freeholders' Book.

At a Supreme Court of Judicature held for the Province of New York, before the Honorable James De Lancey, Esq., Chief Justice of the said Province; and the Honorable Frederick Philipse, Esq., Second Justice of the said Province.

On Tuesday the 29th of July, 1735, the Court opened, and *on motion of Mr. Chambers for a struck jury pursuant to the rule of the preceding term, the Court were of opinion that I was entitled to have a struck jury;* and that evening at five of the clock some of my friends attended the Clerk for striking the jury; when to their surprise, the Clerk instead of producing the Freeholders' Book to strike the jury out of it in their presence as usual, he produced a list of 48 persons, who, he said he had taken out of the Freeholders' Book; my friends told him, that a great number of these persons were not freeholders; that others were persons holding commissions and offices at the Governor's pleasure; that others were of the late displaced Magistrates of this city, who must be supposed to have resentment against me for what I had printed concerning them; that others were the Governor's baker, tailor, shoemaker, candlemaker, joiner, etc.; that as to the few indifferent men that were upon the list, they had reason to believe (as they had heard) that Mr. Attorney had a list of them, to strike them out; and therefore requested that he would either bring the Freeholders' Book and choose out of it 48 unexceptionable men in their presence, as usual; or else that he would hear their objections particularly to the list he offered, and that he would put impartial men in the place of those against whom they could show just objections. Notwithstanding this, the Clerk refused to strike the jury out of the Freeholders' Book, and refused to hear any objections to the persons on his list, but told my friends, if any objections they had to any persons, they might strike those persons out; to which they answered, there would not remain a jury if they struck out all the exceptionable men, and according to the custom they had only a right to strike out 12.

But finding no arguments could prevail with the Clerk to hear their objections to his list, nor to strike the jury as usual, Mr. Chambers told him he must apply to the Court, which the next morning he did, and the Court upon his motion *ordered that the 48 should be struck out of the Freeholders' Book as usual, in the presence of the parties, and that the Clerk should hear objections to persons proposed to be of the 48, and allow of such exceptions as were just.* In pursuance of that order a jury was that evening struck, to the satisfaction of both parties, though my friends and counsel insisted on no objections but *want of freehold;* and though they did not insist that Mr. Attorney General (who was assisted by Mr. Blagge)[17] should show any particular cause against any persons he disliked, but acquiesced that *any person he disliked* should be left out of the 48.

Before James De Lancey, Esq., Chief Justice of the Province of New York, and Frederick Philipse, Second Judge, came on my trial, on the fourth day of August, 1735, upon an information for printing and publishing two newspapers, which were called libels against our Governor and his administration.

The Defendant John Peter Zenger being called appeared.

And the Sheriff returned his *venire*[18] for the trial of the said cause.

Mr. Chambers, of counsel for the Defendant. I humbly move Your Honors that we may have justice done by the Sheriff, and that he may return the names of the jurors in the same order as they were struck.

Chief Justice. How is that? Are they not so returned?

Mr. Chambers. No they are not: For some of the names that were last set down in the panel are now placed first.

Chief Justice. Make out that and you shall be righted.

Mr. Chambers. I have the copy of the panel in my hand, as the jurors were struck, and if the Clerk will produce the original signed by Mr. Attorney and myself, Your Honor will see our complaint is just.

Chief Justice. Clerk, is it so? Look upon that copy; is it a true copy of the panel as it was struck?

Clerk. Yes, I believe it is.

Chief Justice. How came the names of the jurors to be misplaced in the panel annexed to the venire?

Sheriff. I have returned the jurors in the same order in which the Clerk gave them to me.

Chief Justice. Let the names of the jurors be ranged in the order they were struck, agreeable to the copy here in Court.

Which was done accordingly. And the jury, whose names were as follows, were called and sworn.[19]

Hermanus Rutgers	Samuel Weaver	Benjamin Hildreth
Stanly Holmes	Andries Marschalk	Abraham Keteltas
Edward Man	Egbert van Borsom	John Goelet
John Bell	Thomas Hunt, *Form.*	Hercules Wendover

Mr. Attorney General opened the information, which was as follows:

Mr. Attorney. May it please Your Honors, and you, gentlemen of the jury; the information now before the Court, and to which the Defendant Zenger has pleaded *not guilty,* is an information for printing and publishing *a false, scandalous and seditious libel,* in which His Excellency the Governor of this Province, who is the King's immediate representative here, is greatly and unjustly scandalized as a person that has no regard to law nor justice; with much more, as will appear upon reading the information. This of libeling is what has always been discouraged as a thing that tends to create differences among men, ill blood among the people, and oftentimes great bloodshed between the party libeling and the party libeled. There can be no doubt but you gentlemen of the jury will have the same ill opinion of such practices as the judges have always shown upon such occasions: But I shall say no more at this time until you hear the information, which is as follows:

New York, Supreme Court.

Of the term of January, in the eighth year of the reign of our sovereign lord King George the Second, etc.

New York, Ss. Be it remembered that Richard Bradley, Esq., Attorney General of our sovereign lord the King, for the Province of New York, who for our said lord the King in this part prosecutes, in his own proper person comes here into the Court of our said lord the King, and for our said lord the King gives the Court here to understand and be informed that John Peter Zenger, late of the City of New York, printer (being a seditious person and a frequent printer and publisher of false news and seditious libels, and wickedly and maliciously devising the government of our said lord the King of this His Majesty's Province of New York under the administration of His Excellency William Cosby, Esq.; Captain General and Governor-in-Chief of the said Province, to traduce, scandalize and vilify, and His Excellency the said Governor and the ministers and officers of our said lord the King, of and for the said Province to bring into suspicion and the ill opinion of the subjects of our said lord the King residing within the said Province) the twenty-eighth day of January, in the seventh year of the reign of our sovereign lord George the Second, by the grace of God of Great Britain, France and Ireland, King, Defender of the Faith, etc., at the City of New York, *did falsely, seditiously and scandalously* print and publish, and cause to be printed and published, a certain *false, malicious, seditious scandalous* libel, entitled *The New York Weekly Journal, containing the Freshest Advices, Foreign and Domestic;* in which libel (of and concerning His Excellency the said Governor, and the ministers and officers of our said lord the King, of and for the said Province) among other things therein contained are these words:

Your appearance in print at last gives a pleasure to many, though most wish you had come fairly into the open field, and not appeared behind *retrenchments* made of the supposed laws against libeling and of what other men have said and done before; these *retrenchments,* gentlemen, may soon be shown to you and all men to be weak, and to have neither law nor reason for their foundation, so cannot long stand you in stead: Therefore, you had much better as yet leave them, and come to what *the people of this City and Province* (the City and Province of New York meaning[20]) think are the points in question (*to wit*) *They* (the people of the City and Province of New York meaning) *think as matters now stand that their* LIBERTIES *and* PROPERTIES *are precarious, and that* SLAVERY *is like to be entailed on them and their posterity if some past things be not amended, and this they collect from many past proceedings.* (Meaning many of the past proceedings of His

Excellency the said Governor, and of the ministers and officers of our said lord the King, of and for the said Province.)

And the said Attorney General of our said lord the King, for our said lord the King, likewise gives the Court here to understand and be informed that the said John Peter Zenger afterwards (*to wit*) the eighth day of April, in the seventh year of the reign of our said lord the King, at the City of New York aforesaid, did *falsely, seditiously and scandalously* print and publish, and cause to be printed and published, another *false, malicious seditious and scandalous* libel entitled *The New York Weekly Journal, containing the Freshest Advices, Foreign and Domestic.* In which libel (of and concerning the government of the said Province of New York, and of and concerning His Excellency the said Governor and the ministers and officers of our said lord the King, of and for the said Province) among other things therein contained as these words:

One of our neighbors (one of the inhabitants of New Jersey meaning) *being in company, observing the strangers* (some of the inhabitants of New York meaning) *full of complaints, endeavored to persuade them to remove into Jersey; to which it was replied, that would be leaping out of the frying pan into the fire, for, says he, we both are under the same Governor* (His Excellency the said Governor meaning) *and your Assembly have shown with a witness what is to be expected from them; one that was then moving to Pennsylvania,* (meaning one that was then removing from New York with intent to reside at Pennsylvania) *to which place it is reported several considerable men are removing* (from New York meaning) *expressed, in terms very moving, much concern for the circumstances of New York* (the bad circumstances of the Province and people of New York meaning) *seemed to think them very much owing to the influence that some men* (whom he called tools) *had in the administration* (meaning the administration of government of the said Province of New York) *said he was now going from them, and was not to be hurt by any measures they should take, but could not help having some concern for the welfare of his countrymen, and should be glad to hear that the Assembly* (meaning the General Assembly of the Province of New York) *would exert themselves as became them, by showing that they have the interest of their country more at heart than the gratification of any private view of any of their members, or being at all affected by the smiles or frowns of a governor* (His Excellency the said Governor meaning), *both which ought equally to be despised when the interest of their country is at stake. You, says he, complain of the lawyers, but I think the law itself is at an end;* WE (the people of the Province of New York meaning) SEE MEN'S DEEDS DESTROYED, JUDGES ARBITRARILY DISPLACED, NEW COURTS ERECTED WITHOUT CONSENT OF THE LEGISLATURE (within the Province of New York meaning) BY WHICH, IT SEEMS TO ME, TRIALS BY JURIES ARE TAKEN AWAY WHEN A GOVERNOR PLEASES (His Excellency the said Governor meaning), MEN OF KNOWN ESTATES DENIED THEIR VOTES CONTRARY TO THE RECEIVED PRACTICE, THE BEST EXPOSITOR OF ANY LAW: *Who is then in that Province* (meaning the Province of New York) *that call* (can call meaning) *anything his own, or enjoy any libery* (liberty meaning) *longer than those in the administration* (meaning the administration of government of the said Province of New York) *will condescend to let them do it, for which reason I have left it* (the Province of New York meaning), *as I believe more will.*

To the great disturbance of the peace of the said Province of New York, to the great scandal of our said lord the King, of His Excellency the said Governor, and of all others concerned in the administration of the government of the said Province, and against the peace of our sovereign lord the King his crown and dignity, etc. Whereupon the said Attorney General of our said lord the King, for our said lord the King, prays the advisement of the Court here, in the premises, and the due process of the law, against him the said John Peter Zenger, in this part to be done, to answer to our said lord the King of and in the premises, etc.

R. Bradley, Attorney General.

To this information the Defendant has pleaded *not guilty,* and we are ready to prove it.

> [*Mr. Chambers* has not been pleased to favor me with his notes, so I cannot, for fear of doing him injustice, pretend to set down his arguments; but here *Mr. Chambers* set forth very clearly the nature of a libel, the great allowances that ought to be made for what men speak or write, that in all libels there must be some particular persons so clearly pointed out that no doubt must remain about who is meant; that he was in hopes *Mr. Attorney* would fail in his proof as to this point; and therefore he desired that he would go on to examine his witnesses.] [21]

Then *Mr. Hamilton,* who at the request of some of my friends was so kind as to come from Philadelphia to assist me on the trial, spoke.

Mr. Hamilton. May it please Your Honor; I am concerned in this cause on the part of Mr. Zenger the Defendant. The information against my client was sent me a few days before I left home, with some instructions to let me know how far I might rely upon the truth of those parts of the papers set forth in the information and which are said to be libelous. And though I am perfectly of the opinion with the gentleman who has just now spoke on the same side with me as to the common course of proceedings, I mean in putting Mr. Attorney upon proving that my client printed and published those papers mentioned in the information; yet I cannot think it proper for me (without doing violence to my own principles) to deny the publication of a complaint which I think is the right of every free-born subject to make when the matters so published can be supported with truth; and therefore I'll save Mr. Attorney the trouble of examining his witnesses to that point; and I do (for my client) confess that he both printed and published the two newspapers set forth in the information, and I hope in so doing he has committed no crime.[22]

Mr. Attorney. Then if Your Honor pleases, since Mr. Hamilton has confessed the fact, I think our witnesses may be discharged; we have no further occasion for them.

Mr. Hamilton. If you brought them here only to prove the printing and publishing of these newspapers, we have acknowledged that, and shall abide by it.

> [Here my journeyman and two sons (with several others subpoenaed by Mr. Attorney, to give evidence against me) were discharged, and there was silence in the Court for some time.]

Mr. Chief Justice. Well Mr. Attorney, will you proceed?

Mr. Attorney. Indeed sir, as Mr. Hamilton has confessed the printing and publishing these libels, I think the jury must find a verdict for the King;[23] for supposing they were true, the law says that they are not the less libelous for that; nay indeed the law says their being true is an aggravation of the crime.

Mr. Hamilton. Not so neither, Mr. Attorney, there are two words to that bargain. I hope it is not our bare printing and publishing a paper that will make it a libel: You will have something more to do before you make my client a libeler; for the words themselves must be libelous, that is, *false, scandalous, and seditious* or else we are not guilty.

[As Mr. Attorney has not been pleased to favor us with his argument, which he read, or with the notes of it, we cannot take upon us to set down his words, but only to show the book cases he cited and the general scope of his argument which he drew from those authorities. He observed upon the excellency as well as the use of government, and the great regard and reverence which had been constantly paid to it, both under the law and the gospel. That by government we were protected in our lives, religion and properties; and that for these reasons great care had always been taken to prevent everything that might tend to scandalize magistrates and others concerned in the administration of the government, especially the supreme magistrate. And that there were many instances of very severe judgments, and of punishments inflicted upon such, as had attempted to bring the government into contempt; by publishing false and scurrilous libels against it, or by speaking evil and scandalous words of men in authority; to the great disturbance of the public peace. And to support this, he cited 5 Coke 121 (suppose it should be 125), Wood's Instit. 430, 2 Lilly 168, 1 Hawkins 73.11.6.[24] From these books he insisted that a libel was a malicious defamation of any person, expressed either in printing or writing, signs or pictures, to asperse the reputation of one that is alive or the memory of one that is dead; if he is a private man, the libeler deserves a severe punishment, but if it is against a magistrate or other public person, it is a greater offense; for this concerns not only the breach of the peace, but the scandal of the government; for what greater scandal of government can there be than to have corrupt or wicked magistrates to be appointed by the King to govern his subjects under him? And a greater imputation to the state cannot be than to suffer such corrupt men to sit in the sacred seat of justice, or to have any meddling in or concerning the administration of justice; And from the same books Mr. Attorney insisted that whether the person defamed is a private man or a magistrate, whether living or dead, whether the libel is true or false, or if the party against whom it is made is of good or evil fame, it is nevertheless a libel: For in a settled state of government the party aggrieved ought to complain for every injury done him in the ordinary course of the law. And as to its publication, the law had taken so great care of men's reputations that if one maliciously repeats it, or sings it in the presence of another, or delivers the libel or a copy of it over to scandalize the party, he is to be punished as a publisher of a libel. He said it was likewise evident that libeling was an offense against the law of God. *Act. XXIII. 5. Then said Paul, I wist not brethren, that he was the High Priest: For it is written, thou shalt not speak evil of the ruler of the People. 2 Pet. X. II. Despise government, presumptuous are they, self-willed, they are not afraid to speak evil of dignitaries, etc.*[25] He then insisted that it was clear, both by the law of God and man, that it was a very great offense to speak evil of or to revile those in authority over us; and that Mr. Zenger had offended in a most notorious and gross manner in scandalizing His Excellency our Governor, who is the King's immediate representative and the supreme magistrate of this Province: For can there be anything more scandalous said of a Governor than what is published in those papers? Nay, not only the Governor, but both the Council and Assembly are scandalized; for there it is plainly said that *as matters now stand, their liberties and properties are precarious, and that slavery is like to be entailed on them and their posterity.* And then again Mr. Zenger says *the Assembly ought to despise the smiles or frowns of a governor; that he thinks the law is at an end; that we see men's deeds destroyed, judges arbitrarily displaced, new courts erected without consent of the legislature;* and *that it seems trials by juries are taken away when a governor pleases; that none can call anything their own longer than those in the administration will condescend to let them do it.*—And Mr. Attorney added that he did not know what could be said in defense of a man that had so notoriously scandalized the Governor and principal magistrates and officers of the government by charging them with depriving the people of their rights and liberties, and taking away trials by juries, and in short, putting an end to the law itself.—If this was not a libel, he said, he did not know what was one. Such persons as will take those liberties with governors and magistrates he thought ought to suffer for stirring up sedition and discontent among the people. And concluded by saying that the government had been very much traduced and exposed by Mr. Zenger before he was taken notice of; that at last it was the opinion of the Governor and Council that he ought not to be suffered to go on to disturb the peace of the government by publishing such libels against the

Governor and the chief persons in the government; and therefore they had directed this prosecution to put a stop to this scandalous and wicked practice of libeling and defaming His Majesty's government and disturbing His Majesty's peace.

Mr. Chambers then summed up to the jury, observing with great strength of reason on Mr. Attorney's defect of proof that the papers in the information were *false, malicious, or seditious,* which was incumbent on him to prove to the jury, and without which they could not on their oaths say *that they were so, as charged.*]

Mr. Hamilton. May it please Your Honor; I agree with Mr. Attorney, that government is a sacred thing, but I differ very widely from him when he would insinuate that the just complaints of a number of men who suffer under a bad administration is libeling that administration. Had I believed that to be law, I should not have given the Court the trouble of hearing anything that I should say in this cause. I own when I read the information I had not the art to find out (without the help of Mr. Attorney's *innuendoes*) that the Governor was the person meant in every period of that newspaper; and I was inclined to believe that they were wrote by some who from an extraordinary zeal for liberty had misconstrued the conduct of some persons in authority into crimes; and that Mr. Attorney out of his too great zeal for power had exhibited this information to correct the indiscretion of my client; and at the same time to show his superiors the great concern he had lest they should be treated with any undue freedom. But from what Mr. Attorney has just now said, *to wit,* that this prosecution was directed by the Governor and Council, and from the extraordinary appearance of people of all conditions which I observe in Court upon this occasion, I have reason to think that those in the administration have by this prosecution something more in view, and that the people believe they have a good deal more at stake, than I apprehended: And therefore as it is become my duty to be both plain and particular in this cause, I beg leave to bespeak the patience of the Court.

I was in hopes, as that terrible Court, where those dreadful judgments were given and that law established which Mr. Attorney has produced for authorities to support this cause, was long ago laid aside as the most dangerous court to the liberties of the people of England that ever was known in that kingdom; that Mr. Attorney knowing this would not have attempted to set up a Star Chamber [26] here, nor to make their judgments a precedent to us: For it is well known that what would have been judged treason in those days for a man to speak, I think, has since not only been practiced as lawful, but the contrary doctrine has been held to be law.

In Brewster's case for printing *that the subjects might defend their rights and liberties by arms, in case the King should go about to destroy them,* he was told by the Chief Justice that it was a great mercy he was not proceeded against for his life; for that to say the King could be resisted by arms in any case whatsoever was express treason.[27] And yet we see since that time Dr. Sacheverell was sentenced in the highest court in Great Britain for saying *that such a resistance was not lawful.* Besides, as times have made very great changes in the laws of England, so in my opinion there is good reason that places should do so too.

Is it not surprising to see a subject, upon his receiving a commission from the King to be a governor of a colony in America, immediately imagining himself to be vested with all the prerogatives belonging to the sacred person of his Prince? And which is yet more astonishing, to see that a people can be so wild as to allow of and acknowledge those prerogatives and exemptions, even to their own destruction? Is it so hard a matter to distinguish between the majesty of our Sovereign and the power of a governor of the plantations? Is not this making very free with our Prince, to apply that regard, obedience and allegiance to a subject which is due only to our Sovereign? And yet in all the cases which Mr. Attorney has cited to show the duty and obedience we owe to the supreme magistrate, it is the King that is there meant and understood, though Mr. Attorney is pleased to urge them as authorities to prove the heinousness of Mr. Zenger's offense against the Governor of New York. The several plantations are compared to so many large corporations, and perhaps not improperly; and can anyone give an instance that the mayor or head of a corporation ever put in a claim to the sacred rights of majesty? Let us not (while we are pretending to pay a great regard to our Prince and his peace) make bold to transfer that allegiance to a subject which we owe to our King only. What strange doctrine is it to press everything for law here which is so in England? I believe we should not think it a favor, at present at least, to establish this practice. In England so great a regard and reverence is had to the judges,* that if any man strikes another in Westminster Hall while the judges are sitting, he shall lose his right hand and forfeit his land and goods for so doing. And though the judges here claim all the powers and authorities within this government that a Court of King's Bench has in England, yet I believe Mr. Attorney will scarcely say that such a punishment could be legally inflicted on a man for committing such an offense in the presence of the judges sitting in any court within the Province of New York. The reason is obvious; a quarrel or riot in New York cannot possibly be attended with those dangerous consequences that it might in Westminster Hall; nor (I hope) will it be alleged that any misbehavior to a governor in the plantations will, or ought to be, judged of or punished as a like undutifulness would be to our Sovereign. From all which, I hope Mr. Attorney will not think it proper to apply his law cases (to support the cause of his Governor) which have only been judged where the King's safety or honor was concerned. It will not be denied but that a freeholder in the Province of New York has as good a right to the sole and separate use of his lands as a freeholder in England, who has a right to bring an action of trespass against his neighbor for suffering his horse or cow to come and feed upon his land, or eat his corn, whether enclosed or not enclosed; and yet I believe it would be looked upon as a strange attempt for one man here to bring an action against another, whose cattle and horses feed upon his grounds not enclosed, or indeed for eating and treading down his corn, if that were not enclosed.[28] Numberless are the instances of this kind that might be given, to show that what is good law at one time and in one place

* C[oke] 3 *Inst.* 140.

is not so at another time and in another place; so that I think the law seems to expect that in these parts of the world men should take care, by a good fence, to preserve their property from the injury of unruly beasts. And perhaps there may be as good reason why men should take the same care to make an honest and upright conduct a fence and security against the injury of unruly tongues.

Mr. Attorney. I don't know what the gentleman means, by comparing cases of freeholders in England with freeholders here. What has this case to do with actions of trespass, or men's fencing their ground? The case before the Court is whether Mr. Zenger is guilty of libeling His Excellency the Governor of New York, and indeed the whole administration of the government? Mr. Hamilton has confessed the printing and publishing, and I think nothing is plainer than that the words in the information are *scandalous, and tend to sedition, and to disquiet the minds of the people of this Province.* And if such papers are not libels, I think it may be said there can be no such thing as a libel.

Mr. Hamilton. May it please Your Honor; I cannot agree with Mr. Attorney: For though I freely acknowledge that there are such things as libels, yet I must insist at the same time that what my client is charged with is not a libel; and I observed just now that Mr. Attorney in defining a libel made use of the words *scandalous, seditious, and tend to disquiet the people;* but (whether with design or not I will not say) he omitted the word *false.*

Mr. Attorney. I think I did not omit the word *false:* But it has been said already that it may be a libel notwithstanding it may be true.

Mr. Hamilton. In this I must still differ with Mr. Attorney; for I depend upon it, we are to be tried upon this information now before the Court and jury, and to which we have pleaded *not guilty,* and by it we are charged with printing and publishing *a certain false, malicious, seditious and scandalous libel.* This word *false* must have some meaning, or else how came it there? I hope Mr. Attorney will not say he put it there by chance, and I am of opinion his information would not be good without it. But to show that it is the principal thing which, in my opinion, makes a libel, I put the case, if the information had been for printing and publishing a certain *true* libel, would that be the same thing? Or could Mr. Attorney support such an information by any precedent in the English law? No, the falsehood makes the scandal, and both make the libel. And to show the Court that I am in good earnest and to save the Court's time and Mr. Attorney's trouble, I will agree that if he can prove the facts charged upon us to be *false,* I'll own them to be *scandalous, seditious* and *a libel.* So the work seems now to be pretty much shortened, and Mr. Attorney has now only to prove the words *false* in order to make us guilty.

Mr. Attorney. We have nothing to prove; you have confessed the printing and publishing; but if it was necessary (as I insist it is not) how can we prove a negative? But I hope some regard will be had to the authorities that have been produced, and that supposing all the words to be true, yet that will not help them, that Chief Justice Holt in his charge to the jury in the case of Tutchin made no distinction whether Tutchin's papers were *true* or *false;* and as Chief Justice Holt has made no distinction in that case, so none ought to be made here; nor can it be shown in all that case there was any question made about their being *false* or *true.*[29]

Mr. Hamilton. I did expect to hear that a negative cannot be proved; but everybody knows there are many exceptions to that general rule: For if a man is charged with killing another, or stealing his neighbor's horse, if he is innocent in the one case, he may prove the man said to be killed to be really alive; and the horse said to be stolen, never to have been out of his master's stable, etc., and this I think is proving a negative. But we will save Mr. Attorney the trouble of proving a negative, and take the *onus probandi* upon ourselves, and prove those very papers that are called libels to be *true.*

Mr. Chief Justice. You cannot be admitted, Mr. Hamilton, to give the truth of a libel in evidence. A libel is not to be justified; for it is nevertheless a libel that it is *true.*

Mr. Hamilton. I am sorry the Court has so soon resolved upon that piece of law; I expected first to have been heard to that point. I have not in all my reading met with an authority that says we cannot be admitted to give the truth in evidence upon an information for a libel.

Mr. Chief Justice. The law is clear, that you cannot justify a libel.

Mr. Hamilton. I own that, may it please Your Honor, to be so; but, with submission, I understand the word *justify* there to be a justification by plea, as it is in the case upon an indictment for *murder,* or an *assault and battery;* there the prisoner cannot justify, but plead *not guilty:* Yet it will not be denied but he may, and always is admitted, to give the truth of the fact or any other matter in evidence, which goes to his acquittal; as in murder, he may prove it was in defense of his life, his house, etc., and in assault and battery, he may give in evidence that the other party struck first, and in both cases he will be acquitted. And in this sense I understand the word *justify,* when applied to the case before the Court.

Mr. Chief Justice. I pray show that you can give the truth of a libel in evidence.

Mr. Hamilton. I am ready, both from what I understand to be the authorities in the case, and from the reason of the thing,[30] to show that we may lawfully do so. But here I beg leave to observe that informations for libels is a child if not born, yet nursed up and brought to full maturity, in the Court of Star Chamber.

Mr. Chief Justice. Mr. Hamilton you'll find yourself mistaken; for in *Coke's Institutes* you'll find informations for libels long before the Court of Star Chamber.

Mr. Hamilton. I thank Your Honor; that is an authority I did propose to speak to by and by: But as you have mentioned it, I'll read that authority now. I think it is in 3 *Co. Inst.* under title *Libel;* it is the case of John de Northampton for a letter wrote to Robert de Ferrers, one of the King's Privy Council,* concerning Sir William Scot, Chief Justice, and his fellows; but it does not appear to have been upon information; and I have good grounds to say it was upon indictment, as was the case of Adam de Ravensworth, just

* Coke 3 *Inst.* 174.

mentioned before by Lord Coke under the same title; and I think there cannot be a greater, at least a plainer authority for us, than the judgment in the case of John de Northampton, which my Lord has set down at large. *Et quia praedictus Johannes cognovit dictam litteram per se scriptam Roberto de Ferrers, qui est de Concilio Regis, qua littera continet in se nullam veritatem,* etc.[31] Now sir, by this judgment it appears the libelous words were utterly false, and there the falsehood was the crime and is the ground of that judgment: And is not that what we contend for? Do not we insist that the falsehood makes the scandal, and both make the libel? And how shall it be known whether the words are libelous, *that is, true* or *false,* but by admitting us to prove them *true,* since Mr. Attorney will not undertake to prove them *false?* Besides, is it not against common sense that a man should be punished in the same degree for a *true libel* (if any such thing could be) as for a *false one?* I know it is said *that truth makes a libel the more provoking, and therefore the offense is the greater, and consequently the judgment should be the heavier.* Well, suppose it were so, and let us agree for once *that truth is a greater sin than falsehood:* Yet as the offenses are not equal, and as the punishment is arbitrary, *that is,* according as the judges in their discretion shall direct to be inflicted; is it not absolutely necessary that they should know whether the libel is *true* or *false,* that they may by that means be able to proportion the punishment? For would it not be a sad case if the judges, for want of a due information, should chance to give as severe a judgment against a man for writing or publishing a lie as for writing or publishing a truth? And yet this (with submission), as monstrous and ridiculous as it may seem to be, is the natural consequence of Mr. Attorney's doctrine *that truth makes a worse libel than falsehood,* and must follow from his not proving our papers to be *false,* or not suffering us to prove them to be *true.* But this is only reasoning upon the case, and I will now proceed to show what in my opinion will be sufficient to induce the Court to allow us to prove the truth of the words which in the information are called libelous. And first, I think there cannot be a greater authority for us than the judgment I just now mentioned in the case of John de Northampton, and that was in early times, and before the Star Chamber came to its fullness of power and wickedness. In that judgment, as I observed, the *falsehood* of the letter which was wrote is assigned as the very ground of the sentence. And agreeable to this it was urged by Sir Robert Sawyer in the trial of the seven bishops,* *that the falsity, the malice, and sedition of the writing were all facts to be proved.* But here it may be said Sir Robert was one of the bishops' counsel, and his argument is not to be allowed for law: But I offer it only to show that we are not the first who have insisted that to make a writing a libel, it must be *false.* And if the argument of a counsel must have no weight, I hope there will be more regard shown to the opinion of a judge, and therefore I mention the words of Justice Powell in the same trial, where he says (of the petition of the bishops, which was called a libel, and upon which they were prosecuted by information) that *to make it a libel, it must be false and malicious and tend to sedition;* and declared, *as he saw no falsehood or malice in it, he was of opinion that it was no libel.* Now I should think this opinion alone, in the case of the King, and in a case which that King had so much at heart and which to this day has never been contradicted, might be a sufficient authority to entitle us to the liberty of proving the *truth* of the papers which in the information are called *false, malicious, seditious and scandalous.* If it be objected *that the opinions of the other three judges were against him,* I answer that the censures the judgments of these men have undergone, and the approbation Justice Powell's opinion, his judgment and conduct upon that trial has met with, and the honor he gained to himself for daring to speak truth at such a time, upon such an occasion, and in the reign of such a King, is more than sufficient in my humble opinion, to warrant our insisting on his judgment as a full authority to our purpose, and it will lie upon Mr. Attorney to show that this opinion has since that time been denied to be law, or

* *State Trials,* Vol. 4 [Trial of the seven bishops, June 29, 1688, King's Bench. IV *State Trials* 300–392. For the most famous account of the trial, see Macaulay, *History of England,* II, 990–1039].

that Justice Powell who delivered it has ever been condemned or blamed for it in any law book extant at this day, and this I will venture to say Mr. Attorney cannot do. But to make this point yet more clear, if anything can be clearer, I will on our part proceed and show that in the case of Sir Samuel Barnardiston, his counsel, notwithstanding he stood before one of the greatest monsters that ever presided in an English court (Judge Jeffreys) insisted on the want of proof to the *malice* and *seditious intent* of the author of what was called a libel.[32] And in the case of Tutchin, which seems to be Mr. Attorney's chief authority, that case is against him; for he was upon his trial put upon showing the truth of his papers, but did not; at least the prisoner was asked by the King's counsel whether he would say they were *true?* * And as he never pretended that they were true, the Chief Justice was not to say so. But the point will still be clearer on our side from Fuller's case, *for falsely and wickedly causing to be printed a false and scandalous libel, in which (amongst other things) were contained these words,* "Mr. Jones has also made oath that he paid £5000 more by the late King's order to several persons in places of trust, that they might complete my ruin, and invalidate me forever. Nor is this all; for the same Mr. Jones will prove by undeniable witness and demonstration that he has distributed more than £180,000 in eight years last past by the French King's order to persons in public trust in this kingdom." † Here you see is a scandalous and infamous charge against the late King; here is a charge no less than high treason against the *men in public trust* for receiving money of the French King, then in actual war with the Crown of Great Britain; and yet the Court were far from bearing him down with that Star Chamber doctrine, *to wit, that it was no matter whether what he said was true or false;* no, on the contrary, Lord Chief Justice Holt asks Fuller, "Can you make it appear they are true? Have you any witnesses? You might have had subpoenas for your witnesses against this day. If you take

* *State Trials,* Vol. V, 549 [Case of John Tutchin].

† *State Trials,* Vol. V, 445 [Case of William Fuller, May 20, 1702, King's Bench. V *State Trials* 445–449].

upon you to write such things as you are charged with, it lies upon you to prove them true, at your peril. If you have any witnesses, I will hear them. How came you to write those books which are not true? If you have any witnesses, produce them. If you can offer any matter to prove what you have wrote, let us hear it." Thus said and thus did that great man Lord Chief Justice Holt upon a trial of the like kind with ours, and the rule laid down by him in this case is *that he who will take upon him to write things, it lies upon him to prove them at his peril.* Now, sir, we have acknowledged the printing and publishing of those papers set forth in the information, and (with the leave of the Court) agreeable to the rule laid down by Chief Justice Holt, we are ready to prove them to be true, at our peril.

Mr. Chief Justice. Let me see the book.

[Here the Court had the case under consideration a considerable time, and everyone was silent.]

Mr. Chief Justice. Mr. Attorney, you have heard what Mr. Hamilton has said, and the cases he has cited, for having his witnesses examined to prove the truth of the several facts contained in the papers set forth in the information, what do you say to it?

Mr. Attorney. The law in my opinion is very clear; they cannot be admitted to justify a libel; for, by the authorities I have already read to the Court, it is not the less a libel because it is true. I think I need not trouble the Court with reading the cases over again; the thing seems to be very plain, and I submit it to the Court.

Mr. Chief Justice. Mr. Hamilton, the Court is of opinion, you ought not to be permitted to prove the facts in the papers: These are the words of the book, "It is far from being a justification of a libel, that the contents thereof are true, or that the person upon whom it is made had a bad reputation, since the greater appearance there is of truth in any malicious invective, so much the more provoking it is." [33]

Mr. Hamilton. These are Star Chamber cases, and I was in hopes that practice had been dead with the Court.

Mr. Chief Justice. Mr. Hamilton, the Court have delivered their opinion, and we expect you will use us with good manners; you are not to be permitted to argue against the opinion of the Court.

Mr. Hamilton. With submission, I have seen the practice in very great courts, and never heard it deemed unmannerly to—

Mr. Chief Justice. After the Court have declared their opinion, it is not good manners to insist upon a point in which you are overruled.

Mr. Hamilton. I will say no more at this time; the Court I see is against us in this point; and that I hope I may be allowed to say.

Mr. Chief Justice. Use the Court with good manners, and you shall be allowed all the liberty you can reasonably desire.

Mr. Hamilton. I thank Your Honor. Then, gentlemen of the jury, it is to you we must now appeal for witnesses to the truth of the facts we have offered and are denied the liberty to prove; and let it not seem strange that I apply myself to you in this manner, I am warranted so to do both by law and reason. The law supposes you to be summoned *out of the neighborhood where the fact is alleged to be committed;* and the reason of your being taken out of the neighborhood is *because you are supposed to have the best knowledge of the fact that is to be tried.*[34] And were you to find a verdict against my client, you must take upon you to say the papers referred to in the information, and which we acknowledge we printed and published, are *false, scandalous and seditious;* but of this I can have no apprehension. You are citizens of New York; you are really what the law supposes you to be, *honest and lawful men;* and, according to my brief, the facts which we offer to prove were not committed in a corner; they are notoriously known to be true; and therefore in your justice lies our safety. And as we are denied the liberty of giving evidence to prove the truth of what we have published, I will beg leave to lay it down as a standing rule in such cases, *that the suppressing of evidence ought always to be taken for the strongest evidence;* and I hope it will have that weight with you. But since we are not admitted to examine our witnesses, I will endeavor to shorten the dispute with Mr. Attorney, and to that end I desire he would favor us with some standard definition of a libel, by which it may be certainly known whether a writing be a libel, yea or not.

Mr. Attorney. The books, I think, have given a very full definition of a libel; they say it is *in a strict sense taken for a malicious defamation, expressed either in printing or writing, and tending either to blacken the memory of one who is dead, or the reputation of one who is alive, and to expose him to public hatred, contempt, or ridicule.* § 2. *But it is said that in a larger sense the notion of a libel may be applied to any defamation whatsoever, expressed either by signs or pictures, as by fixing up a gallows against a man's door, or by painting him in a shameful and ignominious manner.* § 3. *And since the chief cause for which the law so severely punishes all offenses of this nature is the direct tendency of them to a breach of public peace by provoking the parties injured, their friends and families, to acts of revenge, which it would be impossible to restrain by the severest laws, were there no redress from public justice for injuries of this kind, which of all others are most sensibly felt; and since the plain meaning of such scandal as is expressed by signs or pictures is as obvious to common sense, and as easily understood by every common capacity, and altogether as provoking as that which is expressed by writing or printing, why should it not be equally criminal?* § 4. *And from the same ground it seemeth also clearly to follow that such scandal as is expressed in a scoffing and ironical manner makes a writing as properly a libel, as that which is expressed in direct terms; as where a writing, in a taunting manner reckoning up several acts of public charity done by one, says* you will not play the Jew, nor the hypocrite, *and so goes on in a strain of ridicule to insinuate that what he did was owing to his vainglory; or where a writing, pretending to recommend to one the characters of several great men for his imitation, instead of taking notice of what they are generally esteemed famous for, pitched on such qualities only which their enemies charge them with the want of, as by proposing such a one to be imitated for his courage who is known to be a great statesman but no soldier, and another to be imitated for his learning who is known to be a great general but no scholar,* *etc., which kind of writing is as well understood to mean only to upbraid the parties with the want of these qualities as if it had directly and expressly done so.**

Mr. Hamilton. Ay, Mr. Attorney; but what certain standard rule have the books laid down, by which we can certainly know whether the words or the signs are malicious? Whether they are defamatory? Whether they tend to the breach of the peace, and are a sufficient ground to provoke a man, his family, or friends to acts of revenge, especially those of the ironical sort of words? And what rule have you to know when I write ironically? I think it would be hard, when I say *such a man is a very worthy honest gentleman, and of fine understanding,* that therefore I meant *he was a knave or a fool.*

Mr. Attorney. I think the books are very full; it is said in *I Hawk. p. 193,* just now read, *that such scandal as is expressed in a scoffing and ironical manner makes a writing as properly a libel as that which is expressed in direct terms; as where a writing, in a taunting manner says, reckoning up several acts of charity done by one, says,* you will not play the Jew or the hypocrite, *and so goes on to insinuate that what he did was owing to his vainglory, etc. Which kind of writing is as well understood to mean only to upbraid the parties with the want of these qualities, as if it had directly and expressly done so*. I think nothing can be plainer or more full than these words.

Mr. Hamilton. I agree the words are very plain, and I shall not scruple to allow (when we are agreed that the words are *false and scandalous, and were spoken in an ironical and scoffing manner, etc.*) that they are really *libelous;* but here still occurs the uncertainty which makes the difficulty to know what words are *scandalous* and what not; for you say, they may be *scandalous, true* or *false;* besides, how shall we know whether the words were spoke in a *scoffing and ironical manner,* or seriously? Or how can you know whether the man did not think as he wrote? For by your rule, if he did, it is no *irony,* and consequently no *libel.* But under favor, Mr. Attorney, I think the same book and the same section will show us

* 1 Hawk[ins, *Pleas of the Crown*], Chap. LXXIII § 1. & *seq.*

the only rule by which all these things are to be known. The words are these: *which kind of writing is as well* UNDERSTOOD *to mean only to upbraid the parties with the want of these qualities, as if they had directly and expressly done so.*[35] Here it is plain the words are *scandalous, scoffing and ironical* only as they are UNDERSTOOD. I know no rule laid down in the books but this, I mean, as the words are *understood.*

Mr. Chief Justice. Mr. Hamilton, do you think it so hard to know when words are ironical, or spoke in a scoffing manner?

Mr. Hamilton. I own it may be known; but I insist, the only rule to know is, as I do or can *understand* them; I have no other rule to go by, but as I *understand* them.

Mr. Chief Justice. That is certain. All words are libelous or not, as they are *understood.* Those who are to judge of the words must judge whether they *are scandalous* or *ironical, tend to the breach of the peace,* or are *seditious:* There can be no doubt of it.

Mr. Hamilton. I thank Your Honor; I am glad to find the Court of this opinion. Then it follows that those twelve men must *understand* the words in the information to be *scandalous,* that is to say *false;* for I think it is not pretended they are of the *ironical* sort; and when they understand the words to be so, they will say we are guilty of publishing a *false libel,* and not otherwise.

Mr. Chief Justice. No, Mr. Hamilton; the jury may find that Zenger printed and published those papers, and leave it to the Court to judge whether they are libelous; you know this is very common; it is in the nature of a special verdict,[36] where the jury leave the matter of law to the Court.

Mr. Hamilton. I know, may it please Your Honor, the jury may do so; but I do likewise know they may do otherwise. I know they have the right beyond all dispute to determine both the law and the fact, and where they do not doubt of the law, they ought to do so. This of leaving it to the judgment of the Court *whether the words are libelous or not* in effect renders juries useless (to say no worse) in many cases; but this I shall have occasion to speak to by and by; and I will with the Court's leave proceed to examine the inconveniencies that must inevitably arise from the doctrines Mr. Attorney has laid down; and I observe, in support of this prosecution, he has frequently repeated the words taken from the case of *Libel. Famosis* in 5. Co.[37] This is indeed the leading case, and to which almost all the other cases upon the subject of libels do refer; and I must insist upon saying that according as this case seems to be understood by the Court and Mr. Attorney, it is not law at this day: For though I own it to be base and unworthy to scandalize any man, yet I think it is even villainous to scandalize a person of public character, and I will go so far into Mr. Attorney's doctrine as to agree that if the faults, mistakes, nay even the vices of such a person be private and personal, and don't affect the peace of the public, or the liberty or property of our neighbor, it is unmanly and unmannerly to expose them either by word or writing. But when a ruler of a people brings his personal failings, but much more his vices, into his administration, and the people find themselves affected by them, either in their liberties or properties, that will alter the case mightily, and all the high things that are said in favor of rulers, and of dignities, and upon the side of power, will not be able to stop people's mouths when they feel themselves oppressed, I mean in a free government. It is true in times past it was a crime to speak truth, and in that terrible Court of Star Chamber, many worthy and brave men suffered for so doing; and yet even in that Court and in those bad times, a great and good man durst say, what I hope will not be taken amiss of me to say in this place, *to wit, The practice of informations for libels is a sword in the hands of a wicked king and an arrant coward to cut down and destroy the innocent; the one cannot because of his high station, and the other dares not because of his want of courage, revenge himself in another manner.*[38]

Mr. Attorney. Pray Mr. Hamilton, have a care what you say, don't go too far neither, I don't like those liberties.

Mr. Hamilton. Sure, Mr. Attorney, you won't make any applications; all men agree that we are governed by the best of kings, and I cannot see the meaning of Mr. Attorney's caution; my well known principles, and the sense I have of the blessings we enjoy under His present Majesty, makes it impossible for me to err, and I hope, even to be suspected, in that point of duty to my King. May it please Your Honor, I was saying that notwithstanding all the duty and reverence claimed by Mr. Attorney to men in authority, they are not exempt from observing the rules of common justice, either in their private or public capacities; the laws of our Mother Country know no exemption. It is true, men in power are harder to be come at for wrongs they do either to a private person or to the public; especially a governor in the plantations, where they insist upon an exemption from answering complaints of any kind in their own government. We are indeed told and it is true they are obliged to answer a suit in the King's courts at Westminster for a wrong done to any person here: But do we not know how impracticable this is to most men among us, to leave their families (who depend upon their labor and care for their livelihood) and carry evidences to Britain, and at a great, nay, a far greater expense than almost any of us are able to bear, only to prosecute a governor for an injury done here. But when the oppression is general there is no remedy even that way, no, our constitution has (blessed be God) given us an opportunity, if not to have such wrongs redressed, yet by our prudence and resolution we may in a great measure prevent the committing of such wrongs by making a governor sensible that it is his interest to be just to those under his care; for such is the sense that men in general (I mean freemen) have of common justice, that when they come to know that a chief magistrate abuses the power with which he is trusted for the good of the people, and is attempting to turn that very power against the innocent, whether of high or low degree, I say mankind in general seldom fail to interpose, and as far as they can, prevent the destruction of their fellow subjects. And has it not often been seen (and I hope it will always be seen) that when the representatives of a free people are by just representations or remonstrances made sensible of the sufferings of their fellow subjects by the abuse of power in the hands of a governor, they have declared (and loudly too) that they were not obliged by any law to support a governor who goes about to destroy a province or colony, or their privileges, which by His Majesty he was appointed, and by the law he is bound to protect and encourage. But I pray it may be considered of what use is this mighty privilege if every man that suffers must be silent? And if a man must be taken up as a libeler for telling his sufferings to his neighbor? I know it may be answered, *Have you not a legislature? Have you not a House of Representatives to whom you may complain?* And to this I answer, we have. But what then? Is an Assembly to be troubled with every injury done by a governor? Or are they to hear of nothing but what those in the administration will please to tell them? Or what sort of a trial must a man have? And how is he to be remedied; especially if the case were, as I have known it to happen in America in my time, that a governor who has places (I will not say pensions, for I believe they seldom give that to another which they can take to themselves) to bestow, and can or will keep the same Assembly (after he has modeled them so as to get a majority of the House in his interest) for near *twice seven years* together? [39] I pray, what redress is to be expected for an honest man who makes his complaint against a governor to an Assembly who may properly enough be said to be made by the same governor against whom the complaint is made? The thing answers itself. No, it is natural, it is a privilege, I will go farther, it is a right which all freemen claim, and are entitled to complain when they are hurt; they have a right publicly to remonstrate the abuses of power in the strongest terms, to put their neighbors upon their guard against the craft or open violence of men in authority, and to assert with courage the sense they have of the blessings of liberty, the value they put upon it, and their resolution at all hazards to preserve it as one of the greatest blessings heaven can bestow. And when a House of Assembly composed of honest freemen sees the general bent of the people's inclinations, that is it which must and will (I'm sure it ought to) weigh with a legislature, in spite of all the craft, caressing and cajoling made use of by a governor to divert them from hearkening to the voice of their country. As we all very well understand the true reason why gentlemen take so much pains and make such great interest to be appointed governors, so is the design of their appointment not less manifest. We know His Majesty's gracious intentions to his subjects; he desires no more than that his people in the plantations should be kept up to their duty and allegiance to the Crown of Great Britain, that peace may be preserved amongst them, and justice impartially administered; that we may be governed so as to render us useful to our Mother Country, by encouraging us to make and raise such commodities as may be useful to Great Britain. But will any one say that all or any of these good ends are to be effected by a governor's setting his people together by the ears, and by the assistance of one part of the people to plague and plunder the other? The commission which governors bear while they execute the powers given them, according to the intent of the Royal Grantor expressed in their commissions, requires and deserves very great reverence and submission; but when a governor departs from the duty enjoined him by his Sovereign, and acts as if he was less accountable than the Royal Hand that gave him all that power and honor which he is possessed of; this sets people upon examining and enquiring into the power, authority and duty of such a magistrate, and to compare those with his conduct, and just as far as they find he exceeds the bounds of his authority, or falls short in doing impartial justice to the people under his administration, so far they very often, in return, come short in their duty to such a governor. For power alone will not make a man beloved, and I have heard it observed that the man who was neither good nor wise before his being made a governor, never mended upon his preferment, but has been generally observed to be worse: For men who are not endued with wisdom and virtue can only be kept in bounds by the law; and by how much the further they think themselves out of the reach of the law, by so much the more wicked and cruel men are. I wish there were no instances of the kind at this day. And wherever this happens to be the case of a governor, unhappy are the people under his administration, and in the end he will find himself so too; for the people will neither love him nor support him. I make no doubt but there are those here who are zealously concerned for the success of this prosecution, and yet I hope they are not many, and even some of those I am persuaded (when they consider what lengths such prosecutions may be carried, and how deeply the liberties of the people may be affected by such means) will not all abide by their present sentiments; I say *not all:* For the man who from an intimacy and acquaintance with a governor has conceived a personal regard for him, the man who has felt none of the strokes of his power, the man who believes that a governor has a regard for him and confides in him, it is natural for such men to wish well to the affairs of such a governor; and as they may be men of honor and generosity, may, and no doubt will, wish him success, so far as the rights and privileges of their fellow citizens are not affected. But as men of honor I can apprehend nothing from them; they will never exceed that point. There are others that are under stronger obligations, and those are such as are in some sort engaged in support of a governor's cause by their own or their relations' dependence on his favor for some post or preferment; such men have what is commonly called duty and gratitude to influence their inclinations, and oblige them to go his lengths. I know men's interests are very near to them, and they will do much rather than forgo the favor of a governor and a livelihood at the same time; but I can with very just grounds hope, even from those men, whom I will suppose to be men of honor and conscience too, that when they see the liberty of their country is in danger, either by their concurrence, or even by their silence, they will like Englishmen, and like themselves, freely make a sacrifice of any preferment of favor rather than be accessory to destroying the liberties of their country and entailing slavery upon their posterity. There are indeed another set of men of whom I have no hopes, I mean such who lay aside all other considerations, and are ready to join with power in any shapes, and with any man or sort of men by whose means or interest they may be assisted to gratify their malice and envy against those whom they have been pleased to hate; and that for no other reason but because they are men of abilities and integrity, or at least are possessed of some valuable qualities far superior to their own. But as envy is the sin of the devil, and therefore very hard, if at all, to be repented of, I will believe there are but few of this detestable and worthless sort of men, nor will their opinions or inclinations have any influence upon this trial. But to proceed; I beg leave to insist that the right of complaining or remonstrating is natural; and the restraint upon this natural right is the law only, and those restraints can only extend to what is *false:* For as it is truth alone which can excuse or justify any man for complaining of a bad administration, I as frankly agree that nothing ought to excuse a man who raises a false charge or accusation, even against a private person, and that no manner of allowance ought to be made to him who does so against a public magistrate. *Truth* ought to govern the whole affair of libels, and yet the party accused runs risk enough even then; for if he fails of proving every tittle of what he has wrote, and to the satisfaction of the Court and jury too, he may find to his cost that when the prosecution is set on foot by men in power, it seldom wants friends to favor it. And from thence (it is said) has arisen the great diversity of opinions among judges about what words were or were not scandalous or libelous. I believe it will be granted that there is not greater uncertainty in any part of the law than about words of scandal; it would be mispending of the Court's time to mention the cases; they may be said to be numberless; and therefore the utmost care ought to be taken in following precedents; and the times when the judgments were given which are quoted for authorities in the case of libels are much to be regarded. I think it will be agreed that ever since the time of the Star Chamber, where the most arbitrary and destructive judgments and opinions were given that ever an Englishmen heard of, at least in his own country: I say prosecutions for libels since the time of that arbitrary Court, and until the Glorious Revolution, have generally been set on foot at the instance of the Crown or its ministers; and it is no small reproach to the law that these prosecutions were too often and too much countenanced by the judges, who held their places at pleasure (a disagreeable tenure to any officer, but a dangerous one in the case of a judge).[40] To say more to this point may not be proper. And yet I cannot think it unwarrantable to show the unhappy influence that a sovereign has sometimes had, not only upon judges, but even upon Parliaments themselves.

It has already been shown how the judges differed in their opinions about the nature of a libel in the case of the seven bishops.[41] There you see three judges of one opinion, that is, of a wrong opinion in the judgment of the best men in England, and one judge of a right opinion. How unhappy might it have been for all of us at this day if that jury had understood the words in that information as the Court did? Or if they had left it to the Court to judge whether the petition of the bishops was or was not a libel? No they took upon them, to their immortal honor! to determine both *law* and *fact,* and to *understand* the petition of the bishops *to be no libel, that is, to contain no falsehood nor sedition,* and therefore found them *not guilty.* And remarkable is the case of Sir Samuel Barnardiston, who was fined £10,000 for writing a letter in which, it may be said, none saw any scandal or falsehood but the Court and jury; for that judgment was afterwards looked upon as a cruel and detestable judgment, and therefore was reversed by Parliament.[42] Many more instances might be given of the complaisance of court judges about those times and before; but I will mention only one case more, and that is the case of Sir Edward Hales, who though a *Roman Catholic,* was by King James II preferred to be a Colonel of his Army, notwithstanding the statute of 25 *Cha. 2nd. Chap.* 2 by which it is provided, *That every one that accepts of an office, civil or military, etc., shall take the oaths, subscribe the declaration, and take the sacrament, within three months, etc., otherwise he is disabled to hold such office, and the grant for the same to be null and void, and the party to forfeit £500.*[43] Sir Edward Hales did not take the oaths or sacrament, and was prosecuted for the £500 for exercising the office of a colonel by the space of three months without conforming as in the act is directed. Sir Edward pleads, *That the King by his letters patents did dispense with his taking the oaths and sacrament, and subscribing the declaration, and had pardoned the forfeiture of*

£500. And *whether the King's dispensation was good, against the said act of Parliament?* was the question. I shall mention no more of this case than to show how in the reign of an arbitrary prince, where judges hold their seats at pleasure, their determinations have not always been such as to make precedents of, but the contrary; and so it happened in this case where it was solemnly judged, *That, notwithstanding this act of Parliament, made in the strongest terms for preservation of the Protestant religion, that yet the King had by his royal prerogative a power to dispense with that law;* and Sir Edward Hales was acquitted by the judges accordingly. So the King's dispensing power, being by the judges set up above the act of Parliament, this law, which the people looked upon as their chief security against popery and arbitrary power, was by this judgment rendered altogether ineffectual. But this judgment is sufficiently exposed by Sir Edward Atkins, late one of the judges of the Court of Common Pleas, in his *Enquiry into the King's Power of Dispensing with Penal Statutes;* * where it is shown *who it was that first invented dispensations; how they came into England; what ill use has been made of them there; and all this principally owing to the countenance given them by the judges.* He says of the dispensing power,† *The Pope was the inventor of it; our Kings have borrowed it from them; and the judges have from time to time nursed and dressed it up, and given it countenance; and it is still upon the growth, and encroaching 'till it has almost subverted all law, and made the regal power absolute if not dissolute.* This seems not only to show how far judges have been influenced by power, and how little cases of this sort where the prerogative has been in question in former reigns are to be relied upon for law: But I think it plainly shows too, that a man may use a greater freedom with the power of his Sovereign and the judges in Great Britain than it seems he may with the power of a governor in the plantations, who is but a fellow subject.

* Sir Edw. Atkins' *Enquiry into the Power of Dispensing with Penal Statutes* [London, 1689].

† Postscript to the *Enquiry,* page 51.

Are these words with which we are charged like these? Do Mr. Zenger's papers contain any such freedoms with his governor or his Council as Sir Edward Atkins has taken with the regal power and the judges in England? And yet I never heard of any information brought against him for these freedoms.

If then upon the whole there is so great an uncertainty among judges (learned and great men) in matters of this kind; if power has had so great an influence on judges; how cautious ought we to be in determining by their judgments, especially in the plantations and in the case of libels? There is heresy in law as well as in religion, and both have changed very much; and we well know that it is not two centuries ago that a man would have been burnt as an heretic for owning such opinions in matters of religion as are publicly wrote and printed at this day. They were fallible men, it seems, and we take the liberty not only to differ from them in religious opinions, but to condemn them and their opinions too; and I must presume that in taking these freedoms in thinking and speaking about matters of faith or religion, we are in the right: For, though it is said there are very great liberties of this kind taken in New York, yet I have heard of no information preferred by Mr. Attorney for any offenses of this sort. From which I think it is pretty clear that in New York a man may make very free with his God, but he must take special care what he says of his governor. It is agreed upon by all men that this is a reign of liberty, and while men keep within the bounds of truth, I hope they may with safety both speak and write their sentiments of the conduct of men in power. I mean of that part of their conduct only which affects the liberty or property of the people under their administration; were this to be denied, then the next step may make them slaves: For what notions can be entertained of slavery beyond that of suffering the greatest injuries and oppressions without the liberty of complaining; or if they do, to be destroyed, body and estate, for so doing?

It is said and insisted on by Mr. Attorney *that government is a sacred thing; that it is to be supported and reverenced; it is government that protects our persons and estates; that prevents treasons, murders, robberies, riots, and all the train of evils that overturns kingdoms and states and ruins particular persons; and if those in the administration, especially the supreme magistrate, must have all their conduct censured by private men, government cannot subsist.* This is called *a licentiousness not to be tolerated.* It is said *that it brings the rulers of the people into contempt, and their authority not to be regarded, and so in the end the laws cannot be put in execution.* These I say, and such as these, are the general topics insisted upon by men in power and their advocates. But I wish it might be considered at the same time how often it has happened that the abuse of power has been the primary cause of these evils, and that it was the injustice and oppression of these great men which has commonly brought them into contempt with the people. The craft and art of such men is great, and who that is the least acquainted with history or law can be ignorant of the specious pretenses which have often been made use of by men in power to introduce arbitrary rule and destroy the liberties of a free people. I will give two instances; and as they are authorities not to be denied, nor can be misunderstood, I presume they will be sufficient.

The *first* is the statute of *3d.* of *Hen. 7. Cap. I.* The preamble of the statute will prove all, and more than I have alleged. It begins, "The King our sovereign lord remembereth how by unlawful maintenances, giving of liveries, signs and tokens, etc., untrue demeanings of sheriffs in making of panels, and other untrue returns, by taking of money, by injuries, by great riots and unlawful assemblies; the policy and good rule of this realm is almost subdued; and for the not punishing these inconveniences, and by occasion of the premises, little or nothing may be found by enquiry, etc., to the increase of murders, etc., and unsureties of all men living, and losses of their lands and goods." Here is a fine and specious pretense for introducing the remedy, as it is called, which is provided by this act, *that is;* instead of being lawfully accused by 24 good and lawful men of the neighborhood, and afterwards tried by 12 like lawful men, here is a power given to the Lord Chancellor, Lord Treasurer, the Keeper of the King's Privy Seal, or two of them, calling to them a bishop, a temporal lord, and other great men mentioned in the act (who, it is to be observed, were all to be dependents on the court), to receive information against any person for any of the misbehaviors recited in that act, and by their discretion to examine and to punish them according to their demerit.[44]

The second statute I proposed to mention is the *11th* of the same King, *chap. 3d,* the preamble of which act has the like fair pretenses as the former: *for the King calling to his remembrance the good laws made against the receiving of liveries, etc., unlawful extortions, maintenances, embracery, etc., unlawful games, etc., and many other great enormities and offenses committed against many good statutes to the displeasure of almighty God, which,* the act says, *could not, nor yet can, be conveniently punished by the due order of the law, except it were first found by 12 men, etc., which, for the causes aforesaid, will not find nor yet present the truth.* And therefore the same statute directs *that the justices of assize, and justices of the peace, shall, upon information for the King before them made, have full power, by their discretion, to hear and determine all such offenses.* Here are two statutes that are allowed to have given the deepest wound to the liberties of the people of England of any that I remember to have been made, unless it may be said that the statute made in the time of Henry 8th by which his proclamations were to have the effect of laws might in its consequence be worse.[45] And yet we see the plausible pretenses found out by the great men to procure these acts. And it may justly be said that by those pretenses the people of England were cheated or awed into the delivering up their ancient and sacred right of trials by grand and petit juries. I hope to be excused for this expression, seeing my Lord Coke calls it *an unjust and strange act, that tended in its execution to the great displeasure of almighty God, and the utter subversion of the common law.**

These, I think, make out what I alleged, and are flagrant instances of the influences of men in power, even upon the representatives of a whole kingdom. From all which I hope it will be agreed

* 4 *Inst.*

that it is a duty which all good men owe to their country to guard against the unhappy influence of ill men when entrusted with power, and especially against their creatures and dependents, who, as they are generally more necessitous, are surely more covetous and cruel. But it is worthy of observation that though the spirit of liberty was borne down and oppressed in England at that time, yet it was not lost; for the Parliament laid hold of the first opportunity to free the subject from the many insufferable oppressions and outrages committed upon their persons and estates by color of these acts, the last of which, being deemed the most grievous, was repealed in the first year of Henry 8th.[46] Though it is to be observed that Henry 7th and his creatures reaped such great advantages by the grievous oppressions and exactions, *grinding the faces of the poor subjects,* as my Lord Coke says, by color of this statute by information only, that a repeal of this act could never be obtained during the life of that prince. The other statute, being the favorite law for supporting arbitrary power, was continued much longer. The execution of it was by the great men of the realm; and how they executed it, the sense of the kingdom, expressed in the *17th* of *Charles 1st* (by which the Court of Star Chamber, the soil where informations grew rankest) will best declare.[47] In that statute, Magna Charta, and the other statutes made in the time of Edward 3rd, which, I think, are no less than five, are particularly enumerated as acts, by which the liberties and privileges of the people of England were secured to them against such oppressive courts as the Star Chamber and others of the like jurisdiction. And the reason assigned for their pulling down the Star Chamber is *that the proceedings, censures and decrees of the Court of Star Chamber, even though the great men of the realm, nay and a bishop too* (holy man) *were judges, had by experience been found to be an intolerable burden to the subject, and the means to introduce an arbitrary power and government.* And therefore that Court was taken away, with all the other courts in that statute mentioned having like jurisdiction.

I don't mention this statute as if by the taking away the Court of Star Chamber the remedy for many of the abuses or offenses censured there was likewise taken away; no, I only intend by it to show that the people of England saw clearly the danger of trusting their liberties and properties to be tried, even by the greatest men in the kingdom, without the judgment of a jury of their equals. They had felt the terrible effects of leaving it to the judgment of these great men to say what was *scandalous and seditious, false or ironical.* And if the Parliament of England thought this power of judging was too great to be trusted with men of the first rank in the kingdom without the aid of a jury, how sacred soever their characters might be, and therefore restored to the people their original right of trial by juries, I hope to be excused for insisting that by the judgment of a Parliament, from whence no appeal lies, the jury are the proper judges of what is *false* at least, if not of what is *scandalous and seditious.* This is an authority not to be denied, it is as plain as it is great, and to say that this act indeed did restore to the people trials by juries, which was not the practice of the Star Chamber, but that did not give the jurors any new authority or any right to try matters of law, I say this objection will not avail; for I must insist that where matter of law is complicated with matter of fact, the jury have a right to determine both. As for instance; upon indictment for murder, the jury may, and almost constantly do, take upon them to judge whether the evidence will amount to murder or manslaughter, and find accordingly; and I must say I cannot see why in our case the jury have not at least as good a right to say whether our newspapers are a libel or no libel as another jury has to say whether killing of a man is murder or manslaughter. The right of the jury to find such a verdict as they in their conscience do think is agreeable to their evidence is supported by the authority of Bushel's case, in *Vaughan's Reports,* pag. 135, beyond any doubt. For, in the argument of that case, the Chief Justice who delivered the opinion of the Court lays it down for law *that in all general issues, as upon* non cul. *in* trespass, non tort., nul disseizen *in assize, etc., though it is matter of law whether the defendant is a trespasser, a disseizer, etc., in the particular cases in issue, yet the jury find not (as in a special verdict) the fact of every case, leaving the law to* *the Court; but find for the plaintiff or defendant upon the issue to be tried, wherein they resolve both law and fact complicately.** It appears by the same case that though the discreet and lawful assistance of the judge, by way of advice to the jury, may be useful; yet that advice or direction ought always to be *upon supposition, and not positive, and upon coercion.*† The reason given in the same book is *because the judge (as judge) cannot know what the evidence is which the jury have,* that is, *he can only know the evidence given in court; but the evidence which the jury have may be of their own knowledge, as they are returned of the neighborhood. They may also know from their own knowledge that what is sworn in court is not true; and they may know the witnesses to be stigmatized, to which the Court may be strangers.*†† But what is to my purpose is that suppose that the Court did really know all the evidence which the jury know, yet in that case it is agreed *that the judge and jury may differ in the result of their evidence as well as two judges may,* which often happens. And in pag. 148, the judge subjoins the reason why it is no crime for a jury to differ in opinion from the Court, where he says *that a man cannot see with another's eye, nor hear by another's ear; no more can a man conclude or infer the thing by another's understanding or reasoning.* From all which (I insist) it is very plain *that the jury are by law at liberty (without any affront to the judgment of the Court) to find both the law and the fact in our case* as they did in the case I am speaking to, which I will beg leave just to mention, and it was this. Mr. Penn and Mead being Quakers, and having met in a peaceable manner, after being shut out of their meeting house, preached in Grace Church Street in London to the people of their own persuasion, and for this they were indicted; and it was said *that they with other persons, to the number of 300, unlawfully and tumultuously assembled, to the disturbance of the peace, etc.* To which they pleaded *not guilty.* And the petit jury being sworn to try the issue between the King

* *Vaughan's Rep.* p. 150.
† Page 144.
‡ Page 147.

and the prisoners, that is, whether they were guilty, according to the form of the indictment? Here there was no dispute but they were assembled together, to the number mentioned in the indictment; But *whether that meeting together was riotously, tumultuously, and to the disturbance of the peace?* was the question. And the Court told the jury it was, and ordered the jury to find it so; *for* (said the Court) *the meeting was the fact, and that is confessed, and we tell you it is unlawful, for it is against the statute; and the meeting being unlawful, it follows of course that it was tumultuous and to the disturbance of the peace.* But the jury did not think fit to take the Court's word for it, for they could neither find *riot, tumult,* or anything tending to the *breach of the peace* committed at that meeting; and they acquitted Mr. Penn and Mead. In doing of which they took upon them to judge both the *law* and the *fact,* at which the Court (being themselves true courtiers) were so much offended that they fined the jury 40 marks apiece, and committed them till paid. But Mr. Bushel, who valued the right of a juryman and the liberty of his country more than his own, refused to pay the fine, and was resolved (though at a great expense and trouble too) to bring, and did bring, his *habeas corpus* to be relieved from his fine and imprisonment, and he was released accordingly; and this being the judgment in his case, it is established for law *that the judges, how great soever they be, have no right to fine imprison or punish a jury for not finding a verdict according to the direction of the Court.*[48] And this I hope is sufficient to prove that jurymen are to see with their own eyes, to hear with their own ears, and to make use of their own consciences and understandings in judging of the lives, liberties or estates of their fellow subjects. And so I have done with this point.

This is the second information for libeling of a governor that I have known in America. And the first, though it may look like a romance, yet as it is true, I will beg leave to mention it. Governor Nicholson, who happened to be offended with one of his clergy, met him one day upon the road, and as was usual with him (under the protection of his commission) used the poor parson with the worst of language, threatened to cut off his ears, slit his nose, and at last to shoot him through the head.[49] The parson being a reverend man, continued all this time uncovered in the heat of the sun, until he found an opportunity to fly for it; and coming to a neighbor's house felt himself very ill of a fever, and immediately writes for a doctor; and that his physician might the better judge of his distemper, he acquainted him with the usage he had received; concluding that the Governor was certainly mad, for that no man in his senses would have behaved in that manner. The doctor unhappily shows the parson's letter; the Governor came to hear of it; and so an information was preferred against the poor man for saying *he believed the Governor was mad;* and it was laid in the information to be *false, scandalous* and *wicked, and wrote with intent to move sedition among the people, and bring His Excellency into contempt.* But by an order from the late Queen Anne, there was a stop put to that prosecution, with sundry others set on foot by the same Governor, against gentlemen of the greatest worth and honor in that government.

And may not I be allowed, after all this, to say that by a little countenance, almost anything which a man writes may, with the help of that useful term of art called an *innuendo,* be construed to be a libel, according to Mr. Attorney's definition of it, that *whether the words are spoke of a person of a public character, or of a private man, whether dead or living, good or bad, true or false* all make a libel; for according to Mr. Attorney, *after a man hears a writing read, or reads and repeats it, or laughs at it, they are all punishable.* It is true, Mr. Attorney is so good as to allow, *after the party knows it to be a libel,* but he is not so kind as to take the man's word for it.

[Here were several cases put to show that though what a man writes of a governor was true, proper and necessary, yet according to the foregoing doctrine it might be construed to be a libel: But Mr. Hamilton after the trial was over being informed that some of the cases he had put had really happened in this government, he declared he had never heard of any such; and as he meant no personal reflections, he was sorry he had mentioned them, and therefore they are omitted here.]

Mr. Hamilton. If a libel is understood in the large and unlimited sense urged by Mr. Attorney, there is scarce a writing I know that may not be called a libel, or scarce any person safe from being called to an account as a libeler: For Moses, meek as he was, libeled Cain; and who is it that has not libeled the Devil? For according to Mr. Attorney, it is no justification to say one has a bad name. Echard has libeled our good King William: Burnet has libeled among many others King Charles and King James; and Rapin has libeled them all.[50] How must a man speak or write, or what must he hear, read, or sing? Or when must he laugh, so as to be secure from being taken up as a libeler? I sincerely believe that were some persons to go through the streets of New York nowadays, and read a part of the Bible, if it was not known to be such, Mr. Attorney, with the help of his *innuendoes,* would easily turn it into a libel. As for instance, *Is. IX. 16, The leaders of the people cause them to err, and they that are led by them are destroyed.*[51] But should Mr. Attorney go about to make this a libel, he would read it thus; *The leaders of the people* [*innuendo,* the Governor and Council of New York] *cause them* [*innuendo,* the people of this Province] *to err, and they* [the people of this Province meaning] *that are led by them* [the Governor and Council meaning] *are destroyed* [*innuendo,* are deceived into the loss of their liberty] which is the worst kind of destruction. Or if some persons should publicly repeat, in a manner not pleasing to his betters, the 10th and 11th verses of the LVI Chap. of the same book, there Mr. Attorney would have a large field to display his skill, in the artful application of his *innuendoes.* The words are, *His watchmen are all blind, they are ignorant, etc. Yea, they are greedy dogs, that can never have enough.* But to make them a libel, there is according to Mr. Attorney's doctrine no more wanting but the aid of his skill in the right adapting his *innuendoes.* As for instance; *His watchmen* [*innuendo,* the Governor's Council and Assembly] *are all blind, they are ignorant* [*innuendo,* will not see the dangerous designs of His Excellency]. *Yea, they* [the Governor and Council meaning] *are greedy dogs, which can never have enough* [*innuendo,* enough of riches and power]. Such an instance as this is seems only fit to be laughed at; but I may appeal to Mr. Attorney himself, whether these are not at least equally proper to be applied to His Excellency and his ministers as some of the inferences and *innuendoes* in his information against my client.[52] Then if Mr. Attorney is at liberty to come into court, and file an information in the King's name without leave, who is secure whom he is pleased to prosecute as a libeler? And as the Crown law is contended for in bad times, there is no remedy for the greatest oppression of this sort, even though the party prosecuted is acquitted with honor. And give me leave to say as great men as any in Britain have boldly asserted that the mode of prosecuting by information (when a Grand Jury will not find *billa vera*)[53] is a national grievance, and greatly inconsistent with that freedom which the subjects of England enjoy in most other cases. But if we are so unhappy as not to be able to ward off this stroke of power directly, yet let us take care not to be cheated out of our liberties by forms and appearances; let us always be sure that the charge in the information is made out clearly even beyond a doubt; for though matters in the information may be called *form* upon trial, yet they may be and often have been found to be *matters of substance* upon giving judgment.

Gentlemen; the danger is great in proportion to the mischief that may happen through our too great credulity. A proper confidence in a court is commendable; but as the verdict (whatever it is) will be yours, you ought to refer no part of your duty to the discretion of other persons. If you should be of opinion that there is no falsehood in Mr. Zenger's papers, you will, nay (pardon me for the expression) you ought to say so; because you don't know whether others (I mean the Court) may be of that opinion. It is your right to do so, and there is much depending upon your resolution as well as upon your integrity.

The loss of liberty to a generous mind is worse than death; and yet we know there have been those in all ages who for the sake of preferment or some imaginary honor have freely lent a helping hand to oppress, nay to destroy their country. This brings to my mind that saying of the immortal Brutus, when he looked upon the creatures of Caesar, who were very great men but by no means good men. "You Romans," said Brutus, "if yet I may call you so, consider what you are doing; remember that you are assisting Caesar to forge those very chains which one day he will make yourselves wear." This is what every man (that values freedom) ought to consider: He should act by judgment and not by affection or self-interest; for, where those prevail, no ties of either country or kindred are regarded, as upon the other hand the man who loves his country prefers its liberty to all other considerations, well knowing that without liberty, life is a misery.

A famous instance of this you will find in the history of another brave Roman of the same name, I mean Lucius Junius Brutus,[54] whose story is well known and therefore I shall mention no more of it than only to show the value he put upon the freedom of his country. After this great man, with his fellow citizens whom he had engaged in the cause, had banished Tarquin the Proud, the last King of Rome, from a throne which he ascended by inhuman murders and possessed by the most dreadful tyranny and proscriptions, and had by this means amassed incredible riches, even sufficient to bribe to his interest many of the young nobility of Rome to assist him in recovering the crown; but the plot being discovered, and principal conspirators were apprehended, among whom were two of the sons of Junius Brutus. It was absolutely necessary that some should be made examples of, to deter others from attempting the restoring of Tarquin and destroying the liberty of Rome. And to effect this it was that Lucius Junius Brutus, one of the consuls of Rome, in the presence of the Roman people, sat judge and condemned his own sons as traitors to their country: And to give the last proof of his exalted virtue and his love of liberty: He with a firmness of mind (only becoming so great a man) caused their heads to be struck off in his own presence; and when he observed that his rigid virtue occasioned a sort of horror among the people, it is observed he only said, "My fellow citizens, do not think that this proceeds from any want of natural affection: No, the death of the sons of Brutus can affect Brutus only; but the loss of liberty will affect my country." Thus highly was liberty esteemed in those days that a father could sacrifice his sons to save his country. But why do I go to heathen Rome to bring instances of the love of liberty, the best blood in Britain has been shed in the cause of liberty: and the freedom we enjoy at this day may be said to be (in a great measure) owing to the glorious stand the famous Hampden,[55] and other of our countrymen, made against the arbitrary demands and illegal impositions of the times in which they lived; who rather than give up the rights of Englishmen and submit to pay an illegal tax of no more, I think, than 3 shillings, resolved to undergo, and for their liberty of their country did undergo, the greatest extremities in that arbitrary and terrible Court of Star Chamber, to whose arbitrary proceedings (it being composed of the principal men of the realm and calculated to support arbitrary government) no bounds or limits could be set, nor could any other hand remove the evil but a Parliament.

Power may justly be compared to a great river, while kept within its due bounds, is both beautiful and useful; but when it overflows its banks, it is then too impetuous to be stemmed, it bears down all before it and brings destruction and desolation wherever it comes. If then this is the nature of power, let us at least do our duty, and like wise men (who value freedom) use our utmost care to support liberty, the only bulwark against lawless power, which in all ages has sacrificed to its wild lust and boundless ambition the blood of the best men that ever lived.

I hope to be pardoned, sir, for my zeal upon this occasion; it is an old and wise caution *that when our neighbor's house is on fire, we ought to take care of our own.* For though blessed be God, I live in a government where liberty is well understood and freely enjoyed; yet experience has shown us all (I'm sure it has to me) that a bad precedent in one government is soon set up for an authority in another; and therefore I cannot but think it mine and every honest man's duty that (while we pay all due obedience to men in authority) we ought at the same time to be upon our guard against power wherever we apprehend that it may affect ourselves or our fellow subjects.

I am truly very unequal to such an undertaking on many accounts. And you see I labor under the weight of many years,[56] and am borne down with great infirmities of body; yet old and weak as I am, I should think it my duty, if required, to go to the utmost part of the land where my service could be of any use in assisting to quench the flame of prosecutions upon informations set on foot by the government to deprive a people of the right of remonstrating (and complaining too) of the arbitrary attempts of men in power. Men who injure and oppress the people under their administration provoke them to cry out and complain; and then make that very complaint the foundation for new oppressions and prosecutions. I wish I could say there were no instances of this kind. But to conclude; the question before the Court and you gentlemen of the jury is not of small nor private concern, it is not the cause of a poor printer, nor of New York alone, which you are now trying: No! It may in its consequence affect every freeman that lives under a British government on the main of America. It is the best cause. It is the cause of liberty; and I make no doubt but your upright conduct this day will not only entitle you to the love and esteem of your fellow citizens; but every man who prefers freedom to a life of slavery will bless and honor you as men who have baffled the attempt of tyranny; and by an impartial and uncorrupt verdict, have laid a noble foundation for securing to ourselves, our posterity, and our neighbors that to which nature and the laws of our country have given us a right—the liberty—both of exposing and opposing arbitrary power (in these parts of the world, at least) by speaking and writing truth.

[Here Mr. Attorney observed that Mr. Hamilton had gone very much out of the way, and had made himself and the people very merry: But that he had been citing cases not at all to the purpose; he said there was no such cause as Mr. Bushel's or Sir Edward Hales' before the Court; and he could not find out what the Court or jury had to do with dispensations, riots or unlawful assemblies: All that the jury had to consider of was Mr. Zenger's printing and publishing two scandalous libels, which very highly reflected on His Excellency and the principal men concerned in the administration of this government, which is confessed. That is, the printing and publishing of the *Journals* set forth in the information is confessed. And concluded that as Mr. Hamilton had confessed the printing and there could be no doubt but they were scandalous papers, highly reflecting upon His Excellency, and the principal magistrates in the Province. And therefore he made no doubt but the jury would find the Defendant guilty, and would refer to the Court for their direction.]

Mr. Chief Justice. Gentlemen of the jury. The great pains Mr. Hamilton has taken to show how little regard juries are to pay to the opinion of the judges, and his insisting so much upon the conduct of some judges in trials of this kind, is done no doubt with a design that you should take but very little notice of what I might say upon this occasion. I shall therefore only observe to you that as the facts or words in the information are confessed: The only thing that can come in question before you is whether the words as set forth in the information make a libel. And that is a matter of law, no doubt, and which you may leave to the Court.[57] But I shall trouble you no further with anything more of my own, but read to you the words of a learned and upright judge* in a case of the like nature.

To say that corrupt officers are appointed to administer affairs is certainly a reflection on the government. If people should not be called to account for possessing the people with an ill opinion of the government, no government can subsist, for it is very necessary for all governments that the people should have a good opinion of it. And nothing can be worse to any government than to endeavor to procure animosities; as to the management of it, this has been always looked upon as a crime, and no government can be safe without it be punished.

Now you are to consider whether these words I have read to you, do not tend to beget an ill opinion of the administration of the government? To tell us, that those that are employed know nothing of the matter, and those that do know are not employed. Men are not adapted to offices, but

* Ch. J. Holt in Tutchin's Case [XIV *Howell's State Trials* 1128].

offices to men, out of a particular regard to their interest, and not to their fitness for the places; this is the purport of these papers.

Mr. Hamilton. I humbly beg Your Honor's pardon: I am very much misapprehended, if you suppose what I said was so designed. Sir, you know; I made an apology for the freedom I found myself under a necessity of using upon this occasion. I said there was nothing personal designed; it arose from the nature of our defense.

The jury withdrew and in a small time returned and being asked by the Clerk whether they were agreed of their verdict, and whether John Peter Zenger was guilty of printing and publishing the libels in the information mentioned? They answered by Thomas Hunt, their foreman, *Not Guilty,* upon which there were three huzzas in the hall which was crowded with people and the next day I was discharged from my imprisonment.

APPENDIX

City of New York } ss At a Common Council held at the City Hall of the said City, on Tuesday the Sixteenth Day of September, Anno Dom. 1735.

Present

Paul Richards Esq., Mayor.
Gerardus Stuyvesant, Esq., Deputy Mayor.
Daniel Horsmanden, Esq., Recorder.

Aldermen: William Roome, Esq., Simon Johnson, Esq., John Walter, Esq., Christopher Fell, Esq., Stephen Bayard, Esq., Johannes Burger, Esq.

Assistants: Mr. Johannes Waldron, Mr. Ede Myer, Mr. John Moore, Mr. John Fred, Mr. Charles Le Roux, Evert Byvanck.

Ordered, *That Andrew Hamilton, Esq., of Philadelphia, barrister at law, be presented with the freedom of this Corporation; and that*

Alderman Bayard, Alderman Johnson, and Alderman Fell be a committee to bring in a draft thereof.

City of New York } ss At a Common Council held at the City Hall of the said City on Monday the Twenty-ninth Day of September, being the Feast Day of St. Michael the Archangel Anno Dom. 1735.

Present

Paul Richards, Esq., Mayor.
Daniel Horsmanden, Esq., Recorder.

Aldermen: William Roome, Esq., Simon Johnson, Esq., John Walter, Esq., Christopher Fell, Esq., Stephen Bayard, Esq., Johannes Burger, Esq.

Assistants: Mr. Johannes Waldron, Mr. John Fred, Mr. Charles Le Roux, Mr. Evert Byvanck, Mr. Henry Bogert.

Stephen Bayard, Simon Johnson and Christopher Fell, Esqs., Aldermen, to whom it was referred to prepare the draft of the freedom of this Corporation, to be presented to Andrew Hamilton, Esq., make their report thereon, in the words following (to wit) *that they have prepared the form of the grant, to the said Andrew Hamilton, Esq., of the freedom of the City of New York, in these words* (to wit).

City of New York } ss Paul Richards, Esq., Mayor, the Recorder, Aldermen, and Assistants of the City of New York, convened in Common Council, to all to whom these presents shall come greeting.

Whereas, honor is the just reward of virtue, and public benefits demand a public acknowledgment. We therefore, under a grateful sense of the remarkable service done to the inhabitants of this City and Colony by Andrew Hamilton, Esq., of Pennsylvania, Barrister at Law, by his learned and generous defense of the rights of mankind, and the liberty of the press, in the case of John Peter Zenger, lately tried on an information exhibited in the Supreme Court of this Colony do by these presents bear to the said Andrew Hamilton, Esq., the public thanks of the freemen of this Corporation for that signal service, which he cheerfully undertook under great indisposition of body, and generously performed, refusing any fee or reward. And in testimony of our great esteem for his person, and sense of his merit, do hereby present him with the freedom of this Corporation. These are therefore to certify and declare that the said Andrew Hamilton, Esq., is hereby admitted, received and allowed a freeman and citizen of the said City: To have, hold, enjoy and partake of all the benefits, liberties, privileges, freedoms and immunities whatsoever granted or belonging to a freeman and citizen of the same City.[58] In testimony whereof the Common Council of the said City, in Common Council assembled, have caused the seal of the said City to be hereunto affixed this twenty-ninth day of September. *Anno Domini* One Thousand Seven Hundred and Thirty-five.

By Order of the Common Council
William Sharpas. Clerk.

And we do further report, that sundry of the members of this Corporation and gentlemen of this City have voluntarily contributed sufficient for a gold box of five ounces and a half for enclosing the seal of the said freedom; upon the lid of which, we are of opinion should be engraved the arms of the City of New York: Witness our hands this twenty-ninth day of September, 1735.

Stephen Bayard.
Simon Johnson.
Christopher Fell.

Which report is approved by this Court, and ordered, *that the freedom and box be forthwith made, pursuant to the said report, and that Mr. Sharpas, the Common Clerk of this City, do affix the seal to the same freedom, and enclose it in the said box.*

Mr. Alderman Bayard going to Philadelphia and offering to be the bearer of the said freedom to Mr. Hamilton, ordered, *that Mr. Sharpas deliver it to Alderman Bayard for that purpose, and that Alderman Bayard do deliver it to Mr. Hamilton, with assurances of the great esteem that this Corporation have for his person and merit.*

City of New York } ss At a Common Council held at the City Hall of the said City, on Wednesday the Fifteenth Day of October, *Anno Domini* 1735.

Present

Paul Richards, Esq., Mayor.
Daniel Horsmanden, Esq., Recorder.

Aldermen: John Walter, Esq., Simon Johnson, Esq., William Roome, Esq., Johannes Burger, Esq.

Assistants: Mr. Johannes Waldron, Mr. Abraham De Peyster, Mr. Gerardus Beekman, Mr. Peter Stoutenburgh, Mr. Henry Bogert.

Ordered, *that the freedom granted by this Corporation to Andrew Hamilton, Esq., with the report of the committee for preparing a draft of the same and the order of this Court, thereon, may be printed.*

William Sharpas.

Round on the lid of the box mentioned in the abovesaid report and order, there is engraved not only the arms of the City of New York, but also this motto in a garter:

DEMERSAE LEGES—TIMEFACTA LIBERTAS—HAEC TANDEM EMERGUNT.[59]

On the inner side of the lid of the box showing itself at the same time with the certificate of the freedom; there is engraven in a flying garter, these words:[60]

NON NUMMIS—VIRTUTE PARATUR.

As an incentive to public virtue, on the front of the rim of the said box, there is engraven a part of Tully's wish:

ITA CUIQUE EVENIAT, UT DE REPUBLICA MERUIT.[61]

Which freedom and box was presented in the manner that had been directed, and gratefully accepted by the said Andrew Hamilton, Esq.

New York, Printed and sold by John Peter Zenger.

MDCCXXXVI [62]

APPENDICES

APPENDIX A · SELECTIONS FROM ZENGER'S PRESS, 1734

1. The two "scandalous" songs of October 1734. These are the two satirical songs which Zenger printed immediately after the September 29, 1734, municipal elections in New York City to celebrate the Morrisite conquest of the Common Council. They were presented by Chief Justice De Lancey to the October 1734 Grand Jury and ordered to be burned.

A Song Made Upon the Election of New Magistrates for This City [1]

To the tune of, "To you Fair Ladies Now on the Land"

To you good lads that dare oppose
  all lawless power and might,
You are the theme that we have chose,
  and to your praise we write:
You dared to show your faces brave
In spite of every abject slave;
            with a fa la la.

Your votes you gave for those brave men
  who feasting did despise;
And never prostituted pen
  to certify the lies
That were drawn up to put in chains,
As well our nymphs as happy swains;
            with a fa la la.

And though the great ones frown at this,
  what need have you to care?

Still let them fret and talk amiss,
  you'll show you boldly dare
Stand up to save your country dear,
In spite of usquebaugh[2] and beer;
          with a fa la la.

They begged and prayed for one year more,
  but it was all in vain:
No wolawants[3] you'd have, you swore;
  by jove you made in plain:
So sent them home to take their rest,
And here's a health unto the best;
          with a fa la la.

A Song Made Upon the Foregoing Occasion

To the tune of, "Now, Now, You Tories All Shall Stoop"

Come on brave boys, let us be brave
  for liberty and law,[4]
Boldly despise the haughty knave,
  that would keep us in awe.
Let's scorn the tools bought by a sop,
  and every cringing fool.
The man who basely bends's a fop,
  a vile insipid tool.

Our country's rights we will defend,
  like brave and honest men;
We voted right and there's an end,
  and so we'll do again.
We vote all signers out of place
  as men who did amiss.
Who sold us by a false address
I'm sure we're right in this.

Exchequer courts, as void by law,[5]
  great grievances we call;
Though great men do assert no flaw
  is in them; they shall fall,
And be condemned by every man
  that's fond of liberty.
Let them withstand it all they can,
  our laws we will stand by.

Though pettifogging knaves deny
  us rights of Englishmen;
We'll make the scoundrel rascals fly,
  and ne'er return again.
Our judges they would chop and change[6]
  for those that serve their turn,
And will not surely think it strange
  if they for this should mourn.

Come fill a bumper, fill it up,
  unto our Aldermen;
For Common Council fill the cup,
  and take it o'er again.
While they with us resolve to stand
  for liberty and law,
We'll drink their healths with hat in hand,
  whoraa! whoraa! whoraa!

2. *New York Weekly Journal nos. 2 and 3: freedom of the press.* This anonymous essay, printed in two parts in the *Journal* and first reprinted here, initiated the newspaper war between Governor Cosby and the Morrisites. The first essay of the new paper, it represented the Morrisites'

formal credo of freedom of the press during the early stages of the Zenger affair.

The

New York Weekly Journal

Containing the Freshest Advices, Foreign and Domestic

Numb. 2. Monday, November 12, 1733.[7]

Mr. Zenger.

Insert the following in your next, and you'll oblige your friend,

CATO.

Rara temporum felicitate ubi sentiri quae velis, et quae sentias dicere licit.

Tacit.[8]

The liberty of the press is a subject of the greatest importance, and in which every individual is as much concerned as he is in any other part of liberty: Therefore it will not be improper to communicate to the public the sentiments of a late excellent writer upon this point. Such is the elegance and perspicuity of his writings, such the inimitable force of his reasoning, that it will be difficult to say anything new that he has not said, or not to say that much worse which he has said.

There are two sorts of monarchies, an absolute and a limited one. In the first, the liberty of the press can never be maintained, it is inconsistent with it; for what absolute monarch would suffer any subject to animadvert on his actions when it is in his power to declare the crime and to nominate the punishment? This would make it very dangerous to exercise such a liberty. Besides the object against which those pens must be directed is their sovereign, the sole supreme magistrate; for there being no law in those monarchies but the will of the prince, it makes it necessary for his ministers to consult his pleasure before anything can be undertaken: He is therefore properly chargeable with the grievances of his subjects, and what the minister there acts being in obedience to the prince, he ought not to incur the hatred of the people; for it would be hard to impute that to him for a crime which is the fruit of his allegiance, and for refusing which he might incur the penalties of treason. Besides, in an absolute monarchy, the will of the prince being the law, a liberty of the press to complain of grievances would be complaining against the law and the constitution, to which they have submitted or have been obliged to submit; and therefore, in one sense, may be said to deserve punishment; so that under an absolute monarchy, I say, such a liberty is inconsistent with the constitution, having no proper subject to politics on which it might be exercised, and if exercised would incur a certain penalty.

But in a limited monarchy, as England is, our laws are known, fixed, and established. They are the straight rule and sure guide to direct the king, the ministers, and other his subjects: And therefore an offense against the laws is such an offense against the constitution as ought to receive a proper adequate punishment; the several constituents of the government, the ministry, and all subordinate magistrates, having their certain, known, and limited sphere in which they move; one part may certainly err, misbehave, and become criminal, without involving the rest or any of them in the crime or punishment.

But some of these may be criminal, yet above punishment, which surely cannot be denied, since most reigns have furnished us with too many instances of powerful and wicked ministers, some of whom by their power have absolutely escaped punishment, and the rest, who met their fate, are likewise instances of this power as much to the purpose; for it was manifest in them that their power had long protected them, their crimes having often long preceded their much desired and deserved punishment and reward.

That *might overcomes right,* or which is the same thing, that might preserves and defends men from punishment, is a proverb established and confirmed by time and experience, the surest discoverers of truth and certainty. It is this therefore which makes the liberty of the press in a limited monarchy and in all its colonies and plantations proper, convenient, and necessary, or indeed it is rather incorporated and interwoven with our very constitution; for if such an overgrown criminal, or an impudent monster in iniquity, cannot immediately be come at by ordinary justice, let him yet receive the lash of satire, let the glaring truths of his ill administration, if possible, awaken his conscience, and if he has no conscience, rouse his fear by showing him his deserts, sting him with the dread of punishment, cover him with shame, and render his actions odious to all honest minds. These methods may in time, and by watching and exposing his actions, make him at least more cautious, and perhaps at last bring down the great haughty and secure criminal within the reach and grasp of ordinary justice. This advantage therefore of exposing the exorbitant crimes of wicked ministers under a limited monarchy makes the liberty of the press not only consistent with, but a necessary part of, the constitution itself.

It is indeed urged that the liberty of the press ought to be restrained because not only the actions of evil ministers may be exposed, but the character of good ones traduced. Admit it in the strongest light that calumny and lies would prevail and blast the character of a great and good minister; yet that is a less evil than the advantages we reap from the liberty of the press, as it is a curb, a bridle, a terror, a shame, and restraint to evil ministers; and it may be the only punishment, especially for a time. But when did calumnies and lies ever destroy the character of one good minister? Their benign influences are known, tasted, and felt by everybody: Or if their characters have been clouded for a time, yet they have generally shined forth in greater luster: Truth will always prevail over falsehood.

The facts exposed are not to be believed because said or published; but it draws people's attention, directs their view, and fixes the eye in a proper position that everyone may judge for himself whether those facts are true or not. People will recollect, enquire and search, before they condemn; and therefore very few good ministers can be hurt by falsehood, but many wicked ones by seasonable truth: But however the mischief that a few may possibly, but improbably, suffer by the freedom of the press is not to be put in competition with the danger which the KING and the *people* may suffer by a shameful, cowardly silence under the tyranny of an insolent, rapacious, infamous minister.

Numb. 3. Monday, November 19, 1733.

(*The remainder of the letter concerning the liberty of the press begun in our last.*)

Inconveniences are rather to be endured than that we should suffer an entire and total destruction. Who would not lose a leg to save his neck? And who would not endanger his hand to guard his heart? The loss of liberty in general would soon follow the suppression of the liberty of the press; for as it is an essential branch of liberty, so perhaps it is the best preservation of the whole. Even a restraint of the press would have a fatal influence. No nation ancient or modern ever lost the liberty of freely speaking, writing, or publishing their sentiments but forthwith lost their liberty in general and became slaves. LIBERTY and SLAVERY! how amiable is one! how odious and abominable the other! Liberty is universal redemption, joy, and happiness; but servitude is absolute reprobation and everlasting perdition in politics.

All the venal supporters of wicked ministers are aware of the great use of the liberty of the press in a limited free monarchy: They know how vain it would be to attack it openly, and therefore endeavor to puzzle the case with words, inconsistencies, and nonsense; but if the opinion of the most numerous, unprejudiced and impartial part of mankind is an argument of truth, the liberty of the press has that as well as reason on its side. I believe every honest Briton of whatever denomination, who loves his country, if left to his own free and unbiased judgment is a friend to the liberty of the press and an enemy to any restraint upon it. Surely all the independent whigs, to a man, are of this opinion. By an *Independent Whig,* I mean one whose principles lead him to be firmly attached to the present happy establishment, both in church and state, and whose fidelity to the royal family is so staunch and riveted as not to be called in question, tho' his mind is not overswayed, or rather necessitated, by the extraordinary weight of lucrative posts or pensions. The dread of infamy hath certainly been of great use to the cause of virtue, and is a stronger curb upon the passions and appetites of some men than any other consideration moral or religious. Whenever, therefore, the talent of satire is made use of to restrain men by the fear of shame from immoral actions, which either do or do not fall under the cognizance of the law, it is properly, and justly, and commendably applied: On the contrary, to condemn all satire is in effect the same thing as countenancing vice by screening it from reproach and the just indignation of mankind. The use of satire was of great service to the patriot whigs in the reign of King Charles and King James the second, as well as in that of Queen Anne. They asserted the freedom of writing against wicked ministers; and tho' they knew it would signify nothing to accuse them publicly whilst they were in the zenith of their power, they made use of satire to prepare the way and alarm the people against their designs. If men in power were always men of integrity, we might venture to trust them with the direction of the press, and there would be no occasion to plead against the restraint of it; but as they have vices like their fellows, so it very often happens that the best intended and the most valuable writings are the objects of their resentment, because opposite to their own tempers or designs. In short, I think, every man of common sense will judge that he is an enemy to his king and country who pleads for any restraint upon the press; but by the press, when nonsense, inconsistencies, or personal reflections are writ, if despised, they die of course; if truth, solid arguments, and elegant, just sentiments are published, they should meet with applause rather than censure; if sense and nonsense are blended, then, by the free use of the press, which is open to all, the inconsistencies of the writer may be made apparent; but to grant a liberty only for praise, flattery, and panegyric, with a restraint on everything which happens to be offensive and disagreeable to those who are at any time in power, is absurd, servile, and ridiculous; upon which, I beg leave to quote one observation of the ingenious Mr. Gordon, in his excellent discourses upon Tacitus. "In truth," says he,

> where no liberty is allowed to speak of governors besides that of praising them, their praises will be little believed; their tenderness and aversion to have their conduct examined will be apt to prompt people to think their conduct guilty or weak, to suspect their management and designs to be worse perhaps than they are, and to become turbulent and seditious, rather than be forced to be silent.[9]

I shall conclude with a citation from Tacitus, pat to the purpose:

> Socordiam eorum inridere libet, qui praesenti potentia credunt extingui posse etiam sequentia aevi memoriam: Nam contra punitis ingeniis gliscit auctoritas, neque aliud externi reges, aut qui eadem saevitia usi sunt, nisi dedecus sibi, atque illis gloriam peperere.[10]

3. New York Weekly Journal nos. 7, 47, 48, and 49: issues burned by the Sheriff in November 1734. These issues of the *Journal* were selected by Governor Cosby for his first attempt to test the opposition's right to criticize his administration. The provincial Council, forced to act alone by the recalcitrance of the Assembly and the New York City Court of Quarter Sessions, ordered the four papers to be burned, and Sheriff John Symes's servant put them to the torch on noon of November 6th. The portions of each issue which the Cosby administration probably considered to be offensive are reprinted here.

Numb. 7. Monday, December 17, 1733.[11]

It is agreed on all hands that a fool may ask more questions than a wise man can answer, or perhaps will answer if he could; but notwithstanding that, I would be glad to be satisfied in the following points of speculation that the above affidavits afford. And it will be no great puzzle to a wise man to answer with a *yea,* or a *nay,* which is the most that will be required in most of those questions.

Q. 1. Is it prudent in the French governors not to suffer an Englishman to view their fortifications, sound their harbors, tarry in their country to discover their strength?

Q. 2. Is it prudent in an English governor to suffer a Frenchman to view our fortifications, sound our harbors, etc.?

Q. 3. If the above affidavits be true, had the French a bad harvest in Canada? Or do they want provisions?

Q. 4. Was the letter from the Governor of Louisburgh to our Governor true?

Q. 5. Might not our Governor as easily have discovered the falsehood of it as anybody else, if he would?

Q. 6. Ought he not to have endeavored to do it?

Q. 7. Did our Governor endeavor to do it?

Q. 8. Was it not known to the greatest part of the town, before the sloop *Le Caesar* left New York, that the French in the sloop *Le Caesar* had sounded and taken the landmarks from without Sandy Hook up to New York? Had taken the view of the town? Had been in the Fort?

Q. 9. Might not the Governor have known the same thing, if he would?

Q. 10. Is there not great probability that he did know it?

Q. 11. Was it for our benefit or that of the French these soundings and landmarks were taken, and views made?

Q. 12. Could we not, by seizing their papers and confining their persons, have prevented them in great measure from making use of the discoveries they made?

Q. 13. Ought they not to have been so prevented?

Q. 14. Was it prudent to suffer them to pass through Hellgate, and also to discover that way of access to us?

Q. 15. If a French governor had suffered an English sloop and company to do what a French sloop and company has done here, would he not have deserved to be —— ——?

Q. 16. Since it appears by the affidavits there was no such scarcity of provisions as by the letter from the Governor of Louisburgh to our Governor is set forth, since the conduct of the French to the

English that happen to go to Canada shows they think it necessary to keep us ignorant of their state and condition as much as they can. Since the sounding our harbors, viewing our fortifications, and the honorable treatment they have received here (the reverse of what we receive in Canada) has let them into a perfect knowledge of our state and condition. And since their voyage must appear to any man of the least penetration to have been made with an intent to make that discovery, and only with that intent. Whether it would not be reasonable in us to provide as well and as soon as we can for our defense?

Q. 17. Whether that can be done any way so well and effectually as by calling the Assembly very soon together?

Q. 18. If this be not done, and any dangerous consequences follow after so full warning, who is blamable?

Sir; Be pleased to insert in your next paper the following list of the honorable gentlemen members of the Council, usually summoned to Council by His Excellency the Governor, and you'll oblige one of your subscribers.[12]

The Honorable George Clarke, Esq., Secretary of this Province, and, by that office, Clerk of the Council.

The Honorable Francis Harison, Esq., Judge of the Admiralty of the Province of New York and New Jersey, Recorder of the City of New York, Examiner of the high and honorable Court of Chancery before His Excellency the Governor, and Surveyor and Searcher of His Majesty's Customs of the Port of New York.

The Honorable Archibald Kennedy, Esq., His Majesty's Receiver General of the Province of New York, and Collector of His Majesty's Customs for the said Province.

The Honorable James De Lancey, Esq., lately made Chief Justice of this Province in the room of Lewis Morris, Esq., displaced.

The Honorable Daniel Horsmanden, Esq., a gentleman lately come to this Province, and more lately by His Excellency our Governor's recommendation (as is said) appointed one of His Majesty's

Council having first been and still he is, one of His Excellency's counsel in his suit in the king's name against the Honorable Rip Van Dam, Esq.

The Honorable Henry Lane, Esq., recommended and appointed as Mr. Horsmanden.—My intelligence, I must own, is not so good as to be able to inform you what office he as yet has. Besides:

Sundry others of the gentlemen of the Council who have no offices, nor expect any, live also in town; but few of them have often the honor of being summoned to Council; and one of them, it is talked, has not been once summoned since November 1732, tho' it is said he has been in town at the time of every one of the Councils since: But as five do make a quorum, and when five do meet the *majority* of them do determine the point in question, it would seem that it is thought there's no need of those (whom we beg leave to call) INOFFICIOUS GENTLEMEN OF THE COUNCIL, seeing enough of more *fit* members are to be had.

Numb. 47. Monday, September 23d, 1734.[13]

(*A second continuation of the letter from Middletown.*)

Pray (says the Counselor very gravely) if a nullity of laws is to be inferred from the Governor's voting in Council, what will become of the support of government? [14] Our governors (it is said) have always done so, and believe they do so in the neighboring governments of York and Pennsylvania, etc., and I never heard that the Councils (whose business it was) either there or here ever opposed the governor's sitting and acting in Council: And, sir, do you consider the dangerous consequence of a nullity of laws? The support of government, answered the Lawyer, is but temporary and in a little time will expire by its own limitation: But were it perpetual, I can't understand how a government is supported by breaking the constitution of it; that seems a contradiction in terms, and like *shoring up a house by pulling of it down.* But if you mean by the support of the government, the support of the governor and of you officers, I see no reason why that should be at the expense of the constitution and burdens laid upon the subject in a manner not warranted by law; when it can be done with as much ease the right way.—The Council (it is true) are more immediately concerned in opposing this voting because the indignity is more immediately offered to them: But why the Assembly should not be as much concerned in supporting the constitution, and defending any attack made upon it, I cannot see; since the people they represent are in general [15] I see the Journals of the Assembly lying there, search them, you will find an Assembly remonstrating against the mad practices of a governor and the vile implements of his oppression; upon which he was recalled. Look a little farther, and under the administration of General Hunter [16] (who was a man as tenacious of power and knew as well how to use it as most men) you will find the Assembly sending their bills up to the Council, and in particular to the president of the Council; all this he admitted, and never once attempted to dispossess the messengers that brought them on the pretense that they ought to have been delivered to him: If he had; that Assembly consisting of members who had no private left-handed views were not so weak and low-spirited as to suffer such an attempt to pass without remarking in a manner suitable to the violence of such a conduct.—You, sir, may know (tho' I do not) what has been always done by our former governors: Some of them have had impudence enough to call every opposition to their unwarrantable and extravagant actions and the despicable wretches they employed to promote their purposes a resistance and opposition of the royal prerogatives of the Crown: And, sir (with submission), I think their practices ought never among sober and free men to be alleged as precedents fit to follow.—What the governors of the neighboring governments of New York, Pennsylvania, etc., have done, I neither do, nor am concerned to know, any more than they are with what our governors do or have done here: The constitution of their governments may be different from ours; and what is unlawful here may be lawful there for ought I know. I am not concerned and meddle not with them or any of them; nor ought they or any of them to meddle with us, it is of Jersey I speak; and of Jersey I would be understood to speak; and of no other place whatsoever. As to your nullity of laws, I take that to be a sort of bugbear, fit only to be used to frighten children; and can be urged with equal force had the laws been made by any one branch of the legislature: And must a man decline in such case the saying *they are not binding,* lest they lose their unlawful force, and which indeed they ought to lose? The question is not *what are the consequences of a nullity of laws?* But *whether they are null or not?* And, *if made only by one or two branches of the legislature when they ought to be made by three?*—The answer is easy and what every man in duty to his country, himself, and his posterity, ought to give.—And whatever the consequences be in such case, they are chargeable upon those who took upon them to do what they ought not to have done; and not upon those who legally dispute or refuse to obey an illegal command.—Nor do I see the mighty danger of esteeming any laws void that really are so.—If the matter of many of them be convenient or necessary for the community, tho' made by an incompetent authority; the nullity of them is easily and quickly remedied by enacting such of them as are fit to be enacted by a competent authority: But a breaking in and making a nullity of the constitution not only infers but introduces a *nullity of liberty,* which I think every freeman is to guard against as much as he can.

A Gentleman present, who had all this time been very attentive, said to the Lawyer that what had been spoken with respect to the Governor's acting and voting in the passing of bills in Council, and the effect it had upon our laws and constitution, was entirely new to him, as he believed they were to most of his auditors: As he seemed to be acquainted with the nature of our Jersey constitution, he desired leave to ask him *why the late President*[17] *adjourned the Assembly of this province by proclamation in the king's name, and under the seal of the province; since the governors did it by proclamation in their own name, and* (*if sealed at all*) *with their own private seal?* Who replied he could not pretend to know the motives that induced the late President to differ from the practice of former governors: But if the late President could adjourn the Assembly at all, he believed he had taken the right method of doing of it: For tho' the governor had power to call, prorogue, and dissolve Assemblies as he has to make judges and justices, yet he cannot do this in his own name and by his own private seal, but in the king's name and under the seal of the province. So the Assembly are called together, and if they can be adjourned by the governor (which may admit of debate) it must be by something of equal authority with that which called them together, which a proclamation under his hand and private seal is not. It is now held in our books that prorogation can only be by the king, but adjournments must be by each House themselves; see 3d. Salk. 266. But it appears by 1 Anderson 294, 295[18] that Queen Elizabeth did adjourn a Parliament in the 28th year of her reign, but then it was by commission under the Great Seal of England after they were met; and there is not an instance to be given of any Parliament called, or prorogued, or adjourned (if adjourned by the king) but what was done under the Great Seal. And I believe all the lawyers that you can converse with will agree to a man (if they know anything of the matter) that an Assembly cannot be prorogued or continued from one sessions to another by adjournment (if done by the governor) by any less authority than that which gave them a being and called them together, *to wit,* the king's name made use of, and his public seal of his Province of New Jersey tested by the governor for the time being. A practice like this has always been the practice of the regents and guardians of the realm of England, as appears abundantly by the books.—The beginning, continuance, prorogation, etc., of Parliaments are *ex officio* taken notice of by the judges; and in pleading of acts of Parliament, the mistake of a day in either of these is fatal. Proclamations and charters are both of the same equal authority, and both under the Great Seal, 1 Shower 140.[19] A proclamation to adjourn or prorogue a General Assembly in Jersey is one of the highest acts of government here, and should be under the seal of the province and in the king's name; and when a governor issues such a proclamation in his own name and under his own private seal, the practice of his predecessors may perhaps be admitted for an excuse for his vanity, but the law can never justify the presumption of the practice, nor our Assembly be adjourned or prorogued by any such proclamation.

You seemed to make a question (said the Gentleman) *whether the late President could adjourn the Assembly, do you think he had less power than the Governor had?*—I made that question (replied the Lawyer) not from any doubt that I had of the president's power, believing that to be equal with the governor's; but from a belief that I had that neither the one nor the other could do it; which belief was not founded on the want of power in the president (if a governor or president could adjourn—as either could prorogue—which will admit of debate) but from the want of an Assembly in being to be adjourned, which I think pretty clearly appears from what has been already said: The Assembly not having been adjourned or prorogued by the late Governor by any instrument under the seal of the Province of New Jersey; and therefore no Assembly in being to be adjourned or prorogued by the President: But I shall say something more in order to clear this matter farther up, if possible.—A prorogation, if done before the time appointed in the writ for the meeting of the Parliament, is a putting of the time of meeting the Parliament off to a farther time; and this is done by an instrument under the Great Seal. And the beginning of the Parliament is not the day on which the writs are made returnable; but the day of their meeting appointed by the prorogation; Dyer, 203. pl. 72; 2d. Keb. 820. pl. 30.[20] But a prorogation after meeting puts a period to the sessions and discontinues everything unfinished in that sessions; which must begin (if at all) in another *de novo*. The day of the summons is the beginning of that Parliament so prorogued, Raym. 192; 1 Lev. 296;[21] 2d. Keb. 820. pl. 30, 686. pl. 10. An adjournment is made by each House, and is a suspension of their acting and a continuance of their session, and of everything before them to be proceeded on at the time to which they are adjourned. A Parliament prorogued to a day certain and summoned before that day, it was agreed by the judges that the summons was contrary to law, and they were again prorogued to the same day as before, Syderfin

330. pl. 1.[22] A Parliament adjourned to a certain day, but the Crown intending to prorogue before that day consulted the judges, who agreed that they must be prorogued on the very day to which it was adjourned, and a proclamation was published to notify this intention, that no more of the members might meet than what were sufficient to make a House, 1 Syderfin 393. pl. 26. I shall not multiply authorities.—An adjournment (as I take it) *ex vi termini*,[23] necessarily presupposes persons met at the time of adjournment, and that meeting to be adjourned, and a time certain to which it is adjourned, whether this is done by the House or by the king.—King Charles I (a prince as fond of prerogative as any) sent to the House to adjourn themselves; but the House or Sir John Eliot, etc., would not suffer the Speaker to adjourn them, and Sir John Eliot and others were prosecuted for hindering of him and keeping of him in the chair, and was fined severally for doing of it.—That the Parliament adjourn themselves, and that our Assembly adjourn themselves is known to all; and it is impossible to conceive how any assembly of men could adjourn themselves that were not met before they adjourned. Queen Elizabeth is one instance of adjourning a Parliament and possibly there may be some more, but if any, very few; and that of the Queen was, and the other must have been, after they were met, the very term implying so much; and every adjournment being a continuance of the proceedings then before them must presuppose that such procedure there was to be continued.—It is objected that the terms have been adjourned by the king's writ: True it is; but then the judges met at the term and published the king's writ at the Court, and in obedience to the king's command adjourned the Court.—Here is an Assembly meets, put the case on the first of May, pass some acts, and give others, some a first, some a second reading: The Governor commands them to adjourn till the 1st of September; they do so; this continues all before them then unfinished, to that 1st of September; and they may then proceed: But had he prorogued them to that time, everything must have begun *de novo*, on the first of September: But if he by proclamation under the public seal adjourns the Assembly (for his own cannot

do it, whatever the other may) on some day betwixt May and September (say the 1st of July) to some farther day after the 1st of September (say the 1st of October), either these matters are wholly discontinued, or continued from the 1st of July to the 1st of October following, or only from the 1st of September to the 1st of October. That they continued till the 1st of September by their own adjournment, and no longer, is indisputable: The question then will be what meeting was adjourned by the proclamation, admitting it to be such a one as it ought to have been (which it by no means is).—

Numb. 48. Monday September 30th, 1734.

(*A third continuation of the letter from Middletown.*)

—The answer is not the first, for that had been adjourned long before: Nor any meeting on the 1st of July, for there was none such: Nor any on the 1st of September; for that was to be *in futuro,* and could not exist on the 1st of July before: For, as I said before, every adjournment of any assembly or meeting of men (and I add) of the things doing in it by them, cannot (as I conceive) be understood possibly to be made, either by themselves or any other, but while that assembly is in being, met together, and acting. To suppose otherwise seems to me a contradiction in terms, and manifest absurdity: And of consequence our Assembly not meeting at the time to which they were by themselves adjourned, nor at that time prorogued to any farther time: (As I take it) they were of course dissolved and entirely dropped; considering first that they were not adjourned or prorogued by an authority equal to that which called them together, *to wit,* the king's name and seal of the province: Secondly, as not adjourned by themselves nor by anybody else in a proper time nor proper manner; therefore dissolved, or had no being as an assembly, and long before the late President issued any proclamation concerning them.

As to prorogation, it seems to stand pretty nigh upon the like foot: For, an assembly being to be called together by the king's writ returnable at a certain day, it seems clear that no writ afterward issued could assemble them before that day but the power that called them together: As they might have appointed any other day; so it seems reasonable that before that day the same power might prorogue, that is, put their meeting off to a farther day: So, after their meeting, when prorogued to a certain day by the king or by commissioners under the Great Seal, it appears by the authority in Syderfin [24] beforementioned that it was contrary to law to call them together before that day and found necessary to prorogue them to the same day; so when they stood adjourned to a certain day, and the king being willing before that day came to prorogue them, consulted his judges, who told him it could not be done before that very day; and accordingly he issued his proclamation to acquaint the members with his intention of proroguing the Parliament, that no more members might attend than was necessary to make a House for that purpose. And the reason of this seems to be plain; for it is not the several members separated and in their private capacity inhabiting the city and kingdom, and of which a Parliament is to be made up of, but those members convened in their public and legislative capacity, at the time and place appointed, that are to be adjourned; and that seems one reason why so small a number as forty (or a very small number compared with the rest) makes up a quorum of the House of Commons.

A Parliament before they are met cannot be adjourned, because not a Parliament in being to be adjourned; nor anything done to be continued: But the time of their first meeting may be prorogued or put off to a farther day. But after they have met, to adjourn a Parliament at any other time than when they are met, and a Parliament is adjourning of what is not in being at that time to be adjourned: Which is too manifest an absurdity to need more to be said about it.

If this doctrine be true, what comes of the support of government, and the rest of our laws? 'Tis hard to be without laws, said the Gentleman.

I have spoke to that already (answered the Lawyer) and hate repetition. The support of the government is temporary, and but for a small time too, and difficult to be disputed (however lawfully it may be done) before a governor and judges of his own making, and who are made to believe it is in his power to displace them at his pleasure, and consequently all concerned in interest to support that support that maintains them; but may not be averse to the hearing of disputes concerning beneficial perpetual laws; because if not made by a competent authority, there is some prospect of advantage to be acquired by assenting to them when they are, and the price may rise in proportion to the need there is of them: But honest and resolute men will no more buy wholesome and necessary laws than they will sell them.

Admitting that the Assembly be dissolved as you say (replied the Gentleman) and they do not know or believe they are dissolved, or will not believe it, but will notwithstanding sit and act; will not their laws be binding?

If they are dissolved, said the Lawyer (and I believe it will puzzle you or any man to prove that they are not, and have not been so a long time), what reason can you or anyone give me why the laws made by any other equal number of men that will sit and act, and lay burdens upon the subject, shall not be equally binding and compel the subject to pay them: And will they not be very wise people who submit to pay any taxes laid by an unlawful authority?

I am no lawyer, replied the other, and therefore can say little to these matters: But I wish the judges and lawyers of New York, or our Chief Justice had been present at this discourse.

I should have been well pleased if he had (answered the Lawyer), for tho' I know anything I can say before persons of so much learning and knowledge in the law will be like *holding a candle to the sun;* and what I have said would have served only as hints for their more clear and explicit treating of the thing (for I doubt not everyone joins with me in opinion), yet since they are not here, you (said he, turning to me) who have taken this discourse in shorthand (as I suppose, being a great master in that way of writing) may communicate it to the public; whom I hope these learned gentlemen will oblige with their more copious and elaborate handling of this subject.

This, Mr. Zenger, I now do, and am, sir,

your humble servant,

Jeremy Anonymous, junr.

Middletown in New Jersey,
August 16, 1734.

Numb. 49. Monday, October 7th, 1734.

Mr. Zenger;[25]

I have received a copy of a letter of thanks from the people of Goshen to their representative, who lives in that neighborhood, which I think deserves to be made public, with an account of true circumstances that rarely attend addresses of this nature. I am told that only one man refused, and that all the freeholders have signed who were not absent at the time of signing. You will see by the list of names that about 78 have signed, which proves that very few were absent, I am told not above 3 or 4. This address came from those persons who had opposed Col. Mathews' election, and who can be least suspected to have done it from private views to serve him; on the contrary, everyone (with the former single exception) laid aside their private resentments to show their public gratitude: When this is compared with what has happened in other parts of this province, it will be seen how justly the people are said to be fickle and changeable, and whether the people have deserted their patriots, or their patriots have deserted them; for to me the people seem steadily to pursue the same maxims of liberty.

Goshen, August 21, 1734.

To Col. Vincent Mathews.

Sir;

We the subscribing freeholders, inhabitants of the precinct of Goshen and Minisink, in the County of Orange, take this opportunity of returning you our hearty thanks for your conduct in the last sessions of the Assembly, while matters of the greatest consequence for the security of our lives, liberty, and property were under your consideration: But we are surprised those things could have admitted so much debate among the representatives of a free people, that they could not be brought to a conclusion before you parted. For supposing the arguments on both sides of the question were otherwise of equal force, can the lovers of liberty hesitate in determining in favor of liberty, and in opposition to what may be introductory of arbitrary power? The laws themselves being a dead letter, which can do neither good nor hurt, but as they have life and force given them from those who are entrusted with the execution of them; it seems to us essential to our freedom that the authority by which our laws receive their life do not depend upon the will and pleasure of any man, or upon a mere opinion of the judges, who are only entrusted to execute the laws, or any other than the plain and positive authority of those who make them.

The accounts we have of your conduct, so conformable to the sentiments of the people you represent, and of your zeal to remove from all trust in the execution of justice such persons whose characters and actions have laid them under the just suspicion of the people of this province, has endeared you to your constituents. The love and esteem of your neighbors will give more real satisfaction and pleasure than the favor of any man however great, and we hope you will find it a greater security. Governors often smile one day and frown the next; nay, they may make a sacrifice of those that have lost all others' friendship by courting theirs; and at best they are here today and gone tomorrow: But you we hope will remain long with us, and your posterity with ours. Your interest is the same with that of the people amongst whom you live, and therefore the most certain security to preserve what you have and transmit it to your latest posterity is got by preserving and increasing the love, virtue, and freedom of the people where you live.—As we doubt not that you will continue in a dutiful execution of the trust reposed in you, so we assure you that you may depend on all the kind and grateful returns that can be expected from a people sensible of your many services.[26]

New York, Sept. 30.[27]

At a Council held at Fort George in New York. Present, His Excellency William Cosby, Esq., the Honorable Francis Harison, Esq., and some others of His Majesty's Council; when His Excellency was pleased to nominate Robert Lurting, Esq., Mayor, John Hendrick Symes, Esq., Sheriff, and Richard Nicolls, Esq., Coroner, for the ensuing year.

The same day came on the elections of the magistrates for this city, and we are informed that the polls for aldermen and common-councilmen stood as follows:

	Aldermen.	Common Council.
Dock Ward	John Cruger, 6 *Step. Bayard, 77	John Moore, 38 Wessel Wessels, 37
	And many more ready to poll for the new candidate.	
East Ward	John Rosevelt, 12 *John Walter, 107	Petrus Rutgers, 17 *Ch. L'Reaux, 99
	And many more ready to poll for the new candidates.	
Montgomerie Ward	Joh. Hardenbroek, 1 *Christoph. Fell, 30	Abel Hardenbr., 1 *John Fred, 30
	And many more ready to poll for the new candidates.	
Out Ward	Gerard Stuyvesant, no opposition.	Tho. D'Key, none. *Joh. Waldron, no opposition.
West Ward	H. van Guelder, 5 *William Rome, 35	John Chamers, 5 *Hen. Bogert, 35

And many more ready to poll for the new candidates.

South Ward	*Simon Johnson, 49 *Isaac de Peyster, 45	*Ede Myer, 49 *Peter Low, 45
North Ward	Anth. Rutgers, 51 *John Burger, 46	Gerrit Rose, 51 *Evert Byvank, 46

A scrutiny was demanded, and upon the scrutiny the votes stood thus:

Anth. Rutgers, 37 *John Burger, 38	Gerrit Rose, 37 *Evert Byvank, 38

Simon Johnson and Ede Myer carried it against the Governor's interest notwithstanding there voted against them a considerable merchant who was an inhabitant of another ward, and about 15 of the soldiers of His Majesty's garrison, besides the Recorder of the city and his interest.[28]

N.B. Mr. Anthony Duane merchant of this city and a great Governor's man, carried his election for Constable of the East Ward by a great majority.

N.B. *Those marked with an * are new candidates.*

As the transactions concerning the scrutiny are of great consequence to this city, they seem deserving of a particular relation and remarks, which I hope may be given in a future paper.

All the members that are chosen were put up by an interest opposite to the Governor's, except John Moore, in whose favor a great many of the city joined, or he would have lost his election.

All those that were aldermen and common-councilmen before signed the address to the Governor that is printed in Mr. Bradford's *Gazette* No. 449, except Alderman Stuyvesant, for which reason he had no opposition in the new choice.[29]

The virtue and vigor of the inhabitants of this city has been such on this occasion as deserves a better pen than mine to give it its due praise, which I hope some will, which will be a great satisfaction to

Your wellwisher,

Thomas Standby

4. New York Weekly Journal nos. 13 and 23: issues cited in the Attorney General's information against Zenger. Richard Bradley's information against Zenger for seditious libel was based on his interpretation of these two articles in these issues of the *Journal.* Hamilton's defense was premised on the assumption that they contained no statement which was not factually correct. The articles have never before been fully reprinted, however, and the allegedly libelous passages appear in a quite new light when read in their proper context.

Numb. 13. Monday, January 28, 1733.

DOMESTIC AFFAIRS

To the authors of the letter to Mr. Bradford, in his Gazette *of January 21, 1734.*[30]

Gentlemen;

Your appearance in print at last gives a pleasure to many, tho' most wish that you had come fairly into the open field and not appeared behind retrenchments made of the supposed *laws against libeling* and of what other men have said and done before: These retrenchments, *gentlemen,* may soon be shown to you and all men to be weak, and have neither law nor reason for their foundation, so cannot long stand you in stead. Therefore you had much better as yet leave them, and come to what THE PEOPLE of this city and province think are the points in question, *to wit:*

They think, as matters now stand, that their LIBERTIES *and* PROPERTIES *are precarious, and that* SLAVERY *is like to be entailed on them and their posterity, if some past things be not amended. And this they collect from many past proceedings.*

You gentlemen think that things past are right, and that things may go on in the same way without such consequence.

These points, gentlemen, highly concern the PEOPLE of this province, and you as well as the rest; it is your interest as well as theirs to have them fairly searched into by enquiry into facts, and by plain and fair arguments upon them without passion. If you are right in your thoughts, then there will be no harm by or from the fair and thorough enquiry: But should you be wrong, and the consequence dreaded follow for want of a timely enquiry and remedy, your posterity as well as ours will be sufferers; nay, you have most reason to fear that your posterity will be the first that will fall by establishing UNBRIDLED POWER.

As the liberty of the press is now struck at, which is the safeguard of all our other liberties: This starts another point worth discussing, which by many was thought would never have needed to have been handled here more than it has been: And undoubtedly it is one of the first things that ought to be examined into fairly before the world.

What other men have said and done (unless right) can be no justification for following their example; these men ought, and we believe soon will, severally justify what they have said and done, or confess wherein they have erred, and make all reasonable satisfaction for their errors.

If anything has been too stinging in what has been printed here, it is believed your delaying so long in coming to the press in order to a fair enquiry was the cause, and will excuse it.

These are the sentiments of many of this city and province, and it is hoped that passions of neither side will draw the disputants off from the points in question.

Numb. 23. Monday, April 8th, 1734.

New Brunswick, March 27, 1734.[31]

Mr. Zenger;

I was at a public house some days since in company with some persons that came from New York: Most of them complained of the deadness of trade: Some of them laid it to the account of the repeal of the Tonnage Act, which they said was done to gratify the resentment of some in New York in order to distress Governor Burnet;[32] but which has been almost the ruin of that town, by paying the Bermudians about £12,000 a year to export those commodities which might be carried in their own bottoms, and the money arising by the freight spent in New York. They said that the

Bermudians were an industrious frugal people who bought no one thing in New York, but lodged the whole freight money in their own island, by which means, since the repeal of that Act, there has been taken from New York above £90,000 and all this to gratify pique and resentment. But this is not all; this money being carried away which would otherwise have circulated in this province and city, and have been paid to the baker, the brewer, the smith, the carpenter, the shipwright, the boatman, the farmer, the shopkeeper, etc., has deadened our trade in all its branches, and forced our industrious poor [33] to seek other habitations; so that within these three years there has been above 300 persons have left New York; the houses stand empty, and there is as many houses as would make one whole street with bills upon their doors: And this has been as great a hurt as the carrying away the money, and is occasioned by it, and all degrees of men feel it, from the merchant down to the carman. And (adds he) it is the industrious poor is the support of any country, and the discouraging the poor tradesmen is the means of ruining any country. Another replies, it is the excessive high wages you tradesmen take prevents your being employed: Learn to be contented with less wages, we shall be able to build, and then no need to employ Bermudians. Very fine, replied the first, now the money is gone you bid us take less wages, when you have nothing to give us, and there is nothing to do. Says another, I know nobody gets estates with us but the lawyers; we are almost come to that pass that an acre of land can't be conveyed under half an acre of parchment. The fees are not settled by our legislature, and everybody takes what they please; and we find it better to bear the disease than to apply for a remedy that's worse: I hope (said he) our Assembly will take this matter into consideration; especially since our late judge hath proved *no fees are lawful but what are settled by them.*[34] I own a small vessel, and there is a fee for a *let-pass,*[35] which I am told is taken by the Cannon Law, and by no other.—One of our neighbors being in company, observing the strangers full of complaints, endeavored to persuade them to remove into Jersey. To which it was replied, that would be *leaping out of the frying pan into the fire;* for, says he, we both are under the same Governor, and your Assembly have shown with a witness what is to be expected from them. One that was then moving to Pennsylvania (to which place it is reported several considerable men are removing) expressed in terms very moving much concern for the circumstances of New York, seemed to think them very much owing to the influence that some men (whom he called tools) had in the administration; said he was now going from them, and was not to be hurt by any measures they should take; but could not help having some concern for the welfare of his countrymen, and should be glad to hear that the Assembly would exert themselves as became them, by showing that they have the interest of their country more at heart than the gratification of any private view of any of their members, or being at all affected by the smiles or frowns of a governor; both which ought equally to be despised when the interest of their country is at stake. You, says he, complain of the lawyers, but I think the law itself is at an end: We see men's deeds destroyed, judges arbitrarily displaced, new courts erected without consent of the legislature, by which it seems to me trials by juries are taken away when a governor pleases; men of known estates denied their votes contrary to the received practice, the best expositor of any law: Who is then in that province that call anything his own, or enjoy any liberty longer than those in the administration will condescend to let him do it? [36] For which reason I have left it, as I believe more will. One of the company replied; if these are illegal impositions, why don't your Assembly impeach the authors of them. *Impeach!* says a Gentleman (once an officer of the Customs) would you have the mob and canaille impeach gentlemen? American assemblies, that have only the power to make little paltry bylaws, pretend to the power of a British Parliament! But besides should they be mad enough to impeach, that impeachment cannot be tried.—How! not tried! (replied the Gentleman) that's strange indeed! I know this is a way of talking you courtiers have among you, to prevent being dealt with as some of you very well deserve. Give me leave to tell you, Sir, you talk indecently of those that differ from you: There are many among them of equal if not superior knowledge to any of your party, and more of superior estates; and our assemblies are very far from deserving the name of *canaille* or dregs of the people, as some of you, who (bating [37] your commissions, which you would never have had in any other place) much better deserve, are fond of using to them: And should they use their authority as they might, would make the proudest of you tremble. Pray (in order to clear this matter up) let me ask a few questions.

Is there any British subject can commit a crime with impunity, and is (if guilty of it) too big to be accused?

He answered, No.

Is the law and the administration of justice so weak and defective in the plantations that any British subject cannot be tried for any crime, and condemned or acquitted according to the merits of his cause?

He answered, It is not.

Does not a Grand Jury (tho' chose by the Sheriff) represent the county?

Answ. They do.

Cannot a Grand Jury indict (that is accuse) any man a subject within their county (how great soever) of any crime?

Answ. They may.

Does not an Assembly represent the whole province, as much as a Grand Jury does a particular county?

Answ. Yes.

Is it unlawful for an Assembly to impeach (that is accuse) any person of any crime?

Answ. No.

Is the administration so weak as not to be able to try the supposed criminal on the Assembly's accusation; tho' you have allowed they can that of a Grand Jury?

I don't suppose it is, *answered the Courtier.*

Then they can be tried, replied the Gentleman.

Courtier. But will they try?

Gent. *I don't suppose they will or dare deny common justice.*

Courtier. But the king can pardon.

Gent. *You are in some measure mistaken in that too, if you mean before trial; for no pardon under the Great Seal is pleadable to an impeachment by the Commons: And if that Assembly once let the world know that they can and will impeach, they'll teach you courtiers to be a little more cautious than they have been.*

The Gentleman was going on upon the duty of an Assembly: But one of the company desired him to leave his politics to another time; which makes me unable to say more, but that I am,

Sir, etc.

NO COURTIER.

P.S. I had forgot to tell you that the Gentleman called *impeachments* the true and greatest PALLADIUM of the people's LIBERTY.

APPENDIX B · PREPARATIONS FOR THE TRIAL, 1735

1. James Alexander's brief. The following is James Alexander's legal brief for his contemplated defense of Zenger, a defense which was exactly paralleled by the first portions of Hamilton's argument in the trial. It is most interesting for its hints as to the evidence which might have been offered to prove the truth of Zenger's statements, had Chief Justice De Lancey allowed it to be introduced.[1]

Zenger ads Dom Regis	Information for Libeling Method proposed for Defense

[Notes entered in a second column on the page:]

Quere, if should except to the Ch. Justice from judging because:

1st. He was one who supported the argument agt. Zenger's *Journals* in the conference between the Council and Assembly.[2]

2dly. On the argument on Zenger's *habeas corpus* he said on this very case that a jury would go near to perjure themselves if they found Zenger not guilty, and submit whether he be an indifferent judge to try the cause.[3]

Support this by 3d Coke 29 *Institutes;* [4] *safety of prisoner* consisteth in indifferency of the Court, the judges ought not to deliver their opinions beforehand of any criminal case that may come before them judicially, etc.

If except, *quere,* if in writing or *viva voce.*

As it's notorious that *Journals* have been sold at Zenger's house, that many people have paid himself for them and even some of jury, also his sons and servant may possibly be compelled to declare their knowledge of his printing them, etc., I think it may give an ill turn to the minds of the jury to lay any stress on want of proof of his printing or publishing, and I think better acknowledge them, but think stress of the defense ought to be on this point.

Whether those parts of the *Journals* in the information be libels or not?

That they were libel perhaps will be produced 1 Hawkins 194 [5] that it's no justification of a libel that the contents thereof are true.

Supported by the Star Chamber cases on margin; and possibly sundry cases in King Charles the Second and King James 2d's time may be produced to prove the same doctrine.

Answer

The destruction of the Star Chamber and the Revolution succeeding these two reigns and the manifest partiality and exorbitancy of these reigns, as the judges then being at discretion of the ministry and pushed and willed for its purposes,

> [Second column:] But here I think it may not be amiss to give a short view of the exorbitancy of those times and the extraordinary [?] doctrines there propagated by the judges with the cures that have since been applied to those things.
>
> *Abr. State Trials* vol. 1st bottom of page 182 to end of common plea [6] and observe on it, here we see plays strained up to the government and writing against them to be writing against the government and a horrible punishment inflicted for it and numerous were the instances of such cruelties of that Court of Star Chamber from which the chief of the doctrine of libels was wrought.
>
> But this terrible Court of Star Chamber was made an end by the Stat. 17 Car. 1st fo. 1107 read part of 1st., 2d., and 3d. par. circumflexed, but *vid.* the preamble and n.b.
>
> But in King Charles the 2d and King James the 2d's time the Court of King's Bench began to exercise the same cruelties as the Court of Star Chamber had done.
>
> At *State Trials* vol. 3 fol. 854. S.S. Barnardiston fined 10,000, etc., but this was reversed. See *State Trials* vol. 5 page 716. [illegible matter]
>
> But the judges (then at the king's mere will) once in KJ 2d's time did openly claim the whole authority of the Star Chamber and the right to inflict like punishments. As Comberback 36.[7]
>
> But declaration of Lords and Commons put an end to those things and enacted they should never be drawn into consequence.

Stat. 1 W. and M.

State Trials vol. 2d 546 Brewster's trial Ld C.J. to say king's abusing his power the people may resist it expressed truth without more, etc., but after the Revolution that doctrine was so far from being law that the Canbury [?] Dr. Sacheverell suffered for asserting—whose trial *State Trials* vol. 5 page 686. If king invade the people's there of supreme power it's lawful to oppose a past fame.

[The second column ends here.]

leaves no stress on those authorities, on the contrary as in *State Trials* vol. 4, 290 [8] things in ill reigns are to be marked out as rocks for us to avoid rather than patterns to be imitated

That they are not libels.

What a libel is even by Star Chamber law:

1 Hawkins 193 a malicious defamation in printing or writing or any defamation whatsoever.

Now if what's printed be true it cannot be a defamation for defamation must be charging another with something false and scandalous or more nearly to the word, giving another fame that what's agreeable to truth, but giving one's true fame cannot be a defamation.

2d. The information itself and all indictments and informations for libels that ever were do plainly point out what's requisite to make a paper a libel, viz., to be false, malicious, seditious and scandalous, but if a paper be not proved to be these, but on the contrary to be true, twelve upon their oaths could never justly find a defendant guilty of such information.

[In margin:] Subpoena Geo. Clarke to p. the destruction of the Indian deed.[9]

With this agrees:

State Trials vol. 4, 363b (bishops' trial) Sir Robt. Sawyer as to falsity and that it was malicious and seditious are all matters of fact and no proof offered up.

Ibid., 390b Justice Powell: to make it a libel it must be false and malicious and it must tend to sedition and I see nothing to prove falsehood and malice.

State Trials 3. vol. 851 Barnardiston trial 851 No proof of seditious intent but Chief Justice Jeffreys said law supplies proof, but Wms. of counsel for defendant insisted on proof of malice.

Ibid., 854 A verdict against Barnardiston, but *State Trials* vol. 5 page 716 that judgment reversed by House of Lords on writ of error and gave their reasons.[10]

State Trials vol. 5 page 544 Mr. Serg. Darnell of counsel agt. Tutchin says will you say they are true from which may be inferred that if he would have said so and proved so then they would not have been libels seeing they were not false.

State Trials vol. 5 page 448 Fuller's case, L.C.J. Holt: Can you make it appear that books are true?

Ibid., 449 If you can offer any matter to prove what you have written let us hear it.

> [In margin in another hand:] See the [two illegible words] of the L.C. Ju. Holt in several parts of the page where to attaint the deft. may call witnesses to prove the content of the libel. [In margin, Alexander's hand:] Witness: Geo. Clarke, Cornelius Van Horne, Capt. Morris, Rip Van Dam, Joseph Scott, Jere. Tothill, Richard Ashfield.

Objection.

A libel not to be justified upon an indictment or information, tho' the contents be true and for this may be cited many books as Hobart 253 and Coke's *Reports* 125, both Star Chamber cases. 3d Salkeld 225 Holt says deft. may justify in an action not in an indictment for a libel if words be true.[11]

I say that this must mean that a deft. can't plead the justification of the words on an indictment, but cannot mean that deft. can't give it in evidence that they are true.

For to suppose it would make the law contradict itself.

As suppose an action is brought for a libel and deft. justified by pleading that what he wrote was true, as it was lawful for him to do, and proves his justification and is acquitted. Shall deft. for same thing be condemned on an information or indictment when it was admitted before that it was lawful for him to do it?

I think it's absurd to say it and to take off the absurdity, tho' he can't plead the justification, he may give the matter of it in evidence, and agreeable to this is the general cases before listed.

Also:

Law of Evidence 111 When a man cannot take advantage of special matter in pleading, he shall take advantage of it in evidence. *Co. Lit.* 283[12] example 1 Hawk. cap. 29 sect. 25.

1 Hawk. cap. 62 sect. 3 In battery may give it in evidence that other first assaulted him, but in an action for it he must plead it.

2d Hawkins cap. 46 sect. 44 It seems agreed that *son assault demesne* may be given in evidence on the general issue in an indictment but not in an action of battery.

Also, in murder deft. shall not justify by *se defendendo, per infortunium,* etc., but must give it in evidence.

As to that part of no. 13 in the information, that question may be put without any libel or accusation agt. the present administration, seeing no time is prefixed for the many past proceedings, and I shall now assign some past proceedings before this govt. and from which it might be collected, viz.:

1 The erecting a Court of Chancery in Col. Hunter's time and the Exchequer in the present Gov.'s time without consent in General Assembly, which is a thing notorious and the consequences of that thing has been again and again resolved to be oppressive by the acts of the General Assembly which are also notorious.

> [In margin:] *Quere,* if plea to jurisdiction of Chancery in the Equivalent case late filed may not be given in evidence to prove this. Especially as by the King's counsel it was admitted true by coming to hearing thereon without denying the facts thereof by replication.[13]

Judges, justices, sheriffs and coroners, in whose hands are our laws, our liberties and properties, were before this Govr. came appointed by the govr. alone contrary to the royal instructions, and consequently our lives, liberties and properties were at the mere will of a govr. before this Govr. came, and I think no man will say but that this is a state of slavery, and so no libel on the present administration as charged.

But that paper is very modest for afterwards the contrary question is put and only purposes a fair enquiry into facts who is right or not pretending to assert the truth of one side or other of the question.

As to that part of no. 23 in the information, the facts are that they see men's deeds destroyed, judges arbitrarily displaced, new courts erected without consent of the legislature, by which it seems to me trials by juries are taken away when a govr. pleases, men of known estate denied their votes.

> [In margin:] George Clarke was present at destroying deed; the proceedings at Albany are always entered on minutes of Council, and this was so entered. *Quere,* if can't compel clerk of Council to give evidence of it. The *New York Gazette* may be insisted on for a proof because the information says that no. 13 means Govr., etc., but from the face of it it appears to be directed to the writers of paragraph in the *Gazette* the week before, and consequently the Govr., etc., were writers of that paragraph, also because the *Gazette* is printed by the King's printer of New York, who is paid a yearly salary of £50 drawn by the Govr.

If these facts be true then are the facts asserted in that paper not false, malicious, seditious, etc., as in the information.

As to destroying Albany deed, Richard Ashfield and Jeremiah Tuthill to prove as per dispositions of Albany people; also the *New York Gazette* No.[14] which confesses it and endeavors to justify it.

Judges arbitrarily displaced: to wit, the late Chief Justice of this Court, Vincent Matthews to prove the new commission to Orange County,[15] but if he does not, then in general leave it to every man's knowledge whether not only this but former governors have displaced judges at their pleasure (which is doing it arbitrarily).

As to erecting new courts:

Govr. Hunter's erecting Court of Chancery as before, and for other instances leave it to jury's own knowledge from Van Dam's case.

> [In margin:] The preface to the argument of Van Dam's counsel signed by Van Dam; also the further proceedings of Van Dam by which it appears to have been adjudged on demurrer for want of equity, that the King

> might sue in equity without any equity, which is taking away juries in all civil causes of the King if govrs. please.[16]

As to men of known estates denied their votes: the *Journal* no. 9.[17]

Lewis Morris, Junr., Jas Tothill to prove truth of that account of Westchester election.

As to the question put upon these facts, it seems rational to follow from the facts, to conclude with an encomium on the liberty of the press, the danger of cramping it, we see most nations in the world were reduced to slavery and arbitrary power, the freedom of the press is one of the greatest preservatives agt. that. No proof that the *Journals* informed agt. were false, malicious, scandalous and seditious as charged in the information, and how can they upon their oaths say they were so without saying which they cannot say that deft. is guilty as in the information set forth.

Should the Attorney Genll. show authorities which I do not know that he can, that other parts of the same *Journals* may be given in evidence, there is one article in no. 13 immediately before that in the information which is a hearsay[18] that proved not true, but I think it's unreasonable to put deft. on proving anything out of the information, at least without notice that it will be insisted on, but however here is an affidavit of Abraham Vanhorn, one of the Council, who heard that matter from a man who said he was come from Rhode Island, which I think is enough to justify an article of hearsay news, and there's nothing in that article that's scandalous, seditious or malicious nor false, as there it's set forth: viz., only *we hear* for once it was heard, as by that affidavit will appear if necessary to be produced.

2. *Alexander's drafts of speeches for Zenger: "Prologue and Epilogue to the Farce."* The Morrisites, in despair after the disbarment of Alexander and Smith and before the engagement of Hamilton, apparently intended

to have Zenger speak in his own defense. They had little faith in John Chambers as a defense attorney, and hoped that the hapless defendant could sway the jurors. The two brief speeches are in Alexander's hand, and were probably composed by him. He cynically endorsed them "Prologue and Epilogue to the Farce," doubtless in the days of defeat which quickly followed Zenger's acquittal.[19]

I

May it please Your Honors:

On the silencing my counsel the Court have thought proper to assign me Mr. Chambers who I am convinced will do me all the justice in his power. But as by an act of the General Assembly a man may also plead his own cause, I beg Your Honors will allow me to say everything necessary in the course of this trial which I think absolutely necessary for my own justification, and I don't doubt Your Honors will give me all the privileges due to an Englishman and assist me with your counsel, which I am informed the judges are obliged to do.

I must now beg leave to apply myself to Your Honors, the Chief Justice in particular, and I hope what I shall offer will be sufficient to convince Your Honor that you ought not to sit as judge on my trial in this cause.

My 1st reason is Your Honor was one of the honorable Council that ordered a warrant to commit me to gaol and then was one of the managers at a conference with the General Assembly in which conference Your Honor was pleased to insist that all my *Journals* were scandalous libels, and farther was one of the members of the Council that ordered some of them to be burnt by the hands of the Common Hangman.[20] Which I hope Your Honor will think a full declaration of your opinion and as Your Honor has prejudged the cause, I am therefore of opinion that Your Honor can't hear what I have to offer in my own defense with that impartiality that is necessary for my own justification.

My second reason is that upon my being brought down before Your Honor upon my *habeas corpus,* you was pleased to declare that if any jury acquitted me they would go near being perjured. And to show Your Honor that I have law on my side I beg leave to read a part of 3rd Coke's *Institutes* page 29. Read the case.

For these reasons I hope Your Honor won't sit judge in this cause. But should what I have offered have not sufficient weight to induce Your Honor to leave the bench, I hope Your Honor's impartiality during the course of the trial will convince me that I am wrong in what I offered, and that you have not prejudged the cause.

II

May it please Your Honors and you gentlemen of the jury:

I have now made, by my counsel and self, the best defense I can against the heavy charge of His Majesty's Attorney General that I am a seditious person. You gentlemen of the jury know me, that I have lived very peaceably in this province, that I have in this case followed my trade for the support of my family. And think they have not proved that the papers I am prosecuted for are either false, scandalous, fictitious or seditious, but have produced strong proof of the contrary.

Gentlemen, hard is my case. Here I have lain almost a twelve-month in gaol and my family has been supported by the charity of good honest people, which otherwise must have starved. Thus I have been deprived by this long and tedious confinement from following my business and paying my just debts.[21] My parents and self fled from a country where oppression, tyranny and arbitrary power had ruined almost all the people, and by the generous bounty of Her most gracious Majesty, Queen Anne of pious memory, we were provided for in this province where I have since lived. And to you gentlemen I appeal for my just character. 'Tis you that are this day to pronounce me guilty or innocent. And if for declaring the truth I am to suffer still greater punishment than almost a year's imprisonment, let it be such a punishment as will make an end of my life, for I can't bear the thought of having my family starving and my poor little babes crying for bread, and I not in a capacity to relieve them. To punish a man, gentlemen, for telling the truth, no human law can enact because it opposes the divine laws of God set forth in his Holy Scripture. I shall take up no more of your time, gentlemen, only I beg that the Golden Rule of doing as you would be done by will have its due weight in your consideration upon my affair. And to you, gentlemen, I submit myself, and from you expect the justice due to me.

3. John Chambers' brief. The following document is a brief of the argument which Chambers apparently presented in his opening speech at the Zenger trial. The first several pages of the manuscript, which merely set forth the Attorney General's information against Zenger, are omitted here. The court-appointed lawyer's line of reasoning was not so bold as those of Alexander and Hamilton, but it was competent and indicates that he proposed a conscientious defense of his controversial client.[22]

. . . To which information the Defendant hath pleaded not guilty, in manner and form as he is charged in the information, and for his trial thereof, hath put himself upon his country, which country you are, and which issue you are sworn to try. That is, (as I take it) you are sworn to try, whether the Defendant John Peter Zenger did falsely, seditiously and scandalously print and publish two false, malicious, seditious and scandalous libels, as charged in the information or not; and that he did so print and publish them and that they are false, malicious, seditious and scandalous.[23] I conceive it is incumbent on Mr. Attorney fully to prove and make appear, (not by innuendoes, probabilities and farfetched insinuations) but by plain, positive and convincing evidence. Otherwise you will acquit the Defendant and say he is not guilty. I must own, gentlemen, as I know this to be a cause of great expectation and consequence, I was in hopes I should not have been concerned on either side, and that for several reasons: But since this Court on the prayer of the Defendant were pleased to appoint me of counsel for him, I could not refuse, and indeed as the case was circumstanced with him I think I ought not to have declined him. Notwithstanding I was truly sensible that the nicety of the doctrine naturally arising in such causes (I mean the doctrine of libels) was in a manner new among us and that it required a knowledge in the law far superior to mine in order to distinguish the law from the several facts as proved upon the trial, so as to do justice to my client. For I had often of late reflected and thought that the doctrine of libels was very unsettled in our law books, and that several of the leading cases cited in our books for law seem rather to have been calculated for the arbitrary times in which they were made than to be transmitted to posterity for the good of mankind and the preservation of our rights and liberties: As those Star Chamber cases from the third year of Henry VII to the 17th of King Charles I, when that Court of Star Chamber was dissolved for having arbitrarily assumed to itself a power which by law it ought not, and for inflicting heavier punishments than by law were warranted. And most if not all of those Star Chamber cases were founded on informations brought by the Attorney General. For, as an ingenious author well observes, in cases between subject and subject it lies in the power of the Court to refuse an information if they see cause for so doing, and the defendant hath a day allowed to him to show such cause. Yet when the Crown is the prosecutor, the Attorney General comes into court and by his own authority files an information in the King's name which the judges cannot refuse, nor hath the defendant any privilege to show cause against it. By which means the ministers and those in power have opportunities to harass the best designing man with frivolous and vexatious prosecutions. For though he is acquitted by his country, yet the Crown being exempted by prerogative from paying costs, the innocent man may be involved in an insupportable expense and be thus punished without conviction.

I say such and the like reflections on these doctrines as laid down even at this day could not but make me sensible that any person accused of libeling, though never so innocent, required the assistance of the most able counsel, of which I have not the vanity to think myself one. However I hope the innocence of Mr. Zenger in the present case will altogether supply my inabilities, and I am satisfied he will meet with nothing, but what is right and just at the hands of the Court as well as from you gentlemen of the jury, and therefore I proceed the more cheerfully to discharge (in the best manner I am capable of) the duty I owe to my client. In doing of which I shall beg leave again: 1st, to consider the charge he stands accused of; 2ndly, the proofs necessary to convict him thereof; 3rdly, how far the proof offered is deficient herein, and; 4thly, from the whole show that he is not guilty of the charge in manner and form as laid in the information.

And first the charge is for writing and publishing two false and scandalous libels. Now in the first place it will be necessary to consider what is a libel. And for this read 1 *Hawkins* fo. 193 ch. 73, who tells us that a libel in a strict sense is taken for a malicious defamation expressed whether in printing or writing, etc. 5 *Co.* 121; 5 *Mod.* 165.[24] Now by these authorities it appears that every libel must be a malicious defamation. Now to defame is falsely and maliciously to take from a man his good name and character or to endeavor to do so. Therefore, according to this definition, every libel must be false and malicious and consequently tending to defame somebody certain either in their public or private capacity. ⟨I say somebody certain and who certain must be proved and known by something more than bare assertion, for generals are uncertain, and no one can tell who are meant. Therefore let us consider who are or can be meant by these papers called libels.⟩ [25]

2ndly. Now the proof necessary to convict any person of libeling, I take it, must be to prove the person accused to be guilty of writing, printing or publishing the supposed libel, and that it is false, scandalous and malicious, tending to defame. Otherwise, according to the definition before mentioned, it can be no libel. The person or persons meant must be certainly and particularly named, for generally are uncertain and by them no one can tell who are meant.

State Trials vol. 5 page 550, Sir Robert Sawyer 567.[26] I have now done with the second and shall proceed to the 3rd point, which is how far the proof offered is deficient to prove the Defendant guilty . . .[27]

APPENDIX C
THE CONTROVERSY CONTINUED: TWO ESSAYS OF 1737

1. Anglo-Americanus' critique: Remarks on the Trial of John Peter Zenger, Printer. This essay by "Anglo-Americanus" was one of two long letters attacking the Morrisite conduct of the Zenger case which appeared in Keimer's *Barbados Gazette* in July 1737 and which were later reprinted as a single pamphlet in Philadelphia, New York, and London. Anglo-Americanus dissects Hamilton's defense of Zenger from an English lawyer's moderate point of view. His statement that the liberties of the colonist are sufficiently protected by the ordinary executive, legislative, and judicial institutions of the British empire represents the most forceful and convincing criticism of the radical contentions of Hamilton and Alexander.[1]

Sir, it has been a common remark among those who have observed upon the capricious dispensations of fortune that great events are often produced by instruments that are not seemingly adequate; nay, that the same apparent causes have quite contrary effects; and the road that leads one man to wealth, honor, and power, sometimes carries another to poverty, infamy and ruin. Hence comes that confused distribution of axes and coronets, halters and ribbons, which history displays by numerous shocking examples; and thus it is that fate seems to play at cross-purposes with mankind; or to speak in scripture phrase, in this sense as well as many others, *the wisdom of this world is foolishness.*

I find myself drawn into these grave reflections by reading the *Trial of John Peter Zenger, at New York, upon an Information for Printing and Publishing a Libel.* This piece it seems has been lately printed there, and was put into my hands, t'other day, by a friend who has both a general acquaintance and a correspondence with the northern colonies, as a rare production containing many things new and surprising. And in truth I must say it affords a lively specimen, in miniature, of the justness of the foregoing remarks. I mean that part of it which is attributed to Andrew Hamilton, Esq., of Philadelphia, barrister at law; together with the sequel describing the munificent behavior of the citizens in Common Council assembled to the learned gentleman for his singular performance on that occasion.

I must at the same time assure you that if *Zenger's Trial* had been printed by order of the court that tried him, or from a copy taken by a private hand at the trial, or by any other means that excluded Mr. Hamilton's approbation or privity, I should have enjoyed my own opinion without troubling you or anybody else about it, and had the charity to resolve all the extravagancies that occur throughout his declamation into a right discernment of the people he talked to, and a dexterity in captivating them which had its effect in the acquittal of his client. But when a gentleman of the bar takes the pains to write over a long discourse (he being the only lawyer of either side who gave the printer his notes) in order to send it abroad through the world as a specimen of his abilities, sentiments and principles; as a solemn argument in the law, fit to see the light and abide the test in all places; and, above all, *as a task of duty, which he thought himself bound to perform, even by going to the utmost parts of the land* for the purpose; and all this, *without fee or reward, under the weight of many years and great infirmities of body:* * When a barrister, I say, thus becomes a volunteer for error, and presumes to obtrude bad law and false reasoning upon the sense of mankind because the sage magistrates of New York have put their seal to it; I think myself at liberty without using any other apology to exercise the judging privilege of a reader, since the gentleman himself has put me into the possession of it.

In doing this, I shall not in the least gratify a vain itch of writing, for there are no extraordinary talents necessary for refuting gross

* Zeng. *Trial,* pp. 99, 103. [In the 1738 edition of the *Remarks* the citations were to Wilford's edition of the *Brief Narrative* published in London in the same year.]

absurdities; but I shall have the honest merit of endeavoring to undeceive such of my fellow subjects in the plantations as may, from the late uncommon success of the doctrine, mistake the liberty of the press for a license to write and publish infamous things of their superiors and of all others, at their pleasure, provided they write and publish nothing but what is true. In the next place, I would preserve as far as I am able the dignity of the profession of the law in these remote parts of the British dominions; and prevent its learned professors in England, who probably will see the renowned piece above mentioned (if we may judge from the industry used in dispersing it), from suspecting that all their American brethren use the like arts to gain popularity and honorable rewards. The former, having the advantage of going daily to the great school of law at Westminster, are already apt enough to think meanly of the accomplishments of the latter who are far removed from instruction; and their opinion must be strongly confirmed in this respect if such a rhapsody as was uttered at New York should not only be applauded and rewarded publicly there, but printed and scattered in reams through the other colonies without being followed by a suitable animadversion.

Neither will it be amiss to take some notice in this place of the quackery of the profession in general, without any particular application, as it has been practiced with vast success in some of our colonies. You will often see (if common fame may be trusted) a self-sufficient enterprising lawyer, compounded of something between a politician and a broker, who, making the foibles of the inhabitants his capital study and withal taking advantage of the weakness of his judges, the ignorance of some of his brethren, the modesty of others, and the honest scruples of a third sort (without having any of his own), becomes insensibly an oracle in the courts, and acquires by degrees a kind of dominion over the minds as well as the estates of the people. An influence never to be obtained but by the help of qualities very different from learning and integrity. Wherever such a man is found, the wonder is not great if from a long habit of advancing what he pleases and having it received for law, he comes in time to fancy that what he pleases to advance is really law.

I have taken the pains during this short vacation between our monthly courts candidly to examine this new system of *libels* lately composed and propagated on the continent; the discovery of which cost the good city of New York *five ounces and a half of gold, a scrip of parchment, and three Latin sentences.** My intention is to consider things, not persons, having no other knowledge of the gentleman principally concerned than what is derived from the paper now before me; and being wholly a stranger to the merit of those disputes that gave rise to the prosecution of this *printer.*

Much less shall I turn advocate for any lawless *power* in governors. God forbid I should be guilty of such a prostitution, who know by experience of what stuff they are commonly made; the wrong impressions they are apt to receive of themselves and others; their passions, prejudices and pursuits; though when all reasonable allowances are made for certain circumstances that attend their mission from home and their situation abroad, a considerate person may be tempted to think—it is well they are no worse than they are.

But to come to my remarks on Zenger's Trial.

In considering the defense made for the defendant (Mr. Zenger) by his counsel (Mr. Hamilton) upon *not guilty* pleaded to an *information for printing and publishing a libel,* it is not to the purpose to enquire how far the matters charged in the information are in their nature libelous, nor whether the *innuendoes* are properly used to apply the matters to persons, things and places. It is only necessary to examine the truth of this single proposition upon which the whole defense is grounded, and to which the several parts of it refer; namely, *that the several matters charged in the information are not and cannot be libelous because they are true in fact.*

This is the cardinal point upon which the learned gentleman's whole argument turns, and which he lays down over and over as the first principle that governs the doctrine of libels; † and according-

* Pages 103–105.

† Zeng. *Trial,* pp. 62, 65, 84.

ingly he confesses the printing and publishing of the papers laid in the information, and puts it upon the King's counsel to prove the facts contained in them to be false; alleging, at the same time, that unless that were done the defendant could not be guilty; but if the same were proved to be false, he would own the papers containing them to be libels.* To this, it seems, the Attorney General answered *that a negative is not to be proved;* and the other replied in these words, which I choose to set down that I may not be thought to do him wrong.—*I did expect to hear that negative cannot be proved; but everybody knows there are many exceptions to that general rule: For if a man is charged with killing another, or stealing his neighbor's horse; if he is innocent in the one case, he may prove the man said to be killed to be still alive; and the horse said to be stolen, never to have been out of his master's stable, etc. And this I think is proving a negative.*† Now I must think that it is strange a gentleman of his sagacity, who owns he was prepared for the objection, could not yet hit upon some of these many exceptions which everybody knows. For he does not more than give two instances of one affirmative being destroyed by another that infers a negative of the first; at which rate most negatives may be proved, and then the old rule may be discarded. Thus if it is shown that a man is alive, it follows clearly that he was not killed; and if a horse is proved to have been always in his master's stable (for this is what must be understood of his being never out of the stable) it certainly follows that he could not be stolen. So that, according to this new scheme of proof, he who is accused of killing a man or stealing a horse is to be put upon proving that he did not kill or steal; because it is possible that such proof may be had sometimes: And so in the principal case, if a question arises whether a certain magistrate has done particular acts of injustice or not, the method is to show that he did not do such acts, not that he did them. I have touched upon this, not for its importance, but as a specimen of the

* Page 69.
† Page 69.

learned barrister's manner of reasoning, and of the spirit with which he sets out from the beginning.

At length, however, he takes the *onus probandi* upon himself * and rather than the thing should go unproved, generously undertakes, at his client's peril, to prove the matters charged in the information as libelous to be true. But I would be glad to know, by the way, how this undertaking gentleman could have proved the truth of divers facts contained in the paper which the defendant published, supposing the Court had been so much overseen as to let him into a proof of this sort. Could he prove, for example, that judges were arbitrarily displaced and new courts erected in the Province of New York, without consent of the legislature? For I am credibly informed there never was a pretense or surmise of more than *one judge* being displaced, or more than one court erected under Mr. Cosby's administration, both which happened upon one and the same occasion.[2] Now I would not have this esteemed a captious exception, when I have to deal with a man of law, who must or ought to know that if such a justification as he offered were at all allowable, it ought to be full and express, so as to leave no room for a libeler to multiply and exaggerate facts at his pleasure when he is disposed to traduce persons in authority; there being a manifest difference between a single act of power without or against law (from which perhaps few governments have been free) and an habitual abuse of power in repeated instances of the same species. I would further ask how he could prove *that the law itself was at an end, and that trials by juries were taken away when a governor pleased;* for if I mistake not, he was at that time speaking to a jury in a regular court of law, and in a prosecution which the Governor had much at heart (as the gentleman himself insinuates) and would have been highly pleased to convict his client, yet would not attempt it but in the ordinary course of trial by a jury, and then too could not find a jury that would convict him. I think I am warranted in putting these questions even by the authority of the barrister himself,

* Page 69.

who says— *Truth ought to govern the whole affair of libels, and yet the party accused runs risk enough even then; for if he fails of proving every tittle he has wrote, and to the satisfaction of the court and jury too, he may find to his cost, etc.**

But for the present I will suppose Mr. Hamilton was able to prove all these things, nay, that the jury knew them all to be true. I will go farther and allow that juries in criminal cases may determine both law and fact when they are complicated, if they will take such a decision upon their consciences (which is almost the only point in which I can have the honor of agreeing with him); yet after all these concessions, the main question rests still between us, *viz., whether a writing can be a libel, in legal acceptation, if the matter contained in it be true.* He is pleased indeed, to express his dislike of infamous papers, even when they are true, if leveled against private vices and faults; and in this case he calls them *base, unworthy, scandalous, unmanly and unmannerly.*† But surely it might be expected, when a point of law was in question, that he would have told us whether they were lawful or unlawful, innocent or criminal, since these last are the only epithets that were relative to his subject, though the first might have their weight in a sermon or moral essay. But it is plain he was aware of the consequence of being explicit upon this head; for had he owned such writings to be lawful, because true, he would have alarmed the common sense of mankind by opening a door for exposing at mercy the frailties, vices, defects and misfortunes of every person high and low, which must inevitably destroy the peace of families, and beget ill blood and disorders. If on the other hand, he had acknowledged such writings to be unlawful inasmuch as they concerned private miscarriages and transactions; but that every man might write as much truth as he pleased about the administration of the government, not only by pointing out faults and mistakes, but by publishing his own comment and inferences in order to fill the minds of the people with all the jealousies and apprehensions his imagination can form; it must have shocked men

* Page 84.
† Page 79.

of understanding to be thus told that the law had provided against private quarrels and breaches of the peace occasioned by virulent writing, but had taken no care to prevent sedition and public disturbance arising from the same cause.

His favorite position, however, was to be maintained at all events; and therefore when the Chief Justice rightly instructed him that he could not be admitted to give the truth of a libel in evidence, *that the law was clear that he could not justify a libel; for it is nevertheless a libel that it is true;* * the discerning gentleman was pleased to understand by the word *justify, a justification by plea, as it is in the case of an indictment for murder, or an assault and battery; there* (says he) *the prisoner cannot justify, but plead not guilty; yet in murder, he may prove it was in defense of his life, his house, etc., and in assault and battery, he may give in evidence that the other party struck first, and in both these cases he will be acquitted.*[3]

If the party in either case is acquitted, the reason is I presume because the matter given in evidence amounts to a justification in law of the fact charged on him, and is equivalent to a confession and avoidance in pleading. In like manner, if truth be a sufficient justification of a libel, the defendant will be acquitted upon proving the contents of his paper to be true. Now let it be observed that the words of the book which the Chief Justice relied on are these.† —*It is far from being a justification of a libel, that the contents thereof are true—since the greater appearance there is of truth in any malicious invective, so much the more provoking it is.* That this is good law I hope I shall be able to show fully hereafter, as I shall show, in the meantime, that it is an express authority against the well-read barrister, who declares *he has not in all his reading met with an authority that says he cannot be admitted to give the truth in evidence, etc.*††

He seems to take it for granted (and I shall not dispute it with him

* Page 69.

† Page 74. [The "book" cited by the Chief Justice was Hawkins, *Pleas of the Crown,* I, 194.]

‡ Page 70.

now) that matter of justification cannot, in any case, be pleaded specially to an indictment of *assault* or *murder;* but the party is to take advantage of it in evidence upon *not guilty* pleaded. Let it be so; yet still this matter must be a sufficient justification, or the party can have no benefit from it any way. In an action of assault and battery where the *first assault* must be pleaded specially, the matter of justification is just the same as an indictment for the same offense where it must be given in evidence upon the general issue. I ask then, whether the *first assault* is a justification in an indictment of assault and battery? If the barrister should answer negatively, such answer is against all sense, for the party is acquitted by virtue of the justification only. If he should answer affirmatively, he is inconsistent with himself, for he has but just affirmed that when the book says, *truth is no justification,* it must be understood of a justification by plea, by which he must mean that nothing else is a justification but what is pleaded, or he must mean nothing at all. For the words of the book are—*it is far from being a justification, etc.* It is not said—*you are far from being at liberty to plead it in bar.* In truth, the author is not there speaking of the forms and rules of proceedings upon libels, but upon the substance and nature of the crime, what shall and what shall not excuse or justify it.* This is manifest from the reason subjoined to support his assertion, *viz., since the greater appearance there is of truth, etc.,* which is a solid reason grounded on the wisdom of the law, which punishes libels even against private persons as public offenses because they provoke men to acts of revenge and breaches of the peace. I hope it will not be said that libel is less provoking because the truth of it is to be given in evidence than if it was to be pleaded in bar.

But all this is *Star Chamber doctrine* with the barrister, and the very mention of that court serves him for an answer to everything for which he has no other answer; because the memory of that tribunal is justly detested on account of many illegal and exorbitant proceedings. No; this is the authority of Mr. Serjeant Hawkins (though he uses marginal references to some Star Chamber cases)

* 1 Hawk. Ch. 73. § 5, 6, 7.

whose name is too great to receive any addition from this paper, and who after a long and studious search in the Crown law laid down this proposition for law at the time he wrote his book; and I believe it will appear in the sequel that he was not mistaken.[4] And now I come to join issue with the barrister upon this point, whether Mr. Serjeant or he is in the right; or in other words, whether falsity in fact be essential to a libel, so that the truth of the fact may be given in evidence to prove a writing to be no libel.

He maintains the affirmative of the question, *both from what he understands to be the authorities in the case, and from the reason of the thing*.* All which shall be considered in their order.

The authorities cited by Mr. Hamilton to support the proposition formerly stated consist principally of four cases, which I shall consider in the order as they were produced.

The first is the *Case of John de Northampton,* 18 Ed. III, 3 Inst. 174,[5] which he observes does not appear to have been a case upon an information, but that *he has good grounds to say it was upon an indictment*.† This is what I shall not contest with him, because it is not material, or indeed easy to be determined without seeing the record; though I conceive there are grounds to say it was not upon an indictment, as was the *Case of Adam de Ravensworth* mentioned by Lord Coke in the same chapter. The case, however, stands thus;

> John de Northampton, an attorney of the King's Bench, wrote a letter to one Ferrers, one of the King's Council, that neither Sir William Scot, Chief Justice, nor his fellows the King's justices, nor their clerks, any great thing would do by the commandment of our lord the King, etc., which said John being called, confessed the letter, etc. *Et quia praedictus Johannes cognovit dictam literam per se scriptam, Roberto de Ferrers, qui est de Concilio Regis, quae litera continet in se nullam veritatem: Praetextu cujus Dom. Rex erga curiam, et justiciarios suos habere posset indignationem, quod esset in scandalum justic. et curiae. Ideo dictus Johannes committitur, etc.*[6]

Here says the barrister, *by this judgment it appears the libelous words were utterly false, and there the falsehood was the crime, and*

* Page 70.
† Zeng. *Trial,* p. 70.

is the ground of the judgment. For my own part, I can neither see *truth nor falsehood* in the words at the time they were wrote, for they refer to a future contingency that might or might not be as he said; and in this respect, they were the same as if the man had said the roof of Westminster Hall would fall upon Sir William Scot and his fellows. Besides, the words taken by themselves have no ill meaning; for I imagine it will be allowed that most of *the great things* which judges do, as judges, are such as ought neither to be done nor left undone by the King's commandment. Where then was the offense? The record, I think, shows that in the following words; *praetextu cujus Dom. Rex erga curiam et justic. suos habere posset indignationem, etc. Ideo dictus Johannes committitur, etc.* It is observable that the author of this letter was an attorney of the court, and by the contents thereof he presumes to undertake for the behavior of the judges in some great matters that concerned their office. The letter was addressed to a person who was of the King's Council and might possibly communicate the contents of such a letter to the King; the consequence of which might naturally be that *Dom. Rex habere posset indignationem erga curiam, etc.* For great things were sometimes done in those days by the King's commandment; and the judges, besides, held their posts at will and pleasure.

The words *quae litera continet in se nullam veritatem* were therefore proper for the judges to insert in order to acquit themselves to the King; but they are no more the ground of the judgment than these other words, *qui est de Concilio Regis;* both being only incidental clauses that come in by way of description: For it is not said; *Quia litera praedicta continet in se nullam veritatem.* After all, I would not have this construction of the case, plain and natural as it is, pass merely upon my own credit; for I shall show that this case was so understood by one of the greatest lawyers of his time, before Lord Coke's 3d Inst. appeared in the world.

21 Jac. B. R. Tanfield v. Hiron. Godb. 405, 6.[7]

The plaintiff brought an action upon the case against the defendant for delivering of a scandalous writing to the Prince, etc. Noy for the plaintiff cited 18 Ed. III: a letter was sent to Ferrers, one of the King's Council, the effect of which was that Scot, Chief Justice, and his companions of the same bench would not do a vain thing at the command of the King; *yet because he sent such a letter to the King's Council, although he spake no ill, yet because it might incense the King against the judges, he was punished.* If no ill was said, will it be pretended that the falsehood of what was said could be a reason for punishing a man? Is it not ridiculous to say that the falsehood of innocent or insignificant words can be criminal? This book therefore follows the record of *Northampton's Case,* and says; because it might incense the King against the judges he was punished; which is almost a translation of *praetextu cujus,* etc., which was the ground of the judgment, *ideo committitur.*[8]

The next case which the barrister called to his aid is that of *the seven bishops, State Trials,* Vol. 4,[9] and here he relies on a flourish of one of the counsel for the bishops, and a dubious expression of one of the judges, separated from the rest of his discourse.

Sir Robert Sawyer, it is true, says, *Both the falsity of it* (the libel) *and that it was malicious and seditious, are all matters of fact, which they* (the King's counsel) *have offered to the jury no proof of, etc.* This I must confess proves one point to which the barrister adduced it, viz., *that he was not the first who insisted that to make a writing a libel, it must be false.** And when I have allowed this, I may almost venture to say it is the only point he does prove from the beginning to the ending of his long, elaborate speech. Let me, however, oppose to this the reply of Sir Thomas Powis, in these words; *whether a libel be true or not, as to the matter of fact; was it ever yet permitted in any court of justice to be made a question; or whether the party be punishable for it? And therefore I wonder to hear these gentlemen say that because it is not a false one therefore it is not a libel,* fol. 382.

Mr. Justice Powell also does say *that to make it a libel, it must be false; it must be malicious; and it must tend to sedition.* Upon which words of this learned and worthy judge I would not presume to

* Page 72.

offer any comment, except that which other words of his own afford, that plainly show in what sense he then spoke. His subsequent words are these; *they* (the bishops) *tell His Majesty it is not out of averseness to pay all due obedience; nor want of tenderness to their dissenting fellow subjects; but because they do conceive the thing that was commanded them was against the law of the land; they say they apprehend the declaration is illegal, because it is founded on a dispensing power; I do not remember in any case in all our law that there is any such power in the King; and the case must turn upon that. In short, if there be no such dispensing power in the King, then that can be no libel, which they presented to the King, which says that the declaration, being founded upon such a pretended power, is illegal.* So that the judge put the whole upon that single point, whether it be true that the King had such a dispensing power, or not; which is a question of law, and not of fact; and accordingly the judge appeals to his own reading in the law, not to witnesses or other testimony, for a decision of it. In truth the petition of the bishops is not capable of having falsehood or truth applied to it in any other sense, there being nothing else affirmed or denied in it *but that they thought they could not do what was commanded them because it was against the law.* This was the behavior; these were the sentiments of that upright judge that gained him so much honor among all good men, as the barrister takes notice; not any opinion of his that the contents of a libel must be false in fact to make it a libel; as he would unfairly insinuate.

Sir Samuel Barnardiston's Case is the third that is touched upon; * and here too the gentleman finds nothing that can be strained to his purpose, but the defendant's counsel *insisting on the want of proof to the malice and seditious intent of the author.* He seems to have forgot that the same gentleman insisted also to have it proved *that the defendant was a person of a turbulent and unquiet spirit,* because these words were set forth in the information, and he takes no manner of notice how all this was answered, which I must now do for him, in the words of the Court; *certainly the law supplies*

* Page 73.

the proof, if the thing itself speaks malice and sedition. As it is in murder; we say always in the indictment, he did it by the instigation of the Devil: Can the jury, if they find the fact, find he did it not by such instigation? No, that does necessarily attend the very nature of such an action or thing. So in information for offenses of this nature, we say he did it falsely, maliciously, and seditiously, which are the formal words; but if the nature of the thing be such as necessarily imports malice, reproach and scandal to the government, there needs no proof but of the fact done; the law supplies the rest. How shall any man prove another person's malice, which is a thing that lies only in a man's mind? How should any man know that I am malicious against the government, but by my actions? These words, indeed, were pronounced by the Chief Justice Jeffreys, who was then the mouth of the Court; but though he was really an intemperate judge (or a *monster,* as the barrister, in his bar language, delights to call him) * yet I may safely refer it to all men of law, whether these words could have discredited the best mouth that ever spoke upon that bench. State Trials, vol. 3. 851.

An instance of this sort may not be impertinent, where a Chief Justice (who was no *monster*) [10] addresses himself to a jury that was trying a libel in this manner: *I will not repeat the particulars to you, only something to what the defendant has said, that you may not be misled. He says it does not appear that he did it maliciously or knowingly. There are some things that you that are of the jury are not to expect evidence for, which it is impossible to know but by the act itself. Malice is conceived in the heart, no man knows it, unless he declares it: As in murder, I have malice to a man; no man knows it. I meet this man and kill him; the law calls this malice. If a man speak scandalous words against a man in his calling or trade; he lays his action, malice; though he cannot prove it but by the words themselves; you may see there is malice supposed to a private person in that slander, much more to the King and the state.* State Trials, vol. 2. 537.

Tutchin's Case, the barrister does not properly cite, but endeavors

* Page 73.

to answer as a case urged against him by the King's counsel; and therefore I shall observe upon it in another place.

But the case of cases is still behind, which he reserved for the last, *to make the point clearer on his side* than all the rest put together could do.* It is *Fuller's Case.* State Trials, vol. 5. 445, 6, 7, 8. And it deserves notice that although Fuller was charged with writing a libel, yet *that* was not the gist of the information. He was, in truth, prosecuted for being *a cheat and impostor,* by order of the House of Lords, as the King's counsel declare in the opening.

The information accordingly sets forth,

> That W.F. intending the late King William and his subjects to deceive, and to get several great sums of money fraudulently and deceitfully from the said King; concerning a correspondency between divers officers and subjects of the said late King, and the late King James falsely pretended to be had; did write and print a libel, entitled *Original Letters,* etc., with the deposition of T.J. and T.F. Esqrs., proving the corruption lately practiced in this nation; and the said W.F. afterwards did publish, utter and for truth affirm the said several false and scandalous libels, without any lawful authority; *whereas in truth the said T.J. did not depose upon his oath as is contained in the said false and scandalous libel; but the said scandalous libels are false, feigned, and altogether contrary to truth.* etc.

Here it is manifest he was accused of a cheat in forging *the correspondence and the depositions* just mentioned, with a design of getting money by his pretended discovery. And hence it comes that the Judge very properly asks him, *have you any witnesses? If you take upon you to write such things as you are charged with, it lies upon you to prove them true, at your peril. How come you to write those books that are not true? If you have any witnesses, produce them. Thus said and thus did that great man,* Lord Chief Justice Holt; † but not upon a trial of the like kind with Mr. Zenger's, as his counsel would have it thought. For in this case the *cheat* and the *imposture* was the offense, which consisted wholly in the falsity; that is, in affirming such things for *realities* when they were naught

* Page 73.
† Page 74.

but *fictions*. On the contrary, had he been able to prove those *letters* and those *depositions* to be authentic, the discovery would have been valuable, and might entitle him perhaps to favor and protection instead of punishment; however irregular he was in taking such a method to publish matters of that high consequence. After this, let the learned barrister, *in all his reading,* show an information or indictment for a *libel* where the *falsity* is assigned in form with an *ubi re vera*[11] as the foundation of the offense; which is done in *Fuller's Case;* and then I will acknowledge that the questions put here by Lord Holt would have been proper upon the trial of his client.

This is the sum of the barrister's law cases. And is it not high time to ask whether such gross misrepresentations of the books can proceed from ignorance or disingenuity? Be that as it will; it might certainly be expected that a proposition advanced with so much assurance, *by a man of years and reading,* should have been supported by some one authority in point rather than by a series of low prevarication and quibble. Could he not find in all the book cases and trials at large concerning *libels* (which are sufficient of themselves to make a large volume) one example of proof being received to the truth or falsity contained in a libelous writing? Indeed there is nothing like it to be found; though the occasions have been many where such proof might be had, if it were proper; nay, where the truth of the thing was notorious to all men, and yet no question ever moved concerning it. This shall fully appear in the sequel.

If anything can be necessary further to expose Mr. Hamilton's doctrine of *libels* after answering his own cases, it is only to subjoin some others that will show how much he is mistaken in almost everything he has offered on the subject. I shall therefore mention a very few that will bear a particular application to his crude notions, without entering into a multitude of others to tire the reader.

16 *Car.* 2 the *King v. Pym,* I Sid. 219, B.R.[12]

Pym was indicted at Exeter for a libel which he delivered to a parson to be published in church there, and was to this effect; *you are desired to bewail the sodomitry, wickedness, whoredom, lewdness, that is of late broken out in this formerly well-governed city; that God would turn their hearts from committing those wickednesses which go unpunished by the magistrates.* Pym confessed the indictment, and was fined £100. He afterwards brought a writ of error, and assigned for error that this was no offense, because though he says *go unpunished by the magistrate;* yet he does not say that the magistrate knew of it, and wickedness unknown cannot be punished. It was answered by the Court that this contains matter of great scandal to the government of the city, for it makes the late government better than the present, etc. Hide, Twisden, Keelyng, Windham, *Just.*[13]

I have pitched upon this case because the barrister is fond of comparing the plantations to large corporations; and he will find here that even those are not left to the mercy of libelers, *although they do not put in a claim to the sacred rights of majesty:* * And that a misbehavior of this kind to the magistrates of a corporation is not entirely innocent, *because it is not to be judged of, or punished, as a like undutifulness would be to our Sovereign.*†

This case was adjudged about four years after the *Restoration,* when the memory of the preceding usurpation was fresh in everybody's mind. It is strange therefore Mr. Pym did not put himself on his trial at Exeter, for it was evident beyond contradiction to the people of that age from their own knowledge, as it is now to us from history, that the wickedness specified in the libel was restrained by a stricter hand before than after the Restoration. But this notorious truth, it seems, did not avail Mr. Pym.

22 *Car.* 2 the *King v. Saunders,* Raym. 201. B.R.[14]

Information for writing a scandalous libel to H. Rich. who was indebted to him, and kept him out of his money three years by obtaining a protection, and at length getting into the prison of

* Zeng. *Trial,* p. 67.
† Page 67.

the King's Bench. Saunders wrote him a letter, wherein he tells him; *that if he had any honesty, civility, sobriety or humanity, he would not deal so by him; and that he would one day be damned, and be in Hell for his cheating;* and cited several places of Scripture to make good his allegations. The defendant was found *guilty,* and moved in arrest of judgment that the substance of the letter is not scandalous, but impertinent and insignificant, etc. *Cur.* [15] The letter is provocative, and tends to the incensing Mr. Rich to break the peace. The Court adjudged the letter scandalous, and fined him 40 Marks. Keelyng, Twisden, Rainsford, Moreton, *Just.*[16]

I would entreat the clear-sighted barrister to look carefully into the words of this libel, and try if he can to discover any truth or falsehood in them that was capable of proof. And I must remark upon both these cases, that though they were adjudged in the reign of K. Charles II, yet neither of them was upon a state prosecution, or at a time when the spirit of *plots and factions* had infested the courts of justice; but they remain unquestionable authorities at this day.

State Trials vol. 5. The *Case of Tutchin* is strong against him; a case adjudged since the Revolution, before that learned and upright Judge Sir John Holt, and plainly shows the fallacy that runs throughout his whole argument.

The points insisted on by this Chief Justice in his charge to the jury were these; *to say that corrupt officers are appointed to administer affairs is certainly a reflection on the government. If people should not be called to an account for possessing the people with an ill opinion of the government, no government can subsist; now you are to consider whether these words I have read to you do not tend to beget an ill opinion of the administration of the government; to tell us that those that are employed know nothing of the matter, and those that do know are not employed. Men are not adapted to offices, but offices to men, out of a particular regard to their interest, and not to their fitness for the places. This is the purport of these papers.* If this was the purport of the papers, and so criminal as hath been just said, it is amazing surely that Mr. Tutchin did not offer to prove the truth of these allegations, and thereby take out their sting! Could not he possibly think of as many corrupt or incompetent officers, ecclesiastical, civil or military in England preferred by interest rather than merit, *as there were judges displaced and courts erected in New York?* Or if he was restrained by the hard-hearted judge from desporting himself in this pleasant and spacious field; could he not apply to the private knowledge which the jurors (as well as the rest of mankind) had of these matters? For I imagine it will be allowed that if no instances of this sort could be shown at the time of Tutchin's trial, it was the only period within the memory of man or the reach of history that wanted the like.

But the misfortune was, the poor man was not blessed with such skillful counsel as is to be had in Philadelphia, to think of these good things for him; otherwise you might have heard an alert advocate (*after returning thanks to his Lordship for nothing*) * address himself to the jury in this or the like eloquent strain; *then, gentlemen of the jury, it is to you we must appeal for witnesses to the truth of the facts we have offered, and are denied the liberty to prove; the law supposes you to be summoned out of the neighborhood where the fact is alleged to be committed; and the reason of your being taken out of the neighborhood is because you are supposed to have the best knowledge of the fact that is to be tried. And were you to find a verdict against my client, you must take upon you to say the papers referred to in the information, and which are proved to be written and published by us, are false, scandalous and seditious. You are citizens of New York, honest and lawful men, and the facts which we offer to prove were not committed in a corner; they are notoriously known to be true. And as we are denied the liberty of giving evidence to prove the truth of what we have published, I will beg leave to lay it down as a standing rule in such cases, that the suppressing of evidence ought always to be*

* Page 75.

taken for the strongest evidence, and I hope it will have that weight with you. Lay your hands upon your hearts, gentlemen, and recollect. Do none of you know; nay, do not all of you know certain persons, who shall be nameless, that have been lately promoted by favor and interest to places of trust and profit both in church and state, army and navy; whom you must know and believe in your consciences to be ill men and no way qualified for such preferment; as my sagacious client has most seasonably remonstrated to the neighbors, by virtue of that right which every free-born subject hath of publishing his complaints, when the matters so published can be supported with truth? * But is Lord Holt asleep all this time? Can any reasonable man, who has but common notions of judicature, imagine that this great judge would suffer such trash as this to be thrown out in any court where he sat in judgment? But what must he have said if the libeler before him had offered to prove *that the law itself was at an end; that trials by juries were taken away when a minister pleased; that no man could call anything his own, or enjoy any liberty longer than those in the administration would condescend to let him do it?* Would he have said that these things did not tend to possess the people with an ill opinion of the government; and that governments might well subsist though men should not be called to an account for publishing the like? Or would he have said it was no matter what opinion the people had of the government, nor whether it subsisted or not, provided these assertions were true; and so have discharged the man as a publisher of precious and useful truths *to put the neighbors on their guard?*

But here also the barrister lays hold of a random question, put by one of the King's counsel to Mr. Montague, who was for the defendant, and was then touching upon the affairs of the navy. Saith the former; *will you say they are true?* Now the latter had hinted as much as that these things were true; but did it with that caution which a man of skill uses when he would say something in support of a lame cause, but does not care to press an impropriety too

* Pages 75, 62, 80–81, etc. [A composite paraphrase.]

far. For that learned gentleman was very sensible that if he had presumed to insist expressly on the truth of the matters contained in his client's papers, a severe reprimand was the best thing that could have befallen him. His words are these; *nobody can say that we never had any mismanagements in the Royal Navy; and whenever that has happened, the merchants of England in all probability have suffered for it.* But does the judge in his charge to the jury vouchsafe to give this matter any answer, or so much as to mention it? Lord Holt did not usually pass by material things that were offered in defense of persons tried before him; yet in this case he makes no question or scruple about the truth or falsehood of Tutchin's papers, although they contained many things which his Lordship, the jury, and all the world knew to be **** This candid judge, however, puts the merits of the whole upon the scandal of the government, and the evil tendency of such writings. And therefore I must once more call upon the northern barrister to show a single instance where witnesses have been produced by counsel, and admitted by the Court to prove the truth of a libel. When he does this, it will deserve consideration; but till then he may talk by the hour without any meaning.

I could mention some cases of a more modern date, that have been adjudged in Westminster Hall, when this wild doctrine was not so much as thought of, and when it would not have been altogether useless had it been practicable; but I have chose to mention such only as are reported, that the books may speak for themselves, and judge between us.

But this lawyer seems to be above having his points of law decided by the authorities of the law; and has something in reserve which may serve to overthrow not only what has been offered in this paper, but even all the books of the law. This is what he calls *the reason of the thing,* but is truly and properly a sketch of his own *politics;* which leads me to show that *the true reason of the thing* here agrees with the *law,* and consequently both these are against this expert master of law and reason.[17]

The reason of the thing, as well as it can be collected from a heap of particulars huddled together without order and method, may be reduced to the three following heads.

1. The form of an information for a libel, and the necessity of knowing the truth or falsehood of its contents in order to direct the judges in awarding arbitrary punishment.

2. The right every man hath of publishing his complaints when the matters so published can be supported with truth.

3. The necessity there is of using this right, in the plantations especially, by reason of the difficulty of obtaining redress against evil governors by any other means.

1. It will not be improper to premise, under the first head, that a gentleman of the law who takes upon him to pronounce so magisterially as the northern barrister has done concerning *libels,* ought to have considered well the nature and extent of his subject. It might be expected that he is not unknowing in any part of learning necessary to fix his idea of *a libel.* And yet the present case would appear to be quite different. This learned gentleman might have informed himself by reading some of the ancient laws before the Conquest that when the *falsity* of virulent writings and speeches was taken into the description of the crime, there was a specific penalty annexed, viz., *cutting out the offender's tongue, Lamb. Sax. Laws.*[18] But this severity seems to have fallen into disuse under the Norman Kings; and accordingly Bracton, who wrote in the reign of Henry III, gives a description of these offenses as they were understood in his days, wherein *falsity* is neither expressed nor implied. These are his words; *Fit autem injuria, non solum cum quis pugno percussus fuerit, verberatus, vulneratus, vel fustibus caesus; verum cum ei convitium dictum fuerit, vel de eo factum carmen famosum et hujusmodi.* Fol. 155.[19] Indeed here is no mention of *libels against the King or the state;* the reason of which seems plainly to be that offenses of this sort were considered as a species of *treason* not only in that age but in several ages after, notwithstanding the statute 25 Ed. III [20] and though they have by happy degrees dwindled into *misdemeanors,* yet nobody except the barrister will say they are come to have a greater indulgence from the law than the like

offenses against private persons. How far therefore Bracton's acceptation of a *libel* has prevailed ever since must be submitted upon what has been offered in the preceding part of the remarks.

Here the barrister throws in a shrewd question arising from the form of the information which charges the libel to be *false. This word* FALSE, says he, *must have some meaning, else how came it there? I hope Mr. Attorney will not say he put it there by chance; and I am of opinion his information would not be good without it.** By way of answer to this, I must take leave to put a question or two in the same strain. Suppose a man brings an action of *trespass* for violating his wife, and he fairly sets forth the truth of the case, *viz.,* that the defendant *by amorous addresses, letters, presents, etc.,* did gain the consent of the plaintiff's wife, and at length debauched her. I would ask whether an action of *trespass* thus laid can be supported? I fancy not; and yet this is a more just account of the matter than when *vi et armis,* viz., *swords, staves, knives, etc.,* are introduced as instruments of invading this tender part of our neighbor's property. Suppose further, a man kills another whom he never saw or heard of before; and he is accused of murdering him *of malice forethought.* How come such words to be put into an indictment for a fact so circumstanced? They must have some meaning; surely they are not put there by chance; and I am of opinion the indictment would not be good without them. Why, there is this short answer to be given to all these childish questions; there are many words used in pleadings of most kinds, sometimes for aggravation, sometimes for comprehension, often in compliance with ancient usage, which are not traversable, and many times are incapable of proof. The form of indictments and informations follows the nature of the fact, and sets it out in its worst dress; and if the fact is made appear to be unlawful, all the hard names are supplied by implication of law.

This is not all quoth the counselor; *it is said that truth makes a libel the more provoking; well, let us agree for once that truth is a greater sin than falsehood: yet as the offenses are not equal, and as*

* Zeng. *Trial,* p. 68.

the punishment is arbitrary; is it not absolutely necessary that they should know whether the libel is true or false, that they may by that means be able to proportion the punishment: for would it not be a sad case if the judges, for want of a due information, should chance to give as severe a judgment against a man for writing or publishing a lie, as for writing or publishing a truth? * Now is it not a sad case that he should want to be told that human laws do not strictly regard the moral pravity of actions, but their tendency to hurt the community, whose peace and safety are their principal objects; so that by this standard only are punishments measured. If this profound sophister is of another opinion, let him give a reason why it should be a greater crime in our law for a man to counterfeit a silver shilling than to cut his father's throat.

2. The right of remonstrating or publishing just complaints the barrister thinks the right of all freemen: and so think I, provided such remonstrances and complaints are made in a lawful way. But when he comes to explain it is not a court of justice, it is not a house of representatives, it is not a legislature that is to be troubled (as he phrases it) with these things. Who then, I pray, is to be troubled with them, for *the King* it seems is out of the question? Let the barrister speak for himself; *they have a right* (says he) *publicly to remonstrate against the abuses of power in the strongest terms to put their neighbors upon their guard, etc.*† and in another place, he speaks of it as a hardship *if a man must be taken up as a libeler for telling his sufferings to his neighbor.* Now though I wish and hope as earnestly as he can do, that a free people may never want the means of uttering their just complaints, and of redressing their wrongs too, when their complaints are not heard; yet I always thought these things were better understood than expressed in a court of law; and I shall probably remain in that opinion till the learned gentleman can produce something from the *common* or *statute law,* to show that a British subject has a right of appealing publicly *to his neighbors* (that is, to the collective body of the people)

* Page 71.
† Page 81.

when he is injured in his person, rights or possessions. When I am assured that he can do this I promise him I shall not grudge a voyage to that country, *where liberty is so well understood and so freely enjoyed,** that I may receive the important discovery from his own instructive mouth.

I know the law books assert the right of complaining to the *magistrates and courts of justice,* to the *Parliament,* to the *King* himself; but a right of complaining to the *neighbors* is what has not occurred to me. After all, I would not be thought to derogate, by anything I have said or shall say, from that noble privilege of a free people, *the liberty of the press.* I think it the bulwark of all other liberty, and the surest defense against tyranny and oppression. But still it is a two-edged weapon, capable of cutting both ways, and is not therefore to be trusted in the hands of every discontented fool or designing knave. Men of sense and address (who alone deserve public attention) will ever be able to convey proper ideas to the people, in a time of danger, without running counter to all order and decency, or crying *fire* and *murder* through the streets if they chance to awake from a frightful dream. But I must again urge that these points are not fit to be discussed in a court of justice, whose jurisdiction is circumscribed by positive and known laws. Besides, they take place properly in a sovereign state which has no superior on earth; and where an injured people can expect no relief but from an appeal to heaven. This is far from being the case of colonies; and therefore I come to show, under the third head, that the barrister's *reason of the thing* is no other than *reason inverted,* which possibly may help the projects of a *demagogue* in America, but can never be reconciled to the sentiments of a lawyer, or the principles of a patriot, considered as a subject of Great Britain.

3. I have hitherto been taught to believe that when a brave and free people have resorted to measures unauthorized by the ordinary course of the laws; such measures have been justified by the extraordinary necessity of the case which excluded all other means of re-

* Page 98.

dress. And as far as I understand the constitution, and have heard accounts of the British colonies, such a case cannot well happen, and has never yet happened among them. But here the barrister is ready to ask, how must we behave when we are oppressed by a governor in a country where the courts of law are said to have no coercive power over his person, and where the representatives of the people are, by his intrigues, made accomplices of his iniquity? Certainly it can't be a new discovery to tell this lawyer; that as the governor is a creature of the *Crown,* so the most natural and easy course is to look up to the hand that made him. And I imagine it may be affirmed (without catching an occasion of offering incense to *majesty*) that if one half of the facts contained in Zenger's papers, and vouched for true by his counsel, had been fairly represented and proved at home, Mr. Cosby would not have continued much longer in his government; [21] and then the City of New York might have applied to itself the inscription of the gold box; *demersae leges, timefacta libertas, haec tandem emergunt;* * with greater propriety and security than could possibly be derived from the impetuous harangue of any lawyer whatsoever. I am the more emboldened to say thus much because though it is my lot to dwell in a colony where *liberty has not always been well understood, at least not freely enjoyed,* yet I have known a governor brought to justice within these last twenty years, who was not only supported by a Council and Assembly, besides a numerous party here, but also by powerful friends at home; all which advantages were not able to screen him from censure, disgrace, and a removal from the trust he had abused.[22]

It is not always necessary that particular persons should leave their affairs and families in the plantations to prosecute a governor in Westminster Hall, unless their fortunes are equal to the expense. For it is seldom seen that the violence of a bad governor terminates in private injuries; inasmuch as he can't find his account in anything less than what is of a general and public nature. And when this is the case, I hope none of our colonies are, even at this time,

* Page 104.

so destitute but that they can find the means of making a regular application to their *Sovereign,* either in person or in his courts at Westminster, as their case may require.

But the wild inconsistency that shines through most parts of this orator's speech is peculiarly glaring in that part of it now before me.* The remedy which he says our constitution prescribes for curing or preventing the diseases of an evil administration in the colonies I shall give in his own words; *has it not been often seen* (*and I hope it will always be seen*) *that when the representatives of a free people are by just representations or remonstrances made sensible of the sufferings of their fellow subjects, by the abuse of power in the hands of a governor, they have declared* (*and loudly too*) *that they were not obliged by any law to support a governor who goes about to destroy a province or colony, etc.* One would imagine, at first sight, that this man had the same notion with the rest of mankind of just representations and remonstrances to the representatives of a free people, which has ever been understood to be by way of petition or address directed and presented to them in form; in which case it is hoped that they being moved by the complaints of the people will stretch forth their arms to help them. But alas! we are all mistaken; for he tells us in the same breath that the right way is by telling our sufferings to our neighbors in gazettes and newspapers; † for the representatives are not to be troubled with every injury done by a governor; besides, they are sometimes in the plot with the governor, and the injured party can have no redress from their hands; so that the first complaint (instead of the last resort) must be to the *neighbors,* and so come about to the representatives through that channel.

Now I would be very glad to know what the *neighbors* can do towards effecting the desired reformation that will be attended with so good success and so few ill consequences as a regular application to His Majesty would be. It would be pleasant, doubtless, to hear this politician speak out and explain himself at large upon this sub-

* Pages 80–81.
† Page 81.

ject. I confess it surpasses my comprehension to conceive what the *neighbors* inspired with weekly revelations from the city journalist can do with their governor and Assembly, unless it be to reform them by those persuasive arguments which the *major vis* never wants good store of. If this be the *patriot's* meaning, his words may possibly be understood; but without this meaning they are mere *jargon.*

In a word; I shall agree with the barrister (and so take my leave of him) that *the liberty of exposing and opposing arbitrary power* is the right of a free people; * and he ought at the same time to admit that the order of things and the peace of society require that extraordinary means should not be used for this purpose till the ordinary have failed in the experiment. The supreme magistrate of an *independent kingdom or state* cannot always be controlled by the one, and then the other is justified by that consideration. But in *colonies* that are from their creation subordinate to their Mother Country, there is no person who is not controllable by regular and well-known methods of proceeding; and consequently there can be no absolute necessity of flying to extremities, at least in the first instance. From all which I conceive it follows that *local considerations,* upon which the gentleman lays so great stress, conclude directly against him; and I hope the security which the British constitution affords to every man's person, property and reputation, as well as to the public tranquillity, is not lessened by any distance from the fountain of power and justice; but that a *libel* is a *libel,* and punishable as such in America as well as in Europe.

I am sensible there is a freedom of expression used in these papers of which I should disapprove in the common cases of controversy; but I found myself under a necessity of showing no respect to the performance under consideration unless I were to forfeit the little that might be due to the *Remarks.* For though a lawyer is free, nay obliged by the duty of his profession, to make the most of the cause he espouses (his real sentiments being suspended for that time by reason of the bias under which he acts), yet when he draws his

* Page 99.

private opinion into the debate, and interests his passions in the success of it, he then departs from his character and becomes a *party* rather than an *advocate.* In short, there is an air of self-sufficiency and confidence mixed with the whole lump, enough to give a disrelish even to good sense and good law, but is nauseous beyond all bearing when neither of these is found. Among lawyers, I was sure this lawyer deserved no answer, and yet an answer seemed indispensable, not only for the reasons given at my setting out, but also in order to save many well-meaning people from reverencing a piece of *buffoonery* that had been thrust into the world with so much florid conceit and a gold box tagged to the end of it. A piece wherein the whole commonplace of popular declamation (equally adapted to all popular occasions) is exhausted, and *the Holy Scriptures* brought in to season his jokes.* But as this last seems designed only for a sally of *wit* and *humor,* I shall not offer to detract from its merit; considering too it had so happy an effect as to set the good people alaughing when they heard *the word of God* most ingeniously burlesqued in a *Christian court.* A piece that hardly shows the author to have been serious when he pronounced it, or his wise benefactors when they rewarded him; but that his solemn professions of *principle* and *duty* compel a charitable mind to suspect his knowledge rather than his sincerity, and *citizens* are ever thought to be in earnest when they part with their *gold* and show their *learning.*†

Sir, I ought to make an apology to you for trespassing so long upon your patience, which might have been better employed, but I flatter myself with the hopes of having some allowance made for an honest though weak attempt to rescue the profession of the law and the interest of lawful liberty from the disgrace thrown upon both in one of our sister colonies. This is the truth, and let it be my excuse.

I am yours, etc.,
Anglo-Americanus.

* Pages 95–96.
† Pages 103–105.

2. *James Alexander's response: the Pennsylvania Gazette essay.* Alexander's essay, signed "X.," was originally published as four articles in Benjamin Franklin's *Pennsylvania Gazette,* nos. 466–469 (November 17 to December 8, 1737). It is a deliberate response to Anglo-Americanus' critique in the *Remarks,* and attempts to support Hamilton's defense of Zenger by reference to history and law. Alexander's essay makes a spirited espousal of the freedom of the press, but does not come to grips with the basic issues raised by his antagonist.

THE PENNSYLVANIA GAZETTE

CONTAINING THE FRESHEST ADVICES FOREIGN AND DOMESTIC

From November 10 to November 17, 1737.

Numb. 466

To the author of the Pennsylvania Gazette.[23]

SIR, THE FREEDOM OF SPEECH is a *principal pillar* in a free government: when this support is taken away the constitution is dissolved, and tyranny is erected on its ruins. Republics and limited monarchies derive their strength and vigor from a *popular examination* into the actions of the magistrates. This privilege in all ages has been and always will be abused. The best of princes could not escape the censure and envy of the times they lived in. But the evil is not so great as it may appear at first sight. A magistrate who sincerely aims at the *good* of the society will always have the inclinations of a great majority on his side; and impartial posterity will not fail to render him justice.

These abuses of the freedom of speech are the excrescences of liberty. They ought to be suppressed; but to whom dare we commit the care of doing it? An evil magistrate entrusted with a POWER to *punish words* is armed with a WEAPON the most *destructive* and *terrible.* Under pretense of pruning off the exuberant branches, he frequently destroys the tree.

It is certain that he who robs another of his moral reputation more richly merits a gibbet than if he had plundered him of his purse on the highway. Augustus Caesar under the specious pretext of preserving the characters of the Romans from defamation introduced the law whereby libeling was involved in the penalties of *treason* against the state. This established his tyranny, and for one mischief it prevented, ten thousand evils, horrible and tremendous, sprung up in the place. Thenceforward every person's life and fortune depended on the vile breath of informers. The construction of words being arbitrary and left to the decision of the judges, no man could write or open his mouth without being in danger of forfeiting his head.

One was put to death for inserting in his history the praises of Brutus; another, for styling Cassius the *last* of the Romans. Caligula valued himself for being a notable dancer; to deny he excelled in that manly accomplishment was high treason. This Emperor advanced his horse Incitatus to the dignity of consul, and, though history is silent, I don't question but it was a capital crime to show the least contempt for that high officer of state. Suppose then, any one had called the Prime Minister *a stupid animal.* The Emperor's counsel might argue that the malice of the libel was aggravated by its being true, and consequently more likely to excite the family of this illustrious magistrate to acts of revenge. Such a prosecution would appear ridiculous; yet, if we may rely on tradition, there have been *formerly* proconsuls in America, though of more malice but hardly superior in understanding to Incitatus, who would have thought themselves *libeled* to be called by their *proper names.*

Nero piqued himself on his fine voice and skill in music; *a laudable ambition this!* He performed in public and carried the prize. It was afterwards resolved by all the judges as good law that whoever should insinuate the least doubt of Nero's pre-eminence in THE NOBLE ART OF FIDDLING ought to be deemed a traitor to the state.

By the help of inferences and innuendoes, treasons multiplied in a prodigious manner. GRIEF was treason. A lady of noble birth was put to death for bewailing the loss of her murdered son. SILENCE was declared an overt act to prove the treasonable purposes of the heart. LOOKS were construed into treason. *A serene open aspect* was an evidence that the person was pleased with the calamities that befell the Emperor. *A severe thoughtful countenance* was urged against the man that wore it as a proof of his *plotting* against the state. DREAMS were often made capital offenses. A new species of informers went about Rome, insinuating themselves in all companies to fish out their dreams, which the holy priests, *O! nefarious wicked-ness!* interpreted into high treason. The Romans were so terrified by this strange method of process that, far from discovering their dreams, they durst not own that they slept. In this terrible situation, when everyone had so much cause to fear, even FEAR itself was made a *crime*. Caligula when he put his brother to death gave it as a reason to the Senate that the youth was afraid of being murdered. To be eminent in any virtue, either civil or military, was the greatest crime a man could be guilty of.—*O virtutes certissimum exitium.*[24]

These were some of the effects of the Roman law against libeling.

THOSE of the British kings who aimed at despotic power or the oppression of the subject constantly encouraged prosecutions for words.

Henry VII, a prince mighty in politics, procured that act to be passed whereby the jurisdiction of the Star Chamber was confirmed and extended. Afterwards Empson and Dudley, two voracious dogs of prey, under the protection of this high court exercised the most merciless acts of oppression.[25] The subjects were terrified from uttering their griefs while they saw the thunder of the Star Chamber pointed at their heads. This caution, however, could not prevent several dangerous tumults and insurrections. For when the tongues of the people are restrained, they commonly discharge their resentments by a more *dangerous organ,* and break out into open acts of violence.

During the reign of Henry VIII, a high-spirited monarch, every light expression which happened to displease him was construed by his supple judges into a libel, and sometimes extended to high treason. When Queen Mary, of bloody memory, ascended the throne, the Parliament, in order to raise a *fence* against the violent prosecutions for words which had rendered the lives, liberties and properties of all men precarious, and perhaps dreading the furious persecuting spirit of this princess, passed an act whereby it was declared *that if a libeler doth go so high as to libel against King or Queen by* *denomination, the judges shall lay no greater fine on him than £100 with two months' imprisonment, and no corporal punishment: Neither was this censure to be passed on him except the accusation was fully proved by two witnesses, who were to produce a certificate of their good demeanor for the credit of their report.* This act was confirmed by another in the seventh year of the reign of Queen Elizabeth, only the penalties were heightened to £200 and three months' imprisonment.[26] Notwithstanding, she rarely punished invectives, though the malice of the papists was indefatigable in blackening the brightest of characters with the most impudent falsehoods. She was often heard to applaud that rescript of Theodosius,* "if any person speak ill of the Emperor, through a foolish rashness and inadvertency, it is to be *despised,* if out of madness it deserves *pity,* if from malice and aversion, it calls for *mercy.*"

Her successor, King James I, was a prince of a quite different genius and disposition. He used to say *that, while he had the power of making judges and bishops, he could have what law and gospel he pleased:* Accordingly, he filled those places with such as prostituted their professions to his strange notions of prerogative. Among this number, and I hope it is no discredit to the law, its great oracle, Sir Edward Coke, appears. The Star Chamber, which in the time of Queen Elizabeth had gained a good repute, became an intolerable grievance in the reign of this learned monarch.

But it did not arrive to its meridian altitude until King Charles I begun to wield the scepter. As he had formed a design to lay aside

* *Si quis imperatori malediceret non statim injuria censetur et eo nomine punitur; sed distinguitur an ex levitate processerit et sic contemnitur, an ex insania et miseratione digna censetur, an ex injuria et sic remittenda declaretur. Note,* a rescript was an answer delivered by the Emperor when consulted on some difficult question or point in law. The judges were wholly to be directed by it, whenever such a case came before them; for *voluntas regis habet vigorem legis* is a fundamental principle in the civil law. The rescript mentioned above was not only delivered by Theodosius, but by two other Emperors, Honorius and Arcadius. [The Latin quotation is a paraphrase from Justinian, c. 9, 7, 1: "If anyone slanders the emperor it is not immediately deemed a crime and punished as such; distinction is made whether it proceeded from frivolity and is thus trivial, or from insanity and thus pitiful, or from a sense of wrong and thus pardonable."]

Parliaments and subvert the constitution, so he very well knew that the form of government could not be altered without laying a restraint on freedom of speech and the liberty of the press. Therefore His Majesty issued out his royal *mandate* under the Great Seal of England whereby he commanded his subjects, under pain of his displeasure, not to prescribe to him any time for Parliaments. My Lord Clarendon upon this occasion is pleased to write "that all men took themselves to be prohibited upon the penalty of censure [the censure of the Star Chamber, which few men cared to incur] so much as to speak of Parliaments, or so much as to mention that Parliaments were again to be called."[27]

His Majesty's ministers, to let the nation see they were absolutely determined to suppress all freedom of speech, caused a prosecution to be carried on by the Attorney General against three of the Commons for words spoken in the House anno 1628.[28] The members pleaded to the information that expressions in Parliament ought only to be examined and punished there: This notwithstanding they were all three condemned as disturbers of the state. One of these gentlemen, Sir John Eliot, was fined £2000 and sentenced to lie in prison till it was paid. His Lady was denied admittance to him, even during his sickness; consequently his punishment comprehended an additional sentence of divorce. This patriot, having endured many years imprisonment, sunk under the oppression, and died in gaol. This was such a *wound* to the constitution that even after the Restoration the judgment was reversed in Parliament.

That Englishmen of all ranks might be effectually intimidated from publishing their thoughts on any subject *except on the side of the Court;* His Majesty's ministers caused an information for several libels to be exhibited in the Star Chamber against Mr. Prynn, Burton and Bastwick.[29] They were, each of them, fined £5000, adjudged to lose their ears on the pillory, to be branded on the cheeks with hot irons, and to suffer perpetual imprisonment. Thus these three gentlemen, each of figure and quality in their several professions, *viz., divinity, law* and *physic,* were, for no other offense than writing on controverted points of church government, exposed on public scaffolds, and stigmatized and mutilated as common signal rogues, or the most mechanic malefactors.

Such corporal punishments, inflicted with all the circumstances of cruelty and infamy, bound down all other gentlemen under a servile fear of the like treatment; so that, for several years, no one durst publicly speak or write in defense of the liberties of the people, which the King's ministers, his Privy Council, and his judges had trampled under their feet.

The SPIRIT of the administration looked HIDEOUS and DREADFUL. The hate and resentment which the people conceived against it for a long time lay smothered in their breasts; where these passions festered and grew venomous, and at last discharged themselves by an armed and VINDICTIVE hand.[30]

From November 17 to November 24, 1737.
Numb. 467

KING CHARLES II aimed at the subversion of the government, but concealed his designs under a deep hypocrisy. A method which his predecessor, *in the beginning of his reign,* scorned to make use of. The father, who affected a high and rigid gravity, discountenanced all barefaced immorality. The son, of a gay luxurious disposition, openly encouraged it. So their inclinations being different, the restraint laid on some authors and the encouragement given to others were managed after a different manner.

In this reign a licenser was appointed for the stage and the press.[31] No plays were encouraged but what had a tendency to debase the minds of the people. The original design of comedy was perverted. It appeared in all the shocking circumstances of immodest *double entendres,* obscene description and lewd representation. Religion was sneered out of countenance, and public spirit ridiculed as an awkward, old-fashioned virtue. The fine gentleman of the comedy, though embroidered all over with wit, was a consummate *débauchée;* and the fine lady, though set off with a brilliant imagination, was a very impudent coquette. *Satire,* which in the hands of Horace,

Juvenal and Boileau was pointed with a generous resentment against vice, now became the declared foe of virtue and innocence. As the city of London in all ages, as well as the time we are speaking of, was remarkable for its opposition to arbitrary power, the poets leveled all their artillery against the metropolis in order to bring the citizens into contempt. An alderman was never introduced on the theater but under the complicated character of a sneaking canting hypocrite, a miser and a cuckold. While the Court wits, with impunity, libeled the most valuable part of the nation; other writers of a different stamp, with great learning and gravity, endeavored to prove to Britons that slavery was *jure divino.* Thus the stage and the press, under the direction of a licenser, became battering engines against religion, virtue and liberty: Those who had courage enough to write in their defense were stigmatized as schismatics, and punished as *disturbers* of the GOVERNMENT.

But when the embargo on wit was taken off, Sir Richard Steele and Mr. Addison soon rescued the stage from the load of impurity it labored under. With an inimitable address they strongly recommended to our imitation the most amiable, rational, manly characters: And this with so much success that I cannot suppose there is any reader today, conversant in the writings of those gentlemen, that can taste with any tolerable relish the comedies of the once admired Shadwell.[32] Vice was obliged to retire and give place to virtue. This will always be the consequence when truth has fair play. Falsehood only dreads the attack, and cries out for auxiliaries. Truth never fears the encounter: She scorns the aid of the secular arm, and triumphs by her natural strength.

But to resume the description of the reign of King Charles II. The doctrine of servitude was chiefly managed by Sir Roger L'Estrange. He had great advantages in the argument, being licenser for the press, and might have carried all before him without contradiction if writings on the other side of the question had not been printed by stealth. The authors were prosecuted as seditious libelers. On all these occasions the King's counsel, particularly Sawyer and Finch,[33] appeared most abjectly obsequious to the ends of the Court.

During this blessed management, His Majesty had entered into a secret league with France to render himself absolute, and enslave his subjects.[34] This fact was discovered to the world by Doctor Jonathan Swift, to whom Sir William Temple had entrusted the publication of his works. The establishment of popery in the three kingdoms must have been the foundation of the league. King Charles could not have the least aversion to such a proposition. He was a private papist. King James II took care to justify that part of the character of his royal brother by incontestable facts.

Sidney,[35] the sworn foe of tyranny, was a gentleman of noble birth, of sublime understanding and exalted courage. The ministry were resolved to remove so great an obstacle out of the way of their designs. He was prosecuted for high treason. The overt fact charged in the indictment was a *libel* found in his private study. Mr. Finch, the King's Solicitor General, urged with great vehemency *to this effect; that the imagining the death of the King is treason, even while that imagination remains covert in the mind, though the law cannot punish such secret treasonable thoughts till it arrives to the knowledge of them by some overt fact. That the matter of the libel composed by Sidney was an imagining how to compass the death of King Charles II and the writing of it was an overt fact of the treason, for that* scribere est agere. It seems the King's counsel in this reign had not received the same direction as Queen Elizabeth gave hers. She told them they were to look upon themselves as retained, not so much *pro domina Regina,* as *pro domina veritate.*[36]

Mr. Sidney made a strong and legal defense. He insisted that all the words in the book contained no more than general speculations of government, free for any man to write down, especially since the same are written in the Parliament rolls and in the statute laws.

He argued on the injustice of applying, by *innuendoes,* general assertions concerning government as overt facts to prove the writer was compassing the death of the King; for then no man could write of things done by our ancestors in defense of the constitution and freedom of Britain without exposing himself to capital danger.

He denied that *scribere est agere,* but allowed that *scribere et publicare est agere;*[37] and therefore he urged that as his book was never published or imparted to any person, it could not be an overt fact within the Statute of Treasons, admitting it contained treasonable positions; that on the contrary it was a covert fact locked up in his private study, as much concealed from the knowledge of any man as if it were locked up in the author's mind. This was the substance of Mr. Sidney's defense. But not law, nor reason, nor eloquence, nor innocence ever availed where Jeffreys sat as judge.[38] Without troubling himself with any part of the defense, he declared *in furore* that Sidney's known principles was a sufficient proof of his intention to compass the death of the King: A packed jury thereupon found him guilty of high treason. Great applications were made for his pardon. He was executed as a traitor. This case is a pregnant instance of the danger that attends a law for punishing words; and of the little security the most valuable men have for their lives in that society where a judge by remote inferences and distant innuendoes may construe the most innocent expressions into capital crimes. Sidney, the British Brutus, the warm, the steady friend of liberty, who from a diffusive love to mankind left them that invaluable legacy, his immortal discourses on government, *was* for those very discourses MURDERED by the hands of lawless power.

After the Revolution, when law and justice were restored, the attainder of this great man was reversed in Parliament.

This paper closes with a quotation from Burnet.

Being in Holland (says the Bishop) the Princess of Orange, afterwards Queen Mary, asked me what had sharpened the King, her father, so much against Mr. Jurieu. I told her he had writ with great indecency of Mary Queen of Scots, which cast reflections on them that were descended from her. The Princess said Jurieu was to support the cause he defended, and to expose those that persecuted it in the best way he could. And, if what he said of Mary Queen of Scots was true, he was not to be blamed who made that use of it: And, she added that if princes would do ill things, they must expect that the world will take revenge on their memory, since they cannot reach their persons: That was but a small suffering, far short of what others suffered at their hands.[39]

From November 24 to December 1, 1737.
Numb. 468

IN the two former papers the writer endeavored to prove by historical facts the fatal dangers that necessarily attend a restraint on freedom of speech and the liberty of the press: Upon which the following reflection naturally occurs, viz., THAT WHOEVER ATTEMPTS TO SUPPRESS EITHER OF THOSE, *OUR NATURAL RIGHTS,* OUGHT TO BE REGARDED AS AN *ENEMY* TO LIBERTY AND THE CONSTITUTION. *An inconveniency is always to be suffered when it cannot be removed without introducing a worse.*

I proceed in the next place to enquire into the nature of the English laws in relation to libeling: To acquire a just idea of them the knowledge of history is necessary, and the genius and disposition of the prince is to be considered, in whose time they were introduced and put in practice.

To infuse into the minds of the people an ill opinion of a just administration is a crime that deserves no mercy: But to expose the evil designs or weak management of a magistrate is the duty of every member of society. Yet King James I thought it an unpardonable presumption in the subject to pry into the *arcana imperii.*[40] He imagined that the people ought to believe the authority of the government infallible, and that their submission should be implicit. It may therefore be reasonably presumed that the judgment of the *Star Chamber* concerning libels was influenced by His Majesty's notions of government. No law could be better framed to prevent people from publishing their thoughts on the administration than that which makes no distinction whether a libel be true or false. It is not pretended that any such decision is to be found in our books before this reign. That is not at all to be wondered at. King James was the first of the British monarchs that laid claim to a *divine right.*

It was a refined piece of policy in Augustus Caesar when he proposed a law to the Senate whereby invectives against private men were to be punished as treason. The pill was finely gilded and easily swallowed. But the Romans soon found that the preservation of their characters was only a pretext; to preserve inviolable the sacred name of Caesar was the real design of the law. They quickly jumped on the intended consequence; if it be treason to libel a private person, *it cannot be less than blasphemy to speak ill of the Emperor.* Perhaps it may not appear a too refined conjecture that the *Star Chamber* acted on the same views with Augustus when they gave that decision which made it criminal to publish truth of a private person as well as of a magistrate. I am the more inclined to this conjecture from a passage in Lord Chief Justice Richardson's speech in the *Star Chamber* against Mr. Prynn, who was prosecuted there for a libel. "If subjects have an ill prince, marry what is the remedy? They must pray to God to forgive him. Mr. Prynn saith they were three *worthy* Romans that conspired to murder Nero. This is most horrible!"[41] Tremendous wickedness! indeed my Lord. Where slept the thunder when these three detestable Romans, unawed by the sacred majesty of the diadem, with hands sacrilegious and accursed took away the precious life of that IMPERIAL WOLF, *the Lord's anointed,* who had murdered his own mother, who had put to death Seneca and Burrhus, his two best friends and benefactors, who was drenched in the blood of mankind, and wished and endeavored to extirpate the human race? I think His Lordship has clearly explained the true intent and meaning of the *Star Chamber* doctrine. It centers in the most abjectively passive obedience.

The punishment for writing truth is pillory, loss of ears, branding the face with hot irons, fine and imprisonment at the discretion of the court. Nay, the punishment is to be heightened in proportion to the truth of the facts contained in the libel. But if this monstrous doctrine could have been swallowed down by that *worthy* jury who were on the trial of the seven bishops prosecuted for a libel in the reign of King James II, the liberties of Britain in all human probability had been lost, and popery and slavery established in the three kingdoms.

This was a cause of the greatest expectation and importance that ever came before the judges in Westminster Hall. The bishops had petitioned the King *that he would be graciously pleased not to insist upon their reading in the churches His Majesty's declaration for liberty of conscience; BECAUSE* IT WAS FOUNDED ON A DISPENSING POWER DECLARED ILLEGAL IN PARLIAMENT. *And they said that they could not, in prudence, honor or conscience, so far make themselves parties to it.* In the information exhibited by the Attorney General, the bishops were charged with writing and publishing a false malicious and seditious libel (*under pretense of a petition*) in diminution of the King's prerogative and contempt of his government.

Sawyer and Finch were among the bishops' counsel. The former had been Attorney, the latter Solicitor, General. In these stations they had served the Court only too well. They were turned out because they refused to support the dispensing power. Powis and Williams, who stood in their places, had great advantages over them by reflecting on the precedents and proceedings while they were of the King's counsel.—*What was good law for Sidney and others ought to be law for the bishops: God forbid that in a court of justice any such distinction should be made.*—Williams took very indecent liberties with the prelates, who were obliged to appear in court. He reproached them with acting repugnant to their doctrine of passive obedience. He remembered them of their preaching against himself, and stirring up their clergy to libel him in their sermons. For Williams had been for many years a bold pleader in all causes against the Court. He had been Speaker in two successive Parliaments, and a zealous promoter of the Bill of Exclusion. Jeffreys fined him £10,000 for having licensed, in the preceding reign, by virtue of an order of the House of Commons, the printing of Dangerfield's *Narrative,* which charged the Duke of York with conspiracies of a *black complexion.*[42] This gentleman had no principles, was guided by his own interests, so wheeled about to the Court.

The King's counsel having produced their evidences as to the publication of the petition, the question then to be debated was whether it contained libelous matter or no.

It was *argued,* in substance, for the bishops, that the matter could not be libelous, because it was true. Sir Robert Sawyer makes use of the words *false* and *libelous* as synonymous terms, through the whole course of his argument, and so does Mr. Finch: Accordingly they proceeded to show by the votes and journals of the Parliament, which were brought from the Tower to the court, that the Kings of England in no age had any power to dispense with or set aside the laws of the land: And consequently the bishops' petition, which denied that His Majesty had a dispensing power, could not be deemed false or libelous, or in contempt or diminution of the King's prerogative, as no such power was ever annexed to it. This was the foundation laid down through the whole course of the debate, and which guided and governed the verdict.

It was strongly *urged* in behalf of the King: That the only point to be looked into was whether the libel be reflecting or scandalous, and not whether it be true or false. That the bishops had injured and affronted the King by presuming to prescribe to him their opinions in matters of government. That under pretense of delivering a petition they come and tell His Majesty he has commanded an illegal thing. That by such a proceeding they threw dirt in the King's face, and so were libelers with a witness.

Previous to the opinions of the judges, it will be necessary to give the reader a short sketch of their characters. Wright was brought on the King's Bench and made Chief Justice, as a proper tool to support the dispensing power. Rapin, mentioning this trial, calls Holloway a creature of the Court; but that excellent historian was mistaken in this particular.[43] Powell was a judge of obstinate integrity. *His obstinacy gained him immortal honor*. Allibone was a professed papist and had not taken the tests, consequently he was no judge and his opinion of no authority. Wright in his charge called the petition a libel, and declared that anything which disturbs the government is within the case de Libellis Famosis [the Star Chamber doctrine]. Holloway told the jury that the end and intention of every action is to be considered, and that as the bishops had *no ill intention* in delivering their petition, it could not be deemed

MALICIOUS OR LIBELOUS. Powell declared that falsehood and malice are two essential qualities of a libel, which the prosecutor is obliged to prove. Allibone replied upon Powell that we are not to measure things from any truth they have in themselves, but from the aspect they have on the government; for that every tittle of a libel may be true and yet be a libel still.

The compass of this paper would not admit me to quote the opinions of the judges at length. But I have endeavored, with the strictest regard to truth, to give the substance and effect of them.

It has been generally said that the judges in this trial were equally divided in their opinions. But we shall find a majority on the bench in favor of the bishops when we consider that the cause as to Allibone was *coram non judice*.[44]

Here then is a *late* authority which sets aside, destroys, and annuls the doctrine of the *Star Chamber* reported by Sir Edward Coke in his case *de Libellis Famosis*.

Agreeable to this late *impartial* decision is the *civil law* concerning libels.[45] It is there said that *calumniari est FALSA crimina dicere,* and not *vera crimina dicere:*[46] And therefore a writing that only insinuates a falsehood, and does not directly assert it, cannot come under the denomination of a libel. *Non libellus famosus quoad accusatum, quia non constat directis assertionibus, in quibus venit verum aut falsum quod OMNINO requirit libellus famosus.*[47] In those cases, where the design to injure does not evidently appear from the nature of the words, it is incumbent on the plaintiff to prove the malice by other circumstances. *Animus injuriandi non praesumitur et incumbit injuriato cum probare.*[48]

These resolutions of the Roman lawyers bear so great a conformity to the sentiments of Powell and Holloway that it seems they had them in view when they gave their opinions: Sir Robert Sawyer makes several glances at them in his argument. But, throwing that *supposition* out of the question, natural equity, on which the *civil law* is founded [*the principle of passive obedience ALWAYS excepted*], would have directed any impartial man of common understanding to the same decision.

From December 1 to December 8, 1737.
Numb. 469

IN civil actions an advocate should never appear but when he is persuaded the merits of the cause lie on the side of his client. In criminal actions it often happens that the defendant in strict justice deserves punishment; yet a counsel may oppose it when a magistrate cannot come at the offender without making a breach in the barriers of liberty, and opening a floodgate to arbitrary power. But when the defendant is innocent and unjustly prosecuted, his counsel may, nay ought to take all advantages and use every strategem that his skill, art and learning can furnish him with. This last was the case of Zenger at New York, as appears by the printed trial and the VERDICT of the jury. It was a popular cause. The LIBERTY OF THE PRESS in that province depended on it. On such occasions the dry rules of strict pleading are never observed. The counsel for the defendant sometimes argues from the known principles of law, then raises doubts and difficulties to confound his antagonist, now applies himself to the affections, and chiefly endeavors to raise the passions. Zenger's defense is to be considered in all those different lights. Yet a gentleman of Barbados assures us that it was published as a solemn argument in the law, and therefore writes a very elaborate confutation of it.

I propose to consider some of his objections as far as they interfere with the *freedom of speech* and the *liberty of the press* contended for in the three former papers.

This author began his remarks by giving us a specimen of Mr. Hamilton's method of reasoning. It seems the Attorney General on the trial objected that a negative could not be proved, to which the counsel for Zenger replied that there are many exceptions to that general rule, and instanced, *where a man is charged with killing another, if he is innocent, he may prove the man said to be killed to be still alive*. The Remarker will not allow this to be a good proof of the negative; *for* (says he) *this is no more than an instance of one affirmative being destroyed by another that infers a negative of the first.*[49] It cost me some trouble to find out the meaning of this superlative nonsense, and I think I have at last discovered it. What he understands by the *first* affirmative is the instance of *the man's being charged with killing another,* the *second* affirmative is *the man's being alive,* which certainly infers that the man was not killed, which is undoubtedly a negative of the *first.* But the Remarker blunders strangely. Mr. Hamilton's words are clear. He says that the party accused is on the negative, viz., *that he did NOT kill,* which he may prove by an affirmative, viz., *that the man said to be killed IS still alive.*

Again, *at which rate* (continues our author) *most negatives may be proved.* Here indeed the gentleman happened to stumble right: For every negative capable of proof can only be proved after the same manner, namely, by an affirmative. *But then,* he adds, *that a man will be put upon proving he did not kill, because such proof may be had sometimes, and so the old rule will be discarded.* This is clearly a *non sequitur.* For though a man may prove a negative if he finds it for his advantage, it does by no means follow he shall be obliged to do it; and so the old rule will be preserved.

After such notable instances of a blundering unlogical head, we are not to be surprised at the many absurdities and contradictions of this author, which occur in the sequel of his no-argument.

But I shall only cite those passages where there is a probability of guessing at his meaning; for he has so preposterously jumbled together his little stock of ideas that even after the *greatest efforts* I could find but very little sense or coherence in them. I should not, however, have discontinued my labor, had I not been apprehensive of the fate of poor Don Quixote, who ran distracted by endeavoring to unbowel the sense of the following passage—"The reason of your unreasonableness, which against my reason is wrought, doth so weaken my reason, as with all reason I do justly complain."—There are several profound passages in the Remarks not a whit inferior to this:* The dissertation on the negative and affirmative I once thought to be an exact counterpart of it.

* *Vid.* p. 17 throughout. [This must be a citation to one of the two editions of 1737, of which only a single copy of Andrew Bradford's Philadelphia edition has

Our author labors to prove that a libel whether true or false is punishable. The first authority for his purpose is the *Case of John de Northampton* adjudged in the reign of Edward III. Northampton had wrote a libelous letter to one of the King's Council, purporting that the judges no great thing would do at the commandment of the King, etc., said John was called and the Court pronounced judgment against him on those grounds that the letter contained no truth in it and might incense the King against his judges. Mr. Hamilton says *that by this judgment it appears the libelous words were utterly false, and there the falsehood was the crime and is the ground of the judgment.* The Remarker rejects this explanation, and gives us an ingenious comment of his own. *First,* he says there is neither truth nor falsehood in the words at the time they were wrote. *2ndly,* that they were the same as if John had said the roof of Westminster Hall would fall on the judges. *3dly,* that the words taken by themselves have no ill meaning. *4thly,* that the judges ought to do their duty without any respect to the King's commandment [They are sworn so to do]. *5thly,* he asks where then was the offense? He answers, *6thly,* the record shows it. *7thly,* he says that the author of the letter was an attorney of the Court and by the contents thereof [*the contents of the letter meaning, not the contents of the Court*], he presumes to undertake for the behavior of the judges. *8thly,* that the letter was addressed to a person of the King's Council. *9thly* that he might possibly communicate it to the King. *10thly,* that it might naturally incense the King against the Court. *11thly,* that great things were done in those days by the King's commandment, for the judges held their posts at will and pleasure. *12thly,* that it was therefore proper for the judges to insert that the letter contained NO TRUTH *in order to acquit themselves to the King. 13thly,* that the judges inserted a falsehood only to acquit themselves to His Majesty, because what they inserted was no grounds of their judgment. *14thly,* and lastly, the commentator avers (*with much modesty*) that all this senseless stuff is a PLAIN and natural construction of the

---

been preserved. Page 17 in that copy, located in the library of the Historical Society of Pennsylvania, corresponds to p. 164 of the present volume. Pp. 159–160, or any one of several other citations would seem more appropriate, however.]

case.[50] But he would not have us take it wholly on his own word, and undertakes to show that the case was so understood by *Noy,* in whose mouth our author puts just such becoming nonsense as he entertained us with from himself.

It requires no great penetration to make this decision in question appear reasonable and intelligible. But it ought first to be observed, that Edward III was *one* of the best and wisest, as well as the bravest of our kings, and that the law had never a freer course than under his reign. Where the letter mentions that the judges would do no great things (*i.e.,* illegal things) by the King's commandment, it was plainly insinuated that the judges suspected that the King might command them to do illegal things. Now by the means of that letter the King, being led to imagine that the judges harbored a suspicion so unworthy of him, might be justly incensed against them. Therefore the record truly says that the letter was utterly false, and that there was couched under it an insinuation (certainly MALICIOUS) that might raise an indignation in His Majesty against the Court.—*qua litera continet in se NULLAM VERITATEM, praetexture cujus Dominus Rex erga curiam et justiciarios suos habere posset indignationem, etc.* Hence it evidently appears that not only the *falsehood* but also the *malice* was the ground of the judgment.

I agree with the Remarker that Noy, citing this case, says *that the letter contained no ill, yet the writer was punished.* But these words are absolutely absurd as they stand in the *Remarks,* detached from the context. Noy adduces Northampton's case to prove that a man is punishable for complaining without a cause, though the words of the complaint (simply considered) should contain no ill in them. It is not material to enquire whether the application is just: It is only an expression of a counsel at the bar. The case was adjourned and we hear no more of it. Yet these words of Noy, the Remarker would pass on to the reader as a good authority. *This book therefore,* quoth he referring to Godbolt's *Reports, follows the record of Northampton's case, and says that because it might incense the King against the judges he was punished, which is almost a translation of* praetextu cujus, etc.[51] I could readily pardon our author's gibberish and want of apprehension, but cannot so easily digest his insincerity.

The Remarker in the next place proceeds to the trial of the seven bishops. I shall quote his own words, though I know they are so senseless and insipid that I run the risk of trespassing on the reader's patience. However, here they be.

> Mr. Justice Powell also does say *that to make it a libel, it must be false, it must be malicious and it must tend to sedition.* Upon which words of this learned and worthy judge I would not presume to offer any comment except that which other words of his own afford, that plainly show in what sense he then spoke. His subsequent words are these, *the bishops tell His Majesty it is not out of averseness, etc.* So that the judge put the whole upon that single point, whether it be true, that the King had a dispensing power or not; which is a question of law and not of fact, and accordingly the judge appeals to his own reading in the law, not to witnesses or other testimonies for a decision of it.[52]

Now the bishops had asserted in the libel they were charged with that the dispensing power claimed by the King in his declaration was illegal. The Remarker by granting that the prelates might prove part of their assertion, viz., that the dispensing power was illegal, which is a question of law, necessarily allows them to prove the other part of their assertion, viz., that His Majesty had claimed such a power, which is a question of fact; for the former could not be decided without proving or admitting the latter. And so in all other cases where a man publishes of a magistrate that he has acted or commanded an illegal thing; if the defendant shall be admitted to prove the *mode* or illegality of the thing, it is evidently implied that he may prove the thing itself. So that on the gentleman's own premises, it is a clear consequence that a man prosecuted for a libel shall be admitted to give the truth in evidence. The Remarker has a method of reasoning peculiar to himself: He frequently advances arguments which directly prove the very point he is laboring to confute.

But in truth Judge Powell's words would not have given the least color to such a ridiculous distinction, if they had been fairly quoted. He affirms with the strongest emphasis *that to make it a libel it*

MUST be false, it MUST be malicious and it MUST tend to sedition. (Let it be observed that these three qualities of a libel against the government are in the conjunctive.) His subsequent words are these, *as to the falsehood, I see nothing that is offered by the King's counsel, nor any thing as to the malice.* Here the judge puts the proof both of the falsehood and malice on the prosecutor; and though the falsehood in this case was a question of law, it will not be denied but that the malice was a question of fact. Now shall we attribute this omission to the inadvertency of the Remarker? No, that cannot be supposed, for the sentence immediately followed. But they were nailing, decisive words, which, if they were fairly quoted, had put an end to the dispute, and left the Remarker without the least room for an evasion; and therefore he very honestly dropped them.

Our author says it is necessary to consult Bracton in order to fix our idea of a libel.[53] Now Bracton throughout his five books *De Legibus et Consuetudinibus Angliae* only once happens to mention libels, very perfunctorily. He says no more than that a man may receive an injury by a lampoon and things of that nature. *Fit injuria cum de eo factum carmen famosum et hujusmodi.* Pray how is any person's idea of a libel the better fixed by this description of it? Our author very sagaciously observes on these words of Bracton that the falsity of a libel is neither expressed nor implied by them. That it is not expressed is self-evident, but that it is not implied we have only the Remarker's *ipse dixit* for it. But it was really idle and impertinent to draw this ancient lawyer into the dispute, as nothing could be learned from him, only that a libel is an injury, which everybody will readily grant. I have good ground to suspect that our author did not consult Bracton on this occasion. The passage cited in the *Remarks* is literally transcribed from Coke's 9th *Report,* fol. 60. By which an unlearned reader might be easily led to believe that our author was well skilled in ancient learning. Ridiculous affectation and pedantry this!

To follow the Remarker through all his incoherencies and absurdities would be irksome; and indeed nothing is more vexatious than to be obliged to refute lies and nonsense. Besides a writer who is convicted of imposing wilful falsehoods on the reader ought to be regarded with abhorrence and contempt. 'Tis for this reason I have treated him with an acrimony of style which nothing but his malice and want of sincerity, and not his ignorance, his dullness or vanity could have justified; however as to the precedents and proceedings against libeling before the case of the seven bishops, he ought to be left undisturbed in the full enjoyment of the honor he has justly acquired by transcribing them from commonplace books and publishing them in gazettes. *Pretty speculations these to be inserted in newspapers,* especially when they come clothed and loaded under the jargon and tackle of the law.

I am sure that by this time the reader must be heartily tired with the little I have offered on the subject, though I have endeavored to speak so as to be understood. Yet it in some measure appeared necessary to expose the folly and ignorance of this author, inasmuch as he seemed to be cherished by some pernicious insects of the profession, who neglecting the noble parts, feed on the rotten branches of the law.

Besides, the liberty of the press would be wholly abolished if the Remarker could have propagated the doctrine of punishing truth. Yet he declares he would not be thought to derogate from that noble privilege of a free people. How does he reconcile these contradictions? Why truly, thus. He says that the liberty of the press is a bulwark and two-edged weapon capable of cutting two ways, and is only to be trusted in the hands of men of wit and address, and not with such fools as rail without art.[54] I pass over the blunder of his calling a bulwark a two-edged weapon, for a lawyer is not supposed to be acquainted with military terms; but is it not highly ridiculous that the gentleman will not allow a squib to be fired from the bulwark of liberty, yet freely gives permission to erect on it a battery of cannon.

Again. *Satire* is painted smiling with a dagger under her gown; the more concealed, the surer and deeper it wounds. Barefaced scurrilities founded on falsehood (such as the *Remarks* are stuffed with) are the most silly harmless things imaginable, that do just as much mischief as the coarse ribaldry of a foul-mouthed waterman, or the gross raillery of a Billingsgate wench. Our author would encourage the former but punish the latter. Mr. Hamilton seems to be of a contrary opinion by the contempt he shows for the Remarker's performance.

I would not, however, by anything I have offered, be understood to draw into question the abilities of our author, considered in his oratorial capacity; for it often happens that the gentlemen, *qui jurgia vendunt,*[55] appear with a *grand éclat* at the bar, though they make but lamentable figures in print.

I pursue him no farther. Much less shall I take any notice of his admirer Indus Britanicus. This fellow is wretchedly ignorant; his little sense, if possible, sinks below contempt. His ignorance is only equalled by his malice. Yet methinks, they ought to have been contented in lashing Mr. Hamilton with their dull strokes of no-wit, and not have libeled the Chief Justice by declaring he knew not his duty; and publishing it through the continent.

Upon the whole. To suppress enquiries into the administration is good policy in an arbitrary government: But a free constitution and freedom of speech have such a reciprocal dependence on each other that they cannot subsist without consisting together.

X.

NOTES

INDEX

NOTES

Introduction

1. James Grahame, *The History of the United States of North America* (Philadelphia, 1852), II, 145, 146.

2. George Bancroft, *History of the United States* (Boston, 1859), III, 393–394.

3. Richard Hildreth, *The History of the United States* (New York, 1882), II, 360; John Fiske, *The Dutch and Quaker Colonies in America* (Boston, 1902), II, 296.

4. Two representative recent texts are: Charles A., Mary, and William Beard, *The Beards' New Basic History of the United States* (New York, 1960), p. 86, and Richard Current, T. Harry Williams, and Frank Freidel, *American History: A Survey* (New York, 1961), p. 52.

5. James Alexander to Alured Popple, December 4, 1733, William A. Whitehead, ed., *Documents Relating to the Colonial History of the State of New Jersey* (Newark, 1882), 1st ser., V, 360.

6. *New York Weekly Journal*, no. 12, January 21, 1734. [Hereafter referred to as *NYWJ*.]

7. The two best contemporary accounts of New York politics during the Cosby administration are: Cadwallader Colden, *History of Gov. William Cosby's Administration and of Lt.-Gov. George Clarke's Administration through 1737* (New York Historical Society, *Collections*, LXVIII [1935], 283–355); and William Smith, *The History of the Province of New-York from its Discovery, to the Appointment of Governor Colden, in 1762* (N.Y. Hist. Soc., *Collections*, 1st ser., IV–V [1826]). The best brief modern treatment is in Herbert L. Osgood, *The American Colonies in the Eighteenth Century* (New York, 1904–1907), II, 443–469. For recent scholarship on the subject, see Beverly McAnear, "Politics in Provincial New York, 1689–1761" (unpub. diss., Stanford University, 1935); Nicholas Varga, "New York Politics and Government in the Mid-Eighteenth Century" (unpub. diss., Fordham University, 1960); Stanley N. Katz, "An Easie Access: Anglo-American Politics in New York, 1732–1753" (unpub. diss., Harvard University, 1961).

8. Julius Goebel, Jr., and T. Raymond Naughton, *Law Enforcement in Colonial New York* (New York, 1944), p. 27; Governor Montgomerie's commission, in E. B. O'Callaghan and Berthold Fernow, eds., *Documents*

Relative to the Colonial History of the State of New York (Albany, 1856–1887), V, 837. In England, the proceeding would have come under Exchequer jurisdiction as a matter of course, but in New York there was apparently no clear precedent for litigation concerning the disposition of private income derived out of the public revenue. Furthermore, the New York Assembly was unsure enough of the status of the Exchequer Court to hold an extraordinary discussion on the subject in June 1734. The issue at stake was whether an Exchequer Court could be established without an act of the New York legislature. William Smith presented the Morrisite argument of the need for a statutory grant of authority. His main point was that the King could not erect a court of equity in England without the consent of the legislature; to erect such a court in New York would be, therefore, to establish an arbitrary authority over the citizens of the colony. The circumstances of provincial political life, moreover, made courts of equity doubly dangerous in America where they would not be subject to the strong checks put upon "every branch of power" in the British constitution. [William Smith], *Mr. Smith's Opinion Humbly Offered to the General Assembly* . . . (New York, 1734). Joseph Murray, representing the Governor, maintained that the courts of New York were not established by acts of the Assembly. New Yorkers, he argued, were entitled to equity courts since they were owed all the liberties and privileges of Englishmen—and the courts are the protectors of constitutional rights. Who, he asked, was most in favor of the liberties of the people: "He who affirms and proves, that they are entitled to those *liberties and privileges, laws and customs of England,* and the *good old original courts,* that are by those laws, without an act? Or, he who argues and says, we are not entitled to them, until an act is passed to establish them?" [Joseph Murray], *Mr. Murray's Opinion Relating to the Courts of Justice in the Colony of New-York* . . . [New York, 1734], pp. 31–32. The issue at stake between Murray and Smith was the same as that which later divided Anglo-Americanus and Hamilton: do the constitutional rights of the colonists rest upon the institutions of England or upon the more popular institutions of America?

9. Berthold Fernow, ed., *Calendar of Council Minutes,* New York State Library, *Bulletin,* 58 (1902), 318–319.

10. Morris' opinion is reprinted in New Jersey Historical Society, *Proceedings,* 55 (1937), 89–116: "The Opinion and Argument of the Chief Justice of the Province of New-York, concerning the Jurisdiction of the Supream Court of the said Province, to determine Causes in a Course of Equity." Zenger printed two editions of the pamphlet in 1733.

11. Although each colony had its own legislature, judiciary, and officialdom, they shared the same governor, who spent nearly all his time in New York. Many New Yorkers owned property in both colonies, and some, like Morris and James Alexander, held office in both.

12. See Colden, *History of Cosby and Clarke,* pp. 305–312.

13. *Ibid.,* p. 299.

14. Zenger described the election in the first issue of the *New York Weekly*

Journal, November 5, 1733. See Nicholas Varga, "Election Procedures and Practices in Colonial New York," *New York History,* 41 (1960), 249–277.

15. E.g., "Articles of Complaint against Governor Cosby by Rip Van Dam, Esq.," *New York Col. Docs.,* V, 975–978. For the generally "popular" pretensions of the Morris group, note the tone of the "No Courtier" article in *NYWJ,* no. 23, April 8, 1734, in Appendix A, 4.

16. *New York Gazette,* no. 469, October 14–21, 1734. (Hereafter referred to as *NYG.*)

17. Cosby to Newcastle, October 26, 1732, *New York Col. Docs.,* V, 937; Cosby to Newcastle, January 24, 1734, W. N. Sainsbury, J. W. Fortescue and Cecil Headlam, eds., *Calendar of State Papers, Colonial Series, America and West Indies* (London, 1860–), 1733, p. 25.

18. *NYG,* no. 489, March 3–11, 1735.

19. For an account of Morris' trip to England by his son, see Beverly McAnear, ed., "R. H. Morris: An American in London, 1735–1736," *Pennsylvania Magazine of History,* 64 (1940), 164–217, 356–406. For an analysis of the significance of the Morris mission, see Katz, "Easie Access," pp. 73–155.

20. See *The Arguments of the Council for the Defendant, . . . Rip Van Dam . . . in the Supream Court of New-York* (New York, 1733); and *The Proceedings of Rip Van Dam, Esq; in order for obtaining Equal Justice of His Excellency William Cosby, Esq.* (New York, 1733). These pamphlets were printed by Zenger.

21. *NYWJ,* no. 7, December 17, 1733; Smith, *History of New York,* II, 15.

22. On Zenger's career, see Irving G. Cheslaw, *John Peter Zenger and the New York Weekly Journal: A Historical Study* (New York, 1952). For Alexander's role, see Vincent Buranelli, "Peter Zenger's Editor," *American Quarterly,* 7 (1955), 174–181.

23. See Elizabeth Christine Cook, *Literary Influences in Colonial Newspapers, 1704–1750* (New York, 1912), pp. 125–126, 139.

24. *NYWJ,* no. 4, November 26, 1733; no. 7, December 10, 1733; no. 20, March 18, 1735.

25. *Ibid.,* no. 10, January 7, 1734.

26. December 6, 1734, *New York Col. Docs.,* VI, 21; Cosby to Lords of Trade, June 19, 1734, *ibid.,* VI, 5, 7; Cosby to Newcastle, December 17, 1733, *ibid.,* V, 974.

27. A letter in the *Journal* (no. 8, December 24, 1733) had asserted that all the good governors of New York and New Jersey had had names beginning with the letter "H" (Hamilton, Hurley, Hunter), while the bad governors had come under the letter "C" (Campbell and Carteret in New Jersey, Coote and Cornbury in New York). The *Gazette's* response, dissociating Cosby from Governors Coote and Cornbury, was carried in *NYG,* no. 428, December 31–January 7, 1734.

28. See Cook, *Literary Influences,* pp. 124–125. In January 1734 Bradford used the *Spectator* essay on "Defamatory Papers and Pamphlets" and in November he printed Addison's *Freeholder* essay, "How Ministers of State

Should bear Undeserved Reproach." *NYG,* no. 431, January 21–28, 1734; *ibid.,* no. 472, November 4–11, 1734.

29. *Ibid.,* no. 432, January 28–February 4, 1734; no. 435, February 18–25, 1734; no. 440, March 25–April 1, 1734.

30. *NYWJ,* nos. 2–3, November 12–19, 1733.

31. Lord Chief Justice Mansfield in the Dean of St. Asaph's case (1784), T. B. Howell, comp., *A Complete Collection of State Trials* (London, 1816–1828), XXI, 1040. Although Mansfield was speaking many years after 1735, his famous dictum accurately describes the state of the law at the time of the Zenger trial. For discussions of the law of the press in eighteenth-century England, see: James F. Stephen, *A History of the Criminal Law of England* (London, 1883), II, 298–375; Laurence Hanson, *Government and the Press, 1695–1763* (London, 1936), esp. pp. 7–35; Fredrick Seaton Siebert, *Freedom of the Press in England, 1476–1776* (Urbana, Ill., 1952), pp. 237–392.

32. Stephen, *Hist. Crim. Law,* II, 348. The law was not statutory, but had been developed in the powerful and juryless Court of Star Chamber by the late sixteenth century, and was so construed as to condemn even truthful speech as criminal. The most famous report of a seditious libel case in the Star Chamber is that of *de Libellis Famosis,* 5 *Coke's Reports* 125 (1606).

33. For an excellent account of the problems of the law of the press in colonial America, see Leonard W. Levy, *Legacy of Suppression: Freedom of Speech and Press in Early American History* (Cambridge, Mass., 1960). For New York, see also Goebel and Naughton, *Law Enforcement.* Leonard Levy and Lawrence Leder have recently stressed the similarity between the English law and that of colonial New York: " 'Exotic Fruit': The Right Against Compulsory Self-Incrimination in Colonial New York," *William and Mary Quarterly,* 3rd ser., 20 (1963), 1–32.

34. On Bradford, see Levy, *Legacy of Suppression,* pp. 28–29; on Mackemie, see "A Narrative of a New and Unusual American Imprisonment of Two Presbyterian Ministers: And Prosecution of Mr. Francis Mackemie" (1707) in Peter Force, ed., *Tracts and Other Papers Relating Principally to the Origin . . . of the Colonies in North America* (Washington, D.C., 1836–1846), IV, no. 4. The jury had been given permission to consider Mackemie's innocence, as he had demanded, because the presiding judge was unfamiliar with the proper procedure for such an unusual crime, and consequently was unsure that he could limit the jury to a special verdict. *Ibid.,* IV, 42–44.

35. *NYG,* no. 432, January 28–February 4, 1734.

36. *NYWJ,* no. 15, February 18, 1734.

37. *NYG,* no. 468, October 7–14, 1734.

38. *Ibid.,* no. 470, October 21–28, 1734.

39. *NYWJ,* no. 53, November 4, 1734. The "Middletown Papers" appeared in nos. 47 and 48 of the *Journal.* See Appendix A, 3.

40. *NYWJ,* no. 18, February 25, 1734, reprinting the letter of June 10, 1721 (no. 32) from [John Trenchard and Thomas Gordon], *Cato's Letters: Or Essays on Liberty, Civil and Religious* (London, 1748, 5th ed.) I, 246–247.

41. *NYWJ,* no. 5, December 3, 1733.

42. *Ibid.,* no. 90, July 28, 1735.

43. *Ibid.,* no. 91, August 2, 1735, reprinting from Sir John Hawles, *A Dialogue Between a Barrister at Law, and a Juryman* (London, 1680).

44. See Appendix A, 1 and 3.

45. *NYWJ,* no. 53, November 4, 1734, Appendix A, 4.

46. *NYWJ,* no. 23, April 8, 1734, Appendix A, 4.

47. Livingston Rutherfurd, *John Peter Zenger* (New York, 1904), p. 40. De Lancey's speeches to the two Grand Juries were reprinted by William Bradford in 1734. *The Charge of the Honorable James De Lancey Esq. Chief Justice of the Province of New-York, to the Gentlemen of the Grand Jury for the City and County of New-York, on Tuesday the 15th Day of January, Annoq Domini, 1733* (New York, 173[4]); *The Charge . . . on Tuesday the 15th of October, 1734 . . .* (New York, 1734). See also [Lewis Morris?], *Some Observations on the Charge Given by the Honorable James De Lancey, Esq, Chief Justice of the Province of New-York, to the Grand Jury, the 15th Day of January, 1733* (New York, 1734).

48. *Journal of the Legislative Council of the Colony of New York, 1691–1775* (Albany, 1861), I, 642. The two broadside songs and the four issues of the *Journal* attacked by the Cosby administration are reprinted in Appendix A, 1 and 3.

49. Zenger's affidavit, November 23, 1734, James Alexander Papers, 1733–1734, no. 21, New York Public Library. The affidavit is endorsed, "Persons Proposed to be Zenger's Bail on Habeas Corpus," and lists the names of twenty prominent New Yorkers on an accompanying sheet. It would seem, therefore, that raising the £400 bail would have presented no real difficulty, had Zenger's friends really desired to have him freed.

50. *The Complaint of James Alexander and William Smith to the Committee of the General Assembly of the Colony of New York, etc.* (New York [1736]). This is their paraphrase, which concludes by saying "or words to that effect."

51. William Smith, Jr., makes the curious mistake of stating that Zenger put up the bail and was set free: ". . . bail was exacted in the penalty of eight hundred pounds; upon this he was enlarged, and being well supported, prosecuted his paper." Smith, *History of New York,* II, 17. The amount of bail would appear to be no more than £400, with two sureties required to guarantee that amount.

52. *NYG,* no. 476, December 2–9, 1734.

53. Philip L. White, *The Beekmans of New York* (New York, 1956), p. 175. Henry Beekman, sheriff of New York since 1728, was replaced by John Symes in October 1734.

54. Smith, *History of New York,* II, 19.

55. Goebel and Naughton suggest that the disbarment incident is an important example of how New York law was established. "No more cogent proof could be desired than the action of the Supreme Court in *King v.*

Zenger when the objections to the judges' commissions were brushed aside. The New York courts could pick what they wished from the books and within the gaunt framework of the founding statute make of the judicial system what seemed most suitable." *Law Enforcement,* p. 323.

56. A plaque in the John Peter Zenger Memorial in Federal Hall (Wall and Nassau Streets, New York City) honors the jurors, listing them as follows: Foreman, Thomas Hunt, mariner; Harmanus Rutgers, brewer; John Bell, clerk (?); John Goelet, artisan; Benjamin Hildreth, tailor; Andries Marschalk, baker; Samuel Weaver, currier; Stanley Holmes, tradesman (?); Egbert Van Borsom, vintner; Hercules Wendover, blacksmith; Edward Man, carpenter; Abraham Kateltas, merchant. For a description of the Memorial, see *New York Times,* April 24, 1953, p. 19.

57. Smith, *History of New York,* II, 21–22.

58. The suggestion to engage Hamilton was doubtless made by Alexander. It was discussed by Smith, Lewis Morris, Jr., and Matthew Norris (Morris' brother-in-law, an English naval captain who commanded the station ship in New York), who agreed to Hamilton. Smith, however, seems to have tried to avoid having his name connected with the request for Hamilton's services. Livingston Rutherfurd, *Family Record and Events* (New York, 1894), pp. 14–15; Rutherfurd, *Zenger,* pp. 57–58.

59. For the Hamilton–Andrew Bradford dispute in Pennsylvania, see Anna Janney DeArmond, *Andrew Bradford* (Newark, Delaware, 1949), pp. 84–113.

60. A fragment of what appears to have been the draft for Chambers' opening address is printed in Appendix B, 3. Before Hamilton's services had been secured by the Morrisites, Alexander was apparently sceptical of Chambers' ability to defend Zenger properly, and planned to have the printer speak in his own behalf. Judging from the MSS in the Alexander Papers (no. 28, New York Public Library), the lawyer-editor composed two speeches for Zenger. The first, intended to be read at the beginning of the trial, acknowledged his gratitude for Chambers' appointment, but asked to be allowed to speak in his own behalf, and went on to question De Lancey's impartiality and to call for the Chief Justice to disqualify himself. The second speech was intended to be used at the end of the trial, and dwelt lugubriously on Zenger's poverty and the hardship of his imprisonment, while emphasizing that he had printed nothing but the truth. It was a strong play for the sympathy of the jury. The two speeches are printed in Appendix B, 2.

61. It is worth remarking that Hamilton was only fifty-nine years old in 1735, not eighty as so many historians have thought. His physical infirmity doubtless made him appear older than he was, and he played upon it to gain the sympathy of the jurors. *Brief Narrative,* p. 99. See Burton Alva Konkle, *The Life of Andrew Hamilton, 1676–1741* (Philadelphia, 1941), pp. 65, 69; Charles Warren, *A History of the American Bar* (Boston, 1911), p. 108.

62. *Brief Narrative,* pp. 63, 68. Bradley's "modern" authority for the law of libel, the standard work of that age, was William Hawkins, *A Treatise of*

the Pleas of the Crown (London, 1716–1721), which merely restated the principles of the earlier case.

63. *Brief Narrative,* pp. 68–69, 72–74. Chambers, in the draft of his defense of Zenger, also argued that every libel must be "false and malicious." He also argued that criminal libels must be specific, for persons named "generally are uncertain and by them no one can tell who are meant." He appears to have intended to go on to argue that Zenger did not "defame somebody certain," and hence was innocent of the charge. This is, of course, a quite mild line of attack, although he, like Hamilton, does strike out at the use of informations and Star Chamber precedents. Hamilton, however, did qualify his attitude toward the falsity of libels by insisting that every "tittle" of an alleged libel be proved true. He also admitted that there was only a limited right to criticize private individuals. *Brief Narrative,* pp. 84, 79.

64. *Brief Narrative,* p. 74. Compare Hamilton's argument with Alexander's in the brief of his projected defense of Zenger in Appendix B, 1. Hamilton's argument up to this point in the trial followed Alexander, who was prepared to admit publication and contended that Zenger's papers were not libels, since they were true. Hamilton cited Alexander's authorities on this point. But Alexander had gone on to argue the truth of Zenger's statements, and Judge De Lancey refused to allow Hamilton to introduce the truth of the statements in evidence. Thereafter, the brief could not have been useful in the trial. Alexander did suggest an argument based on the freedom of the press, but did not elaborate it. Neither did Alexander anticipate Hamilton's argument as to the power of the jury to return a general verdict.

65. *Brief Narrative,* pp. 78, 91.

66. *Ibid.,* pp. 66–68.

67. *Ibid.,* pp. 80–82, 87–88, 84, 89–90.

68. This was the crux of the problem for the Morrisites, and the repeated message of the *Journal.* By implication, the New York opposition was demanding that the colonial executive be held responsible to the citizens under his jurisdiction. In reality, they were doing their best to secure redress through the machinery of the imperial system in London, but Morris' ultimate failure to secure reinstatement must have confirmed them in their view that the rule in America was "self-help." On November 26, 1735, the Privy Council decided that Governor Cosby's reasons for removing Morris from his chief justiceship were insufficient. The New Yorker was given no help in reinstating himself, however, and the Duke of Newcastle appears to have intended that he should not be reinstated. *New York Col. Docs.,* VI, 36–37.

69. *Brief Narrative,* pp. 93, 84.

70. *Ibid.,* pp. 66–67.

71. Hamilton's broad style is perhaps explained by Stephen: "I think that the rhetoric commonly used about the liberty of the press derived some part of its energy and vivacity from the consciousness which the lawyers who employed it must have had of the insecurity of its legal foundations—a cir-

cumstance which exercised influence in more ways than one over much of that inordinate appetite for rhetoric which was characteristic of the eighteenth century." *Hist. Crim. Law,* II, 349–350.

72. For the circumstances of the composition of the *Brief Narrative,* see the Note on the Text.

73. The Barbadian letter of Anglo-Americanus was first published in July, 1737 in the *Barbados Gazette.* It was republished as part of a pamphlet attacking Hamilton's performance in the Zenger trial, entitled *Remarks on Zenger's Tryal.* The essay is reprinted in Appendix C.

74. Anglo-Americanus' orthodoxy should not be overemphasized, however. He also took the advanced position that "juries in criminal cases may determine both law and fact when they are complicated." Appendix C, p. 158. On this point, at any rate, he and Hamilton were in agreement. Sir James Stephen, commenting on the dispute between the two lawyers, said: "The speech of Zenger's counsel, Hamilton, was singularly able, bold, and powerful, though full of doubtful, not to say bad, law, which is brought out in some very able letters published at the end of the case. [In *Howell's State Trials.*] I may observe that the author of those letters would have found it difficult to defend himself on his own principles if he had been tried for a libel on Hamilton." Stephen, *Hist. Crim. Law,* II, 323 n. 4.

75. Appendix C, pp. 172, 175, 176.

76. *Ibid.,* p. 177.

77. Alexander's essay was published pseudonymously in the *Pennsylvania Gazette* during November and December 1737. It is reprinted in Appendix C.

78. Appendix C, pp. 183, 190, 194.

79. Quoted by "Z." (John Webbe?) in the *Pennsylvania Gazette,* no. 492, in DeArmond, *Andrew Bradford,* p. 110.

80. For the McDougall incident, see Levy, *Legacy of Suppression,* pp. 78–82; for a similar case in Massachusetts (Isaiah Thomas), see *ibid.,* pp. 72–73. Levy points out that, with the exception of two minor cases in the decade after the Zenger prosecution, the Zenger case "was the last of its kind under the royal judges." *Ibid.,* pp. 20–21.

81. *Ibid.,* pp. 40–42. For an elaboration of this argument, see Leonard W. Levy, "Did the Zenger Case Really Matter? Freedom of the Press in Colonial New York," *William and Mary Quarterly,* 3rd ser., 17 (1960), 35–50. Professor Levy sums up the situation in this way: "The Zenger case in 1735 gave the press freedom to print as far as the truth carried and a jury's emotions might be sympathetically swayed, if the truth was directed away from the House." *Legacy of Suppression,* p. 44.

82. Mansfield in the Dean of St. Asaph's case, XXI *Howell's State Trials* 1040; Sir William Blackstone, *Commentaries on the Laws of England* (London, 1765–1769), IV, 151.

83. The trial of William Owen for seditious libel, King's Bench, July 6, 1752. XVIII *Howell's State Trials* 1203–1230. See Stephen, *Hist. Crim. Law,* II, 323.

84. For Wilkes's legal difficulties, which revolved about questions of free speech, see XIX *Howell's State Trials* 982–1002, 1075–1138, 1381–1418 (1763–1770); case of William Davies Shipley, Dean of St. Asaph, King's Bench, 1783–1784. *Ibid.,* XXI, 847–1046.

85. Quoted in Stephen, *Hist. Crim. Law,* II, 344–345.

86. *Ibid.,* II, 383.

87. See Stephen's comment. *Ibid.,* II, 300–301.

88. See James Morton Smith, *Freedom's Fetters: The Alien and Sedition Laws and American Civil Liberties* (Ithaca, N.Y., 1956), pp. 421–422.

89. U.S. v. Hudson, 7 *Cranch* 32. See Henry Schofield, "Freedom of the Press in the United States," *Essays on Constitutional Law and Equity and Other Subjects* (Boston, 1921), II, 535, n. 35; 544.

90. Henry Cabot Lodge, ed., *The Works of Alexander Hamilton* (New York, 1885–1886), VII, 368.

A Note on the Text

1. The letter is reproduced in Rutherfurd, *Zenger,* facing p. 128.

2. *Brief Narrative,* pp. 21–24; *NYWJ,* no. 78, May 5, 1735.

3. *NYWJ,* no. 93, August 18, 1735.

4. Thomas Fleet published the Boston edition in 1738. The four London editions of 1738 were all printed for J. Wilford, and an undated fifth edition strongly resembles them. Thomas R. Adams of the John Carter Brown Library, Providence, Rhode Island, has called the editor's attention to the republication of Milton's *Areopagitica,* which was first published in 1644. For an excellent bibliography of the *Brief Narrative,* see Rutherfurd's *Zenger,* pp. 249–255, which lists all editions previous to 1904.

5. Charles R. Hildeburn, *Sketches of Printers and Printing in Colonial New York* (New York, 1895), pp. 25–26.

6. *New York Journal,* March 19 and 26, 1770, quoted in Arthur M. Schlesinger, *Prelude to Independence* (New York, 1958), p. 116.

7. The *Brief Narrative* was twice reprinted in nineteenth-century compendia of criminal trials: XVII *Howell's State Trials* 675–764; Peleg W. Chandler, comp., *American Criminal Trials* (Boston, 1841–1844), I, 151–209. It was also included in a twentieth-century compilation: John D. Lawson, comp., *American State Trials* (St. Louis, 1928), XVI, 1–39.

8. Sutro Branch, California State Library, Occasional Papers, English Series, 7: *The Trial of John Peter Zenger (1734) and the Freedom of the Press* (San Francisco, 1940). The Rutherfurd reprint was issued by Peter Smith (New York, 1941).

9. Frank Luther Mott, ed., *Oldtime Comments on Journalism* (Columbia, Mo., 1954), vol. II; Vincent Buranelli, ed., *The Trial of Peter Zenger* (New York, 1957).

10. For the significance of italicization in eighteenth-century printing, see A. M. Schlesinger, *Prelude to Independence,* p. 59 and n. 12.

A Brief Narrative

1. Above the title in the New York Public Library's copy of the first edition of the *Brief Narrative*, there is the following inscription in James Alexander's hand: "Universal History, vol. 5, page 659. The Emperor Titus abrogated the Law of Majesty and would not suffer any person to be prosecuted for speaking disrespectfully of himself or other Emperors his predecessors—saying—if they blacken my character undeservedly they ought rather to be pitied than punished—If deservedly, it would be a crying power of injustice to punish them for speaking truth. cites Dio. L.LVIII page 354." Alexander is quoting from *An Universal History* (London, 1736–1747). The sixth volume, which Alexander used for his inscription at the end of the pamphlet, was published in 1742; the two quotations were therefore added several years after the publication of the *Brief Narrative*.

2. The Chief Justice at this time was, of course, James De Lancey.

3. Hawkins, *Pleas of the Crown*, I, 193–196 (ch. 73).

4. Thursday, 3 o'clock P.M.

5. Friday, 9 o'clock A.M.

6. Of the twelve members of the New York Council, the three who were absent from this session were Rip Van Dam, James Alexander, and Abraham Van Horne. Cosby's refusal to summon Morrisite sympathizers to Council meetings was one of the principal opposition criticisms of the Governor. "Articles of Complaint Against Governor Cosby by Rip Van Dam, Esq.," *New York Col. Docs.*, V, 976 (nos. 8 and 9); see also *NYWJ*, no. 7, December 17, 1733, Appendix A, 3. Van Dam and Alexander were two of the leading members of the Morrisites, and Van Horne was one of the many Dutch merchants of New York who supported them. His name appears on the list of men who were "proposed" to be Zenger's bail. See the Introduction, n. 49.

7. The apparently "libelous" parts of these issues of the *Journal* are reprinted in Appendix A, 3.

8. Tuesday, 9 o'clock A.M.

9. Saturday, 9 o'clock A.M.

10. The municipal legislature of New York City was bicameral, and the upper house was known as the Court of Quarter Sessions. It comprised the mayor, recorder, and the aldermen, who were also justices of the peace for the City and County of New York. The Common Councilors, members of the lower house, had the same legislative prerogatives as the aldermen, but did not serve with them as magistrates. The Council's order required the aldermen to act in their magisterial capacity. For the government of New York, see A. E. Peterson and G. W. Edwards, *New York as an Eighteenth Century Municipality* (New York, 1917).

11. Henry Sacheverell's case, an impeachment before the House of Lords on February 27, 1710, is included in V *State Trials* 645–858. Except where

noted, I have used the 2nd edition (London, 1730), as that is the edition cited in the *Brief Narrative*. The Alderman was correct: only the sheriffs were directed to attend the burning.

12. Francis Harison, the Recorder, was at least partially in error once again. The letter, which urged Burnet's diocesan clergy to take the oaths, was ordered to be burned by the House of Commons, not the House of Lords, on January 21–23, 1693. Thomas B. Macaulay, *The History of England from the Accession of James the Second* (C. H. Firth, ed., London, 1913–1915), V, 2305–2307. The office of recorder of the City of New York resembled that of the present corporation counsel of a large city. The colonial recorder, however, also sat as a member of the Court of Quarter Sessions and the Common Council, and could exercise some of the mayor's powers in his absence. The recorder, like the mayor, was an appointee of the governor, and Harison was certainly among the closest of Cosby's associates and the one of them most despised by the Morrisites. For the recorder of New York City, see Peterson and Edwards, *New York as an Eighteenth Century Municipality*, pp. 26–27, 39.

13. The name of Jeremiah Dunbar, unlike that of Recorder Francis Harison, does not figure in the history of New York politics. There was a contemporary Dunbar family in the city, and Jeremiah's attendance at this burning seems to mark him as a local supporter of the Governor.

14. Richard Bradley had been the Attorney General of New York since 1722. His colleague, Joseph Warrel, was a minor New York lawyer who later became the Attorney General of New Jersey. He was a satellite of Governor Cosby, who recommended him for places on the New York and New Jersey Councils. Like Francis Harison, he was particularly hated by the Morrisites for his complicity in the more devious strategems of the Governor. *New York Col. Docs.*, VI, 35; Colden, *History of Cosby and Clarke*, p. 309. See also Paul M. Hamlin, *Legal Education in Colonial New York* (New York, 1939), p. 106 n. 27.

15. Hawkins, *Pleas of the Crown*.

16. The *Journal* articles referred to in the information are reprinted in Appendix A, 4.

17. Edward Blagge, a member of a well-known New York family of lawyers, was considered by the Morrisites to be on the same level as Harison and Warrel, "another infamous attorney." He did not take part in the argument of Zenger's case but had been Harison's accomplice in the attempt to remove Vincent Matthews from his position of power in Orange County. Hamlin, *Legal Education*, p. 99. For the Matthews affair, see *NYWJ*, no. 49, in Appendix A, 3.

18. A *venire* was the writ used to summon a person to be arraigned for an alleged misdemeanor.

19. Of this group, only Harmanus Rutgers had served on either the January 1734 or October 1734 Grand Juries which had considered the libelousness of Zenger's publications. There was a *Jacob* Goelet on the January

Grand Jury, however, who may have been related to the John Goelet in the present group of jurors. The names of the Grand Jurors are listed in the printed accounts of De Lancey's charges to them. See the Introduction, n. 47.

20. The explanatory words in parentheses are the prosecution's interpretation of Zenger's language, which is alleged to be libelous. They are preceded or followed by the word "meaning," which was originally written in Latin (*innuendo*) and accounts for the legal designation of such a device.

21. See Chambers' brief in Appendix B, 3.

22. This confession of printing and publishing was a novel and dangerous tack for Hamilton to take; it was suggested in Alexander's brief. A common defense against prosecutions for seditious libel was the claim that the libelous matter had not technically been published, or that the defendant could not be proved responsible for its authorship, printing, or publishing. According to the English law of the day, as Bradley quickly pointed out, the only issues on trial were those of Zenger's responsibility for printing and publishing the libels. It is hard to understand why Judge De Lancey did not direct the jury to find Zenger guilty at this early stage of the trial, and it is even harder to understand why he allowed Hamilton to appeal to the judgment of the jury on the subject of truth. The answer may possibly lie in the fact that De Lancey was so inexperienced, and that the Governor was particularly vulnerable to the charge that his administration condoned abuses of the legal privileges of Englishmen.

23. Bradley asks De Lancey to "find a verdict for the King," since the prosecution was undertaken in the name of the King: *Rex* v. *Zenger*.

24. *Coke's Reports;* Thomas Wood, *Institutes of the Laws of England* (London, 1720); John Lilly, *Practical Register; or General Abridgment of the Law* (London, 1719); Hawkins, *Pleas of the Crown.*

25. The references are to the New Testament: Acts of the Apostles; and Peter 2. The citation from Peter 2 is incorrect; it should be 2:10.

26. The Court of Star Chamber, which was abolished in 1641, is "that terrible Court."

27. Case of Thomas Brewster, February 22, 1664, King's Bench. II *State Trials* 534–540 and 545.

28. This is an interesting variation on Hamilton's major theme, of the difference between the practices of England and America. At common law there was no obligation to fence one's land, for a man was held responsible for trespasses by his horses and cattle. In America, however, the law generally required the landowner to fence his property against the trespasses of his neighbor's cattle. In New York, an act of 1734 required stone fences to be 3′8″ high, whereas rail fences had to be 4′. On this point see Richard B. Morris, *Studies in the History of American Law* (New York, 1930), pp. 208–211. Morris sees the distinction between English and American law in this case to be evidence of "the refusal of the colonial courts to impose responsibility without accompanying fault." *Ibid.*, p. 210.

29. Case of John Tutchin, November 4, 1704, King's Bench. V *State Trials*

532–575. Holt's charge to the jury in Tutchin's case is quoted by De Lancey in his charge to the Zenger jurors.

30. Hamilton's distinction between the authorities and "the reason of the thing" was taken by Anglo-Americanus to be an admission of the fact that Hamilton's argument was essentially political rather than legal. See *Remarks,* Appendix C, p. 172.

31. "And since the aforementioned John admits writing the said letter, to Robert de Ferrers of the King's Council, which letter contains no truth whatever, etc."

32. Case of Sir Samuel Barnardiston, February 14, 1684, King's Bench. III *State Trials* 845–854. George Jeffreys, created Baron Jeffreys of Wem in 1685, was a lawyer, Lord Chancellor (1685) and Chief Justice of King's Bench (1683). He was involved in the prosecution of those accused of participation in the Rye House plot, but his infamy rests upon his conduct of the Bloody Assizes in the summer of 1685, when he condemned over three hundred of Monmouth's rebels to death in a high-handed and arbitrary fashion.

33. Hawkins, *Pleas of the Crown,* I, 194.

34. Hamilton is here contending for a conception of the jury which had, by 1735, long since been obsolete. The jury began in the early medieval period as an inquisitional device, by means of which officers of the Crown could ask questions of a group of local residents, who answered under oath. As the jury came to be used for judicial purposes, the jurors acted as witnesses to facts within their knowledge. The jury of presentment, which came to be the Grand Jury, retained this conception of the jury for a long time. By the end of the Middle Ages, however, the jury was supposed to judge the facts of an accusation impartially, and it was not intended to rely on its own knowledge of the alleged crime. The requirement that the jury be selected from the vicinity in which the crime occurred, to which Hamilton alludes, was designed to ensure the accused that he would not be confronted with twelve alien, uncomprehending jurors. In short, Zenger's jury was supposed to arrive at its verdict on the basis of the evidence introduced at the trial rather than its previous "knowledge of the fact that is to be tried." See T. F. T. Plucknett, *A Concise History of the Common Law* (5th ed., Boston, 1956), pp. 106–138.

35. Hawkins, *Pleas of the Crown,* I, 194.

36. A special verdict allows the jury to find the facts of the case, while leaving to the judges the application of the law to the facts. Hamilton's adversary Indus Britanicus contended that if the Philadelphian "really" believed that Zenger's papers were not libelous, he should have advised "his client to *demur* to [the information], whereby he would have admitted no more than what was avowed at the trial on the general issue. Then indeed it would have fairly come before the Court to be considered whether the papers were libelous or not, and he as counsel for the defendant might regularly have been heard to it." *Remarks on the Trial of John Peter Zenger* (London, 1738), p. 22. The last thing Hamilton wanted, of course, was to have the question of libelousness settled by the judges rather than the jury.

37. 5 *Coke's Reports* 125.

38. The quotation is hard to locate. It appears to pertain to one of the Star Chamber prosecutions for seditious libel during the reign of Charles I, such as the trial of John Lilburne in 1637. III *Howell's State Trials* 1315–1368.

39. It is not clear which American governor and colony Hamilton is referring to here. See E. B. Greene, *The Provincial Governor* (Cambridge, Mass., 1898), p. 155. The jurors would have understood his point, though, for Cosby steadfastly refused to dissolve their own Assembly, which had been elected in 1728. Previously, Governors Hunter and Burnet had kept the same complaisant New York Assembly alive from 1716 to 1726.

40. This attack on the seditious libel prosecutions of Charles II and James II was intended to touch a sensitive nerve in New York, since the leading objection to the commissions of De Lancey and Philipse had been that their commissions were granted at pleasure, rather than during good behavior. See Smith and Alexander's exceptions to the commissions, *supra,* pp. 50–52.

41. *Supra,* pp. 72–73.

42. *Supra,* p. 73. See also Appendix B, n. 10.

43. Case of Sir Edward Hales, 1686, King's Bench, XI *Howell's State Trials* 1165–1315.

44. In other words, the act contravenes the common law process by which a man is accused by a Grand Jury and tried by a "petty" jury of twelve men.

45. 31 Hen. VIII c. 8. This act was later implemented by the act of 34 & 35 Hen. VIII c. 23.

46. 1 Hen. VIII c. 6.

47. Hamilton must have intended to refer to 16 Car. I c. 10, the act which abolished the Court of Star Chamber, expounding the evils of arbitrary justice. The parenthetical phrase probably ought to read: "by which the Court of Star Chamber, the soil where informations grew rankest, *was abolished.*"

48. Bushel's case confirmed the power of the jury to ignore the instructions of the trial judge without fear of punishment for their insubordination. In reality, however, juries had gone unpunished for such independence for many years before this case of 1670. See Mark DeWolfe Howe, "Juries as Judges of Criminal Law," *Harvard Law Review,* 52 (1939), 583. It was still not clear that the jury had the *right* to ignore the judge's instructions, however, but their verdict of not guilty in a criminal case gave them the *power* to acquit the defendant without any fear of retribution. It was this power with which Zenger's verdict was rendered, although the prosecution was doubtless correct in contending that the jury in seditious libel prosecutions did not have the same rights it possessed in other criminal cases.

49. The reference is extremely obscure. Francis Nicholson, who had briefly been the Lieutenant Governor of New York in 1688, was the Governor of Virginia in 1699 when a clergyman named John Gourdon (Gordon?) was

prosecuted by the Attorney General of that colony for "scandalous libel against His Majesty and Government here." Gordon, however, confessed his guilt to Nicholson, who ordered the prosecution to be halted. H. R. McIlwaine, ed., *Executive Journals of the Council of Colonial Virginia* (Richmond, 1925–1930), II, 11. Perhaps this incident was the original source of the colorful story told by Hamilton. Professor Leonard Levy does not believe Hamilton knew of any such case, and thinks that he was probably referring to the New York case of 1707 involving the clergyman Francis Mackemie. If Levy is correct, the reference to the New York case is terribly oblique, since the similarities between it and the supposed libel of Governor Nicholson are very slight. It is not impossible, however, since Hamilton suppressed in the *Brief Narrative* several of the cases he had cited at the trial on the ground that he had not known that they had taken place in New York.

50. L. Echard, *The History of England from the First Entrance of Julius Caesar to 1688* (London, 1707–1718) and *The History of the Revolution and the Establishment of England in 1688* (London, 1725); Gilbert Burnet, *Bishop Burnet's History of His Own Time* (London, 1724–1734); Paul de Rapin-Thoyras, *The History of England,* ed. Nicholas Tindal (London, 1725–1731).

51. Isaiah 9:16.

52. "It is certain here Mr. Hamilton took great liberty but the applause with which it was received by the numerous auditors and the approbation they gave it by their countenances made the Court think proper to pass it over without notice." Colden, *History of Cosby and Clarke,* p. 337.

53. A true bill, *"billa vera,"* is found by a Grand Jury when it is satisfied that the evidence presented in support of an indictment is sufficiently strong to warrant a trial of the case. The Morrisite position was that accusations of criminal offenses ought to be made within the jury system, rather than by information, which brought a man to trial on the initiative of the government rather than his peers.

54. Perhaps a historical figure, described by legend as one of the first two consuls of Rome, 509 B.C. For the story of his sons, see Livy, II, 3.

55. John Hampden (1594–1643), lawyer and member of Parliament who refused to pay the forced loan of 1627 and the ship money writ of 1635. He refused to pay the twenty shillings requested of him for the latter tax, and his trial, the Ship Money Case of 1637–1638 (Court of Exchequer) became one of the focal points in the dispute between Charles I and his subjects. The judges divided seven to five against Hampden, but the prerogative of the Crown and the patience of the English people were sorely strained in the process.

56. On the question of Hamilton's "many years," see the Introduction, n. 61.

57. Alexander Hamilton had a low opinion of De Lancey's charge to the jury. He cited the precedent of Chief Justice John Jay in a comparable case: "The jury are . . . told the law, and the fact is for their determination; I

find him telling them that it is their right. This admits of no qualification. The little, miserable conduct of the judge in Zenger's case, when set against this, will kick the beam." Hamilton's speech in the Croswell case: Hamilton, *Works,* Lodge, ed., VII, 371.

58. "Freemen" were members of the Corporation, and had the right to vote for elective officers and to conduct business in the city. Ordinarily, one had to pay a fee (scaled according to occupational status) before the Common Council would admit him as a freeman. Peterson and Edwards, *New York as an Eighteenth Century Municipality,* pp. 285–286.

59. The gold box was oval, 3″ x 2″, and ¾″ deep. In the present century it was purchased by a New Yorker who was a direct descendant of Hamilton. I. N. Phelps Stokes, *The Iconography of Manhattan Island, 1498–1909* (New York, 1915–1928), IV, 542. A photograph of the box and the certificate of freemanship is reproduced, *ibid.,* IV, 592. The inscription on the lid reads: ". . . though a man oppress the laws and overawe liberty, yet still they will recover . . ." Cicero, *De Officiis,* 2, 7, 24.

60. "Won not by money but virtue."

61. "Let each reap, as he has sown for the Republic."

62. At the foot of the last page of the New York Public Library copy of the *Brief Narrative,* Alexander inscribed: "Universal History, vol. 6 page 423. Theodosius revoked the law of treason for speaking seditious words—if such words proceed from levity they are to be despised, if from folly to be pitied, if from malice they are to be forgiven. The place cited is Cod. Theod: L.IX tit. 4 leg. 3 p. 42." This is a paraphrase of the actual passage in *An Universal History,* VI, 423.

At the conclusion of his lengthy account of the Zenger trial (*History of Cosby and Clarke,* pp. 326–339), which is largely drawn from the *Brief Narrative,* Colden remarked: "As to the merits of the cause it seems probable that falsehood in all cases is not necessary to make a libel but malice is and falsehood is a sure proof of the malice.

"Mr. Hamilton seems to own that if malice appear though accompanied with truth it is criminal when people publish the private faults and failings of men in power which do not affect the public. As to the exposing the public faults or crimes of public officers certainly there can be no fault or crime in doing it in a republic where the people are the supreme judges and as the constitution of England has a considerable share of the democracy in its composition, our constitution allows of considerable latitude for complaints of this nature and of appeals to the people for which reason the people of Great Britain have always been very jealous and their parliaments very tender of the liberty of the press." Colden, *History of Cosby and Clarke,* pp. 339–340.

Appendix A

1. See Rutherfurd, *Zenger,* pp. 39–40. The text is taken from the reproduction of Zenger's broadside, *ibid.,* facing p. 38. The defeated Cosbyite incum-

bents, along with the rest of the Governor's supporters, had attended a banquet in his honor and had presented him with an address thanking him for his efforts to alleviate the decay in the city's trade and to secure the defenses of the city and the province's frontiers. The banquet took place on May 28, 1734, and the address was printed in *NYG*, no. 449, May 27–June 3, 1734. Thus "signers" and "feasters," Cosbyites, become the target of these satirical songs.

2. Whiskey.

3. Presumably "fops," a play on *vol au vent*.

4. "Liberty and law" was the Morrisite slogan at Lewis Morris' Eastchester election in 1733. The counterslogan of De Lancey and Philipse was "No Land Tax," to which the Morrisites replied, "No Excise!" English analogies, clearly, were in men's minds. See *NYWJ*, no. 1, [November] 5, 1733.

5. The reference is to the dispute over the establishment of an Exchequer Court in Van Dam's case. The justification for the establishment of such a court was hotly debated by the Morrisites and the Governor's adherents, the latter arguing that the court existed independent of any act of the legislature. The Morrisites claimed that the Exchequer must have a statutory basis.

6. The song refers to Cosby's removal of Lewis Morris from the chief justiceship, and his replacement by James De Lancey. It also refers, perhaps, to the appointment of safely Cosbyite justices of the peace by the new administration, as in Orange County.

7. The extracts from the *Journal* which are reprinted in this Appendix are drawn from originals and photostats of the newspaper in the possession of the New York Public Library. For a location listing of the extant files of the *Journal*, see Rutherfurd, *Zenger*, pp. 259–267.

8. Tacitus, the "late excellent writer upon" freedom of speech, was greatly admired by the more "liberal" political writers of the eighteenth century in England and America. The identical passage was used by the *Journal*'s idol, Cato, in the essay: "Of Freedom of Speech: That the same is inseparable from public liberty" [Trenchard and Gordon], *Cato's Letters*, I, 99. What appealed to both the *Journal* and Cato was Tacitus' admiration for the free institutions of republican Rome. The passage reads: "It is the rare fortune of these days that you may think what you like and say what you think." Tacitus, *Histories*, I, i.

9. Thomas Gordon, trans., *The Works of Tacitus; To Which are Prefixed Political Discourses Upon That Author* (2nd ed., London, 1737), I, 200–201. "Tacitus" Gordon was also the coauthor of *Cato's Letters*.

10. "One is all the more inclined to laugh at the stupidity of men who think the tyranny of the present can efface the memories of coming generations. On the contrary, the persecution of genius increases its influence: foreign kings, and all who have imitated their brutality, have merely brought obloquy on themselves and glory for their victims." Tacitus, *Annals*, IV, 35. The passage ought to read, "Quo magis socordiam eorum . . ."

11. The first selection from no. 7 is a sarcastic comment on Governor Cosby's wisdom in allowing the French sloop *Le Caesar* to enter New York

harbor for provisions in late 1733. The vessel had come from the French fortress at Louisbourg bearing a letter from the local commander which requested Cosby's permission to take on foodstuffs in New York, as there had been a crop failure in Canada. Cosby explained his compliance by claiming that the existing treaties between France and Canada required him to do so. The Morrisites, however, pointing out that the Governor's brother (who was stationed at Annapolis Royal) had married a French Canadian, suggested that Cosby was in league with the French and had knowingly allowed the *Le Caesar* to sound New York harbor and Long Island Sound. Cosby to Newcastle, December 15, 1733, *New York Col. Docs.*, V. 959; St. Ovide de Brouillan to Cosby, September 11, 1733, *ibid.*, V, 970–971; Lewis Morris to Lords of Trade, December 15, 1733, *ibid.*, V, 958. The earlier pages of this issue of the *Journal* contained several affidavits designed to prove the Morrisite contentions of Cosby's duplicity. One attested to the fact that there was no scarcity of food in Canada, declaring that the French were actually exporting provisions. It also stated that the French officers on *Le Caesar* had been seen taking observations of the harbor and the city. Another told a painful tale of French security-mindedness, alleging that Englishmen were driven out of Canada lest they discover military secrets.

12. This is another example of the *Journal*'s blunt sarcasm. It makes two trusted Morrisite criticisms of the Governor: that he overloaded his friends with the places at his disposal, and that he refused to call the Morrisite members to Council sessions. The members of the opposition party were obviously excluded from the Governor's patronage, but felt that they should at least be allowed to perform the offices which they already held. While they complained about Cosby, the Governor was hard at work to have the English authorities remove the Morrisites from their Council posts. Cosby to Lords of Trade, June 19 and December 6, 1734, *New York Col. Docs.*, VI, 6–7, 23; Lords of Trade to Queen Caroline, August 28, 1735, *ibid.*, VI, 34–35.

13. Numbers 47 and 48 of the *Journal* printed the end of an interminably long essay ("Letter from Middletown") on the power of the colonial executive to regulate the length and time of meeting of the local legislature, a point of some importance in assessing the relative power of the governor and the Assembly. The essay is at pains to emphasize that it concerns the government of New Jersey, but Cosby was governor of both colonies, and the parallel was obvious enough. Even so, it is hard not to agree with Zenger that the essay was not libelous, even by the standards of his day.

14. This refers to another of the complaints against Cosby, that he had sat with the Council in its legislative sessions. The British theory was that the Assembly, the Council, and the governor (through his veto power) constituted three distinct branches of colonial government, and that the branches had to be totally separate from one another. Thus the governor could not sit or vote with the Council when it acted as a legislature, although he was free to do so in its executive sessions. Van Dam complained to the imperial officials that Cosby had interfered with the legislative Council: Articles of Complaint,

December 17, 1733, *New York Col. Docs.*, V, 979–980 (nos. 5 and 6). The Board of Trade subsequently forbade the Governor to continue sitting with the Council when it acted in its legislative capacity. Alured Popple to Cosby, January 23, 1736, *ibid.*, VI, 39–40. Lieutenant Governor Clarke later admitted that Cosby had sat with the Council, but stated that he could not remember *any* governor voting with the Council in all his years as a member. Clarke to Popple, May 28, 1736, *ibid.*, VI, 56–57.

15. "I see the Journals . . ." appears to be the start of a new sentence. The sentence left uncompleted by the printer, therefore, is: "since the people they represent are in general . . ." Zenger's work is frequently marred with errors. He dated the first issue of the *Journal* "October 5, 1733," when the correct date was November 5.

16. General Robert Hunter, the Whig who was governor of New York from 1710–1719.

17. The "late President" would appear to be Lewis Morris. Morris was the senior councilor of New Jersey and became President of the Council (temporary executive of the province in the absence of a governor or lieutenant governor) when Hunter returned to England in 1719. With the advice of the Council, Morris adjourned the New Jersey Assembly on August 8, 1719. Frederick W. Ricord and William Nelson, eds., *Documents Relating to the Colonial History of the State of New Jersey* (Trenton, N.J., 1890), 1st ser., XIV, 117. The drift of this criticism carried all the way to Whitehall, where the Secretary of the Board of Trade read it and reminded Cosby that there was some doubt whether he had the right of adjourning the Assembly, "yet there can be none, but that it must be in His Majesty's name, if done at all." Popple to Cosby, January 23, 1736, *New York Col. Docs.*, VI, 40. The letter arrived after Cosby's death and Clarke replied, admitting that the governors of New York had always adjourned the Assembly in their own names rather than in the name of the King. He begged to be allowed to continue the procedure, however, for fear that the Morrisites would take a proclamation in the King's name as an admission that all former adjournments were illegal, or even that "all acts passed under the former method of adjournment are void . . ." Clarke to Popple, May 28, 1736, *ibid.*, VI, 56–57. Perhaps Clarke's fear is proof that Cosby was right in prosecuting the *Journal*—abstract discussion of government *was* potentially dangerous.

18. 3 *Salkeld's Reports; Anderson's Reports.*

19. *Shower's Reports.*

20. *Dyer's Reports; Keble's Reports.*

21. *Raymond's Reports; Levinz' Reports.*

22. *Siderfin's Reports.* Corrected by hand (by Alexander, apparently) to 338 pl. 1.

23. "by the force of the term" or "on the face of it."

24. See n. 22, *supra.*

25. Vincent Matthews was the leading political figure of Orange County. In 1734 he was the Chief Judge of the county, the County Clerk, and one of

the representatives to the New York Assembly from Orange. The letter thanks him for his conduct in the Assembly which ended on June 22, 1734, in which he outspokenly attacked the machinations of the Governor's henchman, Francis Harison. After this letter was published in the *Journal* (and burned), Cosby and Harison retaliated by having Matthews turned out of his judgeship and clerkship in Orange County, and by making "almost a total change" in the commission of the peace for the county. "And such men were generally put in who were thought not to wish well to me." Among those turned out were the signers of this letter who happened to hold commissions from the Governor for posts in Orange County. "Speech of Vincent Matthews read before the New York Assembly on October 21, 1735," New York Historical Society, *Collections,* 1934, pp. 226–240. See the reference to this affair in Alexander's brief, Appendix B, 1.

26. The letter is signed with 78 names.

27. The *Journal*'s report of the September 29, 1734, New York City municipal elections ought to be read in conjunction with the two songs which celebrate the Morrisite victory in the elections. This was the greatest political achievement of the opposition party, since it gave them domination of the government of the largest city in the Province. All the Morrisite candidates, save the merchant John Moore, were elected, and all the incumbents save Moore and Gerardus Stuyvesant went down to defeat. The success was repeated in 1735, when all the incumbents were returned to office. See the *NYWJ,* no. 100, October 6, 1735.

28. The *Journal*'s complaint that soldiers from the New York garrison and nonresident New Yorkers (Francis Harison, the Recorder of the City) voted in the South Ward raises an interesting question: who had the right to vote in New York City? According to the city's recent Montgomerie charter the franchise was reserved to "the freemen of the said city being inhabitants and the freeholders of each respective ward of the city." This clearly permitted nonresidents of the city who held freeholds to vote in the municipal elections, and there are instances in which we know that they did. Whether New York residents who held freeholds in more than one ward could vote in each is less clear, but it seems that they may have had the right—at least in 1771 the practice was outlawed by a provincial statute. Thus Harison may well have been within his rights, though he was reputed to be a poor man and it seems unlikely that he owned much property in the city. The soldiers, on the other hand, were probably not freemen and almost certainly not freeholders. Indeed, since they were members of the four English companies stationed in New York, they were almost certainly not qualified to participate in the election. The alderman in each ward, however, was in charge of its elections, and in this case he was surely sympathetic to the Governor's cause. For the conduct of elections, see Peterson and Edwards, *New York as an Eighteenth Century Municipality,* pp. 243–250; Nicholas Varga, "Election Procedures and Practices in Colonial New York," *New York History,* 41 (1960), 249–277.

29. The proudest Morrisite boast was that all the incumbents who had

attended the banquet for Cosby on May 28, 1734, and who had signed the address thanking the Governor, had been defeated.

30. The offensive passage in no. 13 was drawn from the *Journal*'s challenge to the *Gazette* to enter into an open discussion of the freedom of the press. It is addressed to the authors of a letter in *NYG,* no. 430, January 14–January 21, 1734. The Cosbyite letter writer claimed to have returned home after hearing De Lancey's charge to the Grand Jury on January 15th, and to have turned in reflection to Lewis Morris' charge to the jurors for 1727. Morris' charge, which was reprinted in the *Gazette,* grew out of Chancery case (Quinby, Alexander, and others v. Philipse), and spoke of the dangers of high treason and of the sacred character of the magistrates. The *Gazette*'s correspondent remarked that, although no libels had yet been printed, Morris had thought it necessary to warn New Yorkers that they were not to speak disrespectfully of their government. The moral was clear: Morris and his friends were only concerned to criticize the government when they were on the outs with the Governor. The *Gazette* thus scored a point against the Governor's opponents, but in doing so it fell in with their plans to conduct a "paper war" against him. For Alexander's justification of the allegedly libelous passage in *NYWJ,* no. 13, see his brief in Appendix B, 1.

31. This letter plays upon one of the most serious problems confronting the Cosby administration—the decay of trade in New York. The economy provided the key to the Morrisite attempt to woo the tradesmen and artisans of New York City, as well as the Indian traders in the Mohawk region, from adherence to the Governor. In more prosperous times, it is doubtful that the opposition would have succeeded even in such a mild manner. See, for instance, Lt. Gov. Clarke to Lords of Trade, December 15, 1741, *New York Col. Docs.,* VI, 207.

32. William Burnet was Governor of New York from 1720 to 1728, when he was replaced by Montgomerie. The New York tonnage act had been designed to levy a duty on all ships (except coasting vessels and whalers) entering provincial ports, which were neither built nor partially or wholly owned by New Yorkers. A new tonnage act was passed in June 1734. Its preamble noted that the disappearance of the previous act had caused the decay of the shipping of the Province to the extent that vessels of other ports were the only carriers. *The Colonial Laws of New York from the Year 1664 to the Revolution* (Albany, 1894–1896), II, 843–847, 867–868.

33. For an example of the recurring Morrisite appeal to the "industrious poor," see the supplementary issue of the *Journal* for September 12, 1734. It contains a letter from a tradesman (Timothy Wheelwright) to a group of his friends (headed by "John Chissel") proffering advice for the forthcoming New York City elections. The writer extols the virtues and political reliability of "a *poor honest man*" or a "midling man" and warns the artisans not to vote for *"courtiers."* Wheelwright's words were apparently heeded on September 29 at the polls, and this "No-Courtier" letter may perhaps be regarded as the opening Morrisite manifesto for the fall contests.

34. This refers to the fact that New York had no statutory enactment of the fees charged by lawyers and officers of the government. Lewis Morris, Jr., twice attempted to secure such legislation (August 1732 and May 1734) but failed each time. *Journal of the Votes and Proceedings of the General Assembly of the Colony of New York, 1691–1765* (New York, 1764–1766), I, 637, 660–662. Regulation of fees was part of the Morris program on the grounds that the people of New York were unfairly charged for the ordinary processes of law and civil administration. The "late judge" is apparently Lewis Morris, Sr.

35. A "let pass" was a certificate given to the master of a merchant vessel, enabling the vessel to proceed if it should be questioned by a ship of war.

36. This long sentence summarizes the major complaints against the Cosby administration. "Men's deeds destroyed" refers to the incident of the Albany Deed; "judges arbitrarily displaced" refers to the replacement of Lewis Morris by James De Lancey, and to the treatment of local judges such as Vincent Matthews; "new courts erected" refers to the Exchequer Court controversy, and perhaps also to Cosby's use of the detested Chancery Court, both cases involving courts which operated without juries; "men of known estates denied their votes" refers to Sheriff Cooper's disqualification of the thirty-eight Quaker freeholders in Lewis Morris' 1733 Eastchester election. See Alexander's defense of this passage in his brief.

37. Excepting.

Appendix B

1. The manuscript of this brief is in the Rutherfurd MSS, II, 35. It has previously been printed in Goebel and Naughton, *Law Enforcement in Colonial New York*, pp. 782–786, and it is here reprinted from their text, which is copyrighted by the Commonwealth Fund. See Introduction, n. 64.

2. See the *Brief Narrative*, p. 43.

3. This refers to the "warm expressions" which Zenger refused to specify in the *Brief Narrative*, p. 49.

4. Coke, *Third Institute*.

5. All references to "Hawk." or "Hawkins" relate to William Hawkins, *Pleas of the Crown*.

6. An unclear citation. It does not refer to either the *State Trials* or the abridgment of state trials published previous to the Zenger trial (London, 1704).

7. *Comerbach's Reports*.

8. Alexander refers throughout to the 1730 edition of the *State Trials*. This citation doubtless ought to read IV *State Trials* 390, the argument amongst the judges in the trial of the seven bishops.

9. A reference to the Albany Deed, which the Mohawk Indians had given to the corporation of Albany for some land near the city. The Indians later claimed they had been defrauded, and at a conference with their sachems in

September 1733, Cosby returned the deed to them. The Indians promptly threw it into the campfire, antagonizing the city fathers and the Morrisites, who depended heavily on such northern, Dutch supporters. George Clarke, Secretary of New York and a Councilor, was present at the Albany meeting when the deed was destroyed. See Cosby to Lords of Trade, December 15, 1733, *New York Col. Docs.*, V, 960; Colden, *History of Cosby and Clarke,* pp. 304–305.

10. Alexander here apparently repeats his confused reference to the Barnardiston case. Sir Samuel Barnardiston's trial for seditious libel took place in the King's Bench on February 14, 1684. III *State Trials* 845–854. See the *Brief Narrative,* p. 73. Barnardiston was found guilty and fined £10,000, and this decision was apparently *not* reversed. V *State Trials* 716 is a reference to the impeachment of Henry Sacheverell in February, 1710. See the *Brief Narrative,* pp. 46–47. The source of Alexander's confusion is the fact that Barnardiston was involved in an earlier trial in which a decision *for* him was reversed. Barnardiston had brought suit against Sir William Soame, the Sheriff of Suffolk County, in the King's Bench in 1674. He charged that Soame had entered a double return in the recent Parliamentary election in spite of the fact that Barnardiston had gained a majority of the votes. Judgment was given for Barnardiston, which the Exchequer Chamber later reversed. After the Revolution, Barnardiston brought a writ of error to the House of Lords, seeking a reversal of the Exchequer decision, but on June 25, 1689, the Lords voted not to reverse the reversal. VI *Howell's State Trials* 1063–1120. Barnardiston thus lost his case, which in any event is not relevant to his previous conviction for seditious libel.

11. *Hobart's Reports; Coke's Reports; Salkeld's Reports.*

12. W. Nelson, *Law of Evidence* (London, 1735); *Coke on Littleton,* or Coke, *First Institute.*

13. Alexander planned to base his defense of the truth of *NYWJ,* no. 13 upon Cosby's reinstatement of New York's courts of equity. The Court of Exchequer was re-established in Van Dam's case, and the Governor's Court of Chancery began to do business once more in the Cosby administration. The Morrisites were especially upset about Chancellor Cosby's acceptance of Francis Harison's petition to him for equitable relief over the land grant known as the Oblong or the Equivalent. The ubiquitous team of Smith and Alexander, representing the New York patentees against Harison, offered exceptions to the Governor's jurisdiction as chancellor. For the Chancery proceedings in the Oblong case, see Colden, *History of Cosby and Clarke,* pp. 311–312.

14. *NYG,* no. 428, December 31 to January 7, 1734, maintained that Governor Cosby's destruction of the Albany Deed "is not such an unjust thing as people imagine," and defended him by arguing that the corporation of Albany had tried to cheat "the Heathen out of their inheritance."

15. See Appendix A, n. 25.

16. See the Introduction, n. 20.

17. An enigmatic reference. *NYWJ,* no. 9, December 31, 1733, is not to the

point. Alexander doubtless intended to cite *NYWJ*, no. 1, with its account of the Eastchester election.

18. Immediately preceding the "libelous" article in no. 13, the *Journal* printed a short (hearsay) news report which began, "We hear from Rhode Island . . ." It went on to say that the people of Rhode Island had sent two armed vessels to cruise off the east end of Long Island in hope of intercepting the French sloop *Le Caesar*. They failed in their mission, however, having sailed too late.

19. The manuscripts are in the James Alexander Papers of the New York Public Library, file 28. The concluding speech has been printed in Cheslaw, *Zenger*, p. 19.

20. The two reasons for requesting De Lancey to withdraw from the case and the citation to Coke's *Third Institute* are drawn from Alexander's brief.

21. Zenger had been imprisoned on November 17, 1734, and was released on August 4, 1735. The printer was the father of five sons, the two eldest of whom assisted him in his print shop. Certainly his imprisonment caused neither the boys nor their mother to cry for bread, since the *Journal* missed only one issue (the day after his arrest) during the whole affair. Cheslaw, *Zenger*, pp. 5–6, 14–15, 25.

22. The manuscript of Chambers' brief is in the Jay Papers of the New-York Historical Society, Box 3, 16F. It has not been printed before and, indeed, was withheld from Alexander when he was compiling the *Brief Narrative*. The brief, or more properly, the draft of Chambers' opening speech, is headed: "The King agt. John Peter Zenger: Upon an Information for Libeling brought by Richard Bradley, Esqr., Attorney General."

23. The whole drift of Chambers' argument is that the archaic language of the indictment must be taken literally, and that Zenger's publications must be shown to be "false, malicious, seditious and scandalous." Hamilton used this logic to bolster his argument that libels must be falsehoods, but Chambers took a much less sweeping strike at current legal opinion by restricting himself to the further contention that Zenger's statements were not specific enough to be libelous. Hamilton and Alexander wanted to argue that the statements were true.

24. Hawkins, *Pleas of the Crown; Coke's Reports; Modern Reports.*

25. The two sentences within the brackets are crossed out in the manuscript. Chambers apparently decided that this thought belonged in the succeeding paragraph.

26. The page reference is to the account of Tutchin's case in the 1730 edition of the *State Trials*. Sawyer had died by the time of Tutchin's trial, however, and Chambers doubtless intended to refer to his argument as defense counsel for the seven bishops.

27. The last page or pages of the brief are missing. Judging from Chambers' outline, they contained the third and fourth points of his argument.

Appendix C

1. The first letter, signed "Anglo-Americanus," was dated July 20, 1737, and appeared in the *Barbados Gazette,* no. 439, while the second, signed "Indus-Britanicus" was dated July 29, 1737, and appeared in no. 446. Both letters subsequently appeared as pamphlets entitled *Remarks on Zenger's Tryal, Taken Out of the Barbados Gazette's For the Benefit of the Students in Law, and Others in North America,* printed by the Bradfords, father and son, in New York and Philadelphia in 1737. A London edition was issued in 1738 and the two letters were included in *Carribeana* (London, 1741). They were later included in volume XVII of *Howell's State Trials* (London, 1816) immediately following the *Brief Narrative.* The present text is derived from the London edition of 1738, which is entitled *Remarks on the Trial of John Peter Zenger.* Charles Evans (*American Bibliography* [New York, 1904], no. 4118) attributes the "Anglo-Americanus" essay to Jonathan Blenman, the King's Attorney of Barbados. The vituperative tone and lack of cogency of the second letter make it seem likely that "Indus-Britanicus" was the nom de plume for a less talented hand. Alexander did not deign to reply to it, and it is not reprinted here.

2. Anglo-Americanus obviously refers to the two outstanding incidents in New York: Morris' removal from the Supreme Court and the establishment of the Exchequer Court. James Alexander, however, thought he could find evidence of more than "one judge" and "one court." See his brief.

3. On the question of "justification," see the comment of Indus-Britanicus, *Remarks* (London, 1738), p. 22.

4. The reference is to Hawkins, *Pleas of the Crown.*

5. Coke, *Third Institute.*

6. "And since the aforementioned John admits writing the said letter to Robert de Ferrers of the King's Council, which letter contains no truth whatever, our lord King had the court and his justices in contempt, which was to the scandal of the justices and the court. Therefore the said John is committed, etc."

7. King's Bench, 1624. *Godbolt's Reports.* Godbolt is the lawyer Anglo-Americanus refers to as having reported the case of John de Northampton before Coke's *Third Institute* was published in 1644.

8. According to Godbolt's report of the case, it was one Thomas Bradbrook who sent the scandalous letter. M. 18 Ed. III Rot. 162 (1344).

9. The *Remarks,* like the *Brief Narrative,* cites the 1730 edition of *State Trials.*

10. Lord Chief Justice Hyde, in Brewster's case.

11. "Whereas in fact."

12. King's Bench, 1664. *Siderfin's Reports.*

13. Anglo-Americanus lists four of the judges of the King's Bench to add weight to his citation.

14. King's Bench, 1670. *Raymond's Reports.*

15. *Curia,* or, "the Court said."

16. Again, the judges are listed.

17. This is the crux of the dispute between Hamilton and Anglo-Americanus. Hamilton appeals to politics ("the reason of the thing") because it seems to him to be more just and rational than the law. His antagonist believes that politics and law are congruent. Since the law was essentially the same in both places, the difference clearly lies in their conceptions of the proper basis for politics.

18. W. Lambarde, *Archaionomia,* a collection of the Anglo-Saxon laws (London, 1568).

19. Henry de Bracton, *De Legibus et Consuetudinibus Angliae* (London, 1569). "Vulneratus" was added by the author, and "etiam" was omitted after "verum." "For a wrong is done, not only when someone is struck by a fist, beaten, wounded or cudgelled, but even more when he is insulted, or lampooned or the like."

20. 25 Ed. III c. 2 (the Statute of Treasons).

21. For the Morrisite attempt to secure relief "at home," see the Introduction, p. 7.

22. Anglo-Americanus refers to Robert Lowther, the Governor of Barbados in 1711 and 1715–1720. A petty tyrant, Lowther was fiercely resisted by the Barbadians, including Jonathan Blenman. Blenman was jailed for undertaking the defense of one of Lowther's victims, and had to go to England to secure redress from the Crown. Lowther was eventually recalled and a prosecution was instituted against him by the Crown, but he escaped when George I died and his son proclaimed an act of grace at his accession. This episode may well have established Anglo-Americanus' faith in the imperial system, if he was actually Blenman. Robert H. Schomburgk, *The History of Barbados* (London, 1848), pp. 314–316.

23. The articles were reprinted as a single essay in the Duane and Sparks editions of Franklin's writings, and attributed to the Philadelphian. Sparks was hesitant in his attribution, but both nineteenth-century editors unselfconsciously revised the paragraphing, spelling, and phraseology of the original, and even omitted three paragraphs of Alexander's conclusion. William Duane, ed., *The Works of Benjamin Franklin* (Philadelphia, 1808–1817), IV, 319–340; Jared Sparks, ed., *The Works of Benjamin Franklin* (Boston, 1836–1840), II, 285–310. Vincent Buranelli (*The Trial of John Peter Zenger,* New York, 1957, pp. 141–143) reprinted short extracts from the essay, but it is reprinted in its complete and accurate form for the first time in this volume. The text is derived from the Library of Congress' file of the *Pennsylvania Gazette.*

24. "O virtues, most certain destruction."

25. Sir Richard Empson and Edmund Dudley, the chief agents of Henry VII's harsh financial policies.

26. Alexander intends to refer to 1 & 2 Ph. & Mary c. 3, and 23 Eliz. I c. 2. The former established a fine of £100 and three months' imprisonment

for a first offense of maliciously slandering the King or Queen, but demanded the loss of the right hand for writing against the King or Queen. The statute of Elizabeth provided for the pillory and the loss of both ears, or a fine of £200 and six months' imprisonment for speaking seditious rumors against the Queen. However, printing, writing or publishing any seditious book against the Queen was to be considered a felony without clergy.

27. Clarendon, *The History of the Rebellion,* [Oxford, 1702–1704] (W. Dunn Macray, ed., Oxford, 1888), I, 5.

28. Nine members of the Parliament of 1628–1629, which produced the Petition of Right and the Three Resolutions of March 2, 1629, were called to account before the Privy Council. Those who refused to apologize for their conduct were proceeded against in the King's Bench, but refused to plead on the grounds that the court had no jurisdiction over words spoken in Parliament. The three who absolutely refused to give in, Eliot, Strode, and Valentine, were imprisoned.

29. William Prynn, Henry Burton, and Dr. John Bastwick were tried by the Star Chamber on June 14, 1737. III *Howell's State Trials* 711–770.

30. The passions of the English people, that is to say, were discharged in the Civil War of 1642–1649.

31. Licensing of the press was begun in 1662, under the Regulating of Printing Act of that year. For licensing, see Siebert, *Freedom of the Press in England,* pp. 237–263.

32. Thomas Shadwell, the Restoration playwright and poet laureate.

33. Sir Robert Sawyer, Attorney General from 1681 to 1687, and Heneage Finch (first Earl of Aylesford), Solicitor General from 1679 to 1686.

34. The Treaty of Dover, 1670, between Charles II and Louis XIV of France, a secret clause of which provided for the re-establishment of Roman Catholicism in England.

35. Algernon Sidney, who was charged with high treason for his supposed complicity in the Rye House plot, and tried before George Jeffreys in the King's Bench, November 21, 1683. IX *Howell's State Trials* 818–950.

36. "for our lady the Queen"; "for our lady truth."

37. "to write is to act"; "to write and to publish is to act."

38. See the *Brief Narrative,* n. 39.

39. Burnet, *History of His Own Times* [1723–1734] (London, 1838), p. 439.

40. "secrets of state."

41. William Prynn's case, Star Chamber, February 7, 1633. I *State Trials* 404.

42. Thomas Dangerfield, *Mr. Tho. Dangerfield's Particular Narrative, of the Late Popish Design . . .* (London, 1679).

43. Rapin-Thoyras, *The History of England* (London, 1731), XV, 143.

44. "beyond the jurisdiction of the court."

45. The civil law is Roman law, *corpus juris civilis,* as opposed to the common law of England and the canon law.

46. "to slander is to bring false accusations"; "to bring true accusations."

47. "It is not a libel as charged, since it does not consist of direct asser-

tions in which truth or falsehood appear, and this is exactly what libel requires."

48. "An intent to harm is not presumed and it is incumbent on the plaintiff to prove it."

49. *Supra*, p. 156.

50. *Supra*, pp. 161–163.

51. *Supra*, p. 163.

52. *Supra*, pp. 163–164.

53. *Supra*, p. 173.

54. *Supra*, p. 176.

55. "who peddle the law."

INDEX

THE JOHN HARVARD LIBRARY

The intent of Waldron Phoenix Belknap, Jr., as expressed in an early will, was for Harvard College to use the income from a permanent trust fund he set up, for "editing and publishing rare, inaccessible, or hitherto unpublished source material of interest in connection with the history, literature, art (including minor and useful art), commerce, customs, and manners or way of life of the Colonial and Federal Periods of the United States . . . In all cases the emphasis shall be on the presentation of the basic material." A later testament broadened this statement, but Mr. Belknap's interests remained constant until his death.

In linking the name of the first benefactor of Harvard College with the purpose of this later, generous-minded believer in American culture the John Harvard Library seeks to emphasize the importance of Mr. Belknap's purpose. The John Harvard Library of the Belknap Press of Harvard University Press exists to make books and documents about the American past more readily available to scholars and the general reader.

JHL